W9-CGX-033

DATE DUE

GAYLORD			PRINTED IN U.S.A.

HENRY WARD BEECHER

Henry Ward Beecher
Beecher Family Papers, Manuscripts and Archives, Yale University Library

HENRY WARD BEECHER

Peripatetic Preacher

Halford R. Ryan

Great American Orators, Number 5

Bernard K. Duffy and Halford R. Ryan,
Series Advisors

Greenwood Press
New York • Westport, Connecticut • London

Library of Congress Cataloging-in-Publication Data

Ryan, Halford Ross.
  Henry Ward Beecher : peripatetic preacher / Halford R. Ryan.
     p.   cm — (Great American orators, ISSN 0898-8277 ; no. 5)
  Includes bibliographical references.
  ISBN 0-313-26389-2 (lib. bdg. : alk. paper)
  1. Beecher, Henry Ward, 1813-1887. 2. Preaching—United States—
History—19th century. 3. Sermons, American. 4. Congregationalist
churches—Sermons. I. Title. II. Series.
BV4208.U6R934   1990
251'.0092—dc20   89-38228

British Library Cataloguing in Publication Data is available.

Library of Congress Catalog Card Number: 89-38228
ISBN: 0-313-26389-2
ISSN: 0898-8277

First published in 1990

Greenwood Press, Inc.
88 Post Road West, Westport, Connecticut 06881

Printed in the United States of America

The paper used in this book complies with the
Permanent Paper Standard issued by the National
Information Standards Organization (Z39.48-1984).

10 9 8 7 6 5 4 3 2 1

Copyright Acknowledgments

Permission granted by Beecher Family Papers, Manuscripts and Archives,
Yale University Library, for letters, diaries, sermons, speeches, photograph,
and other miscellaneous materials.

Contents

Series Foreword

The idea for a series of books on great American orators grew out of the recognition that there is a paucity of book-length studies on individual orators and their speeches. Apart from a few notable exceptions, the study of American public address has been pursued in scores of articles published in professional journals. As helpful as these studies have been, none has or can provide a complete analysis of a speaker's rhetoric. Book-length studies, such as those in this series, will help fill the void that has existed in the study of American public address and its related disciplines of politics and history, theology and sociology, communication and law. In books, the critic can explicate a broader range of a speaker's persuasive discourse than reasonably could be treated in articles. The comprehensive research and sustained reflection that books require will undoubtedly yield many original and enduring insights concerning the nation's most important voices.

Public address has been a fertile ground for scholarly investigation. No matter how insightful their intellectual forebears, each generation of scholars must reexamine its universe of discourse, while expanding the compass of its researches and redefining its purpose and methods. To avoid intellectual torpor new scholars cannot be content simply to see through the eyes of those who have come before them. We hope that this series of books will stimulate important new understandings of the nature of persuasive discourse and provide additional opportunities for scholarship in the history and criticism of American public address.

This series examines the role of rhetoric in the United States. American speakers shaped the destiny of the colonies, the young republic, and the mature nation. During each stage of the intellectual, political, and religious development of the United States, great orators, standing at the rostrum, on the stump, and in the pulpit, used words and gestures to influence their audiences. Usually striving for the noble, sometimes achieving the base, they urged their fellow citizens toward a more perfect Union. The books in this series chronicle and explain the accomplishments of representative American leaders as orators.

A series of book-length studies on American persuaders honors the role men and women have played in U.S. history. Previously, if one desired to assess the impact of a speaker or a speech upon history, the path was, at best, not well marked and, at worst, littered with obstacles. To be sure, one might turn to biographies and general histories to learn about an orator, but for the public address scholar these sources often prove unhelpful. Rhetorical topics, such as speech invention, style, delivery, organizational strategies, and persuasive effect, are often treated in passing, if mentioned at all. Authoritative speech texts are often difficult to locate and the problem of textual accuracy is frequently encountered. This is especially true for those figures who spoke one or two hundred years ago, or for those whose persuasive role, though significant, was secondary to other leading lights of the age.

Each book in this series is organized to meet the needs of scholars and students of the history and criticism of American public address. Part I is a critical analysis of the orator and his or her speeches. Within the format of a case study, one may expect considerable latitude. For instance, in a given chapter an author might explicate a single speech or a group of related speeches, or examine orations that comprise a genre of rhetoric such as forensic speaking. But the critic's focus remains on the rhetorical considerations of speaker, speech, occasion, and effect. Part II contains the texts of the important addresses that are discussed in the critical analysis that precedes it. To the extent possible, each author has endeavored to collect authoritative speech texts, which have often been found through original research in collections of primary source material. In a few instances, because of the extreme length of a speech, texts have been edited, but the authors have been careful to delete material that is least important to the speech, and these deletions have been held to a minimum.

In each book there is a chronology of major speeches that serves more purposes than may be apparent at first. Pragmatically, it lists all of the orator's known speeches and addresses. Places and dates of the speeches are also listed, although this is information that is sometimes difficult to determine precisely. But in a wider sense, the chronology attests to the scope of rhetoric in the United States. Certainly in quantity, if not always in quality, Americans are historically talkers and listeners.

Because of the disparate nature of the speakers examined in the series, there is some latitude in the nature of the bibliographical materials that have been included in each book. But in every instance, authors have carefully described original historical materials and collections and gathered critical studies, biographies and autobiographies, and a variety of secondary sources that bear on the speaker and the oratory. By combining in each book bibliographical materials, speech texts, and critical chapters, this series notes that text and research sources are interwoven in the act of rhetorical criticism.

May the books in this series serve to memorialize the nation's greatest orators.

Bernard K. Duffy
Halford R. Ryan

Preface

I have always thought it strange in the study of public address that the subject of delivery received such scant attention in critical studies of oratory. To be sure, reports of early figures' habits on the platform are sometimes nonexistent or so fulsome that they are little more than uncritical encomia. Yet, these objections are increasingly less applicable in more recent times, and even to a degree for some of the early speakers in the colonial era, at the nation's birth, and during the golden age of American oratory. Especially since the advent of the voice recording, the motion picture newsreel, and most recently the video recording, the materials are at hand to discuss, more than in just passing, an orator's delivery. Granted, a handful of rhetorical scholars have mounted a focused examination of an orator's delivery, or have attempted to integrate delivery into a larger rhetorical study. But most critics, if the professional journals and monographs are any indication of contemporary rhetorical practice, have been content to unfold a speech as if it were not delivered by a human voice or gestures and have assumed that listeners seldom evaluated and reacted to what they saw and heard. In short, critics seem to conceive an address as somehow born on a printed page, which is to be treated as a kind of literary text, but not as a speech that was originally delivered with inflections, hand and facial gestures, vocal pacing, and eye contact.

That complaint informs the following caveat concerning the present study. To the extent possible, I try to assay how the Reverend Henry Ward Beecher delivered a speech or sermon and how Americans responded to his voice and gestures. I contend that Beecher was a successful speaker and preacher in great part due to his skills in delivery. Obviously, delivery cannot be separated from content, but, historically, content has been all too often divorced from delivery. The reason is simple: the speech exists as a text, its delivery is gone with the wind and light waves that carried it, and in Beecher's case, this was over a hundred years ago. In an ironic sense, the "Collected Sermons and Speeches" in the back matter of this book reinforces the practiced tendency in the criticism of public address to elevate the text and to forget about, or to mention in passing, the speech's delivery.

Yet, I try to capture something of Beecher's deportment on the public platform. However elusive that portraiture is, and although at times the composition is sketchy and the canvas is not completely covered with the broad strokes and vibrant pigmentation that one might desire from one who has carped about other critics' ignoring or playing down delivery, I hope to evoke something of the fact that Beecher once addressed his words to the American audience, and that they went to hear him preach in person, paid to listen to his lectures, and in Great Britain during the American Civil War some Englishmen came prepared to stop his voice by whatever means short of physical violence. It is probably true that more people read his famous speeches in the newspapers than listened to them in person, and more people probably read his sermons in his published collections of homilies than heard him preach in Plymouth Church. Yet his various readerships were predicated on the fact that he was a great orator. When the opportunity arose, as his yearly income attested, people paid more money to hear him than to read him. Given that Beecher devoted considerable attention to the development of his delivery, especially in his early ministry so that he could coast on his attainments more or less throughout the rest of his career, it behooves the rhetorical critic to follow his lead.

Acknowledgments

The research for this book was conducted in the Beecher Family Papers, Sterling Memorial Library, and in the Divinity School Library of Yale University, New Haven, Connecticut. I thank the individuals who helped me in those libraries.

I wish to thank John Elrod, Dean of the College, Washington and Lee University, and the advisory committee for a John M. Glenn Grant that was a subvention for my stay in New Haven. The grant also stipulated an allotted time in the summer to complete a major portion of the manuscript. Karen Lyle, religion department, typed the texts of the collected speeches and sermons, and Ruth Floyd helped me with the computer.

The ideas that I present in this book are in some measure indicative of my teaching Beecher's persuasions to students in the history and criticism of American public address. The conversations in those classes are reflected herein, and those discussions warrant the claim that teaching and research can be combined advantageously for student and instructor.

Lastly, I wish to thank the supportive members of my family: Cheryl, my wife and friend through these years, for her encouragement to begin long ago, for her sustenance as writing projects multiplied, and now for her toleration for the clickety-clack of the computer keyboard; and Shawn, my daughter, who accepts a desk-bound father.

I
HENRY WARD BEECHER

Introduction

The Reverend Henry Ward Beecher dominated the pulpit and the public platform from shortly before the Civil War until his death in 1887. "To account for his power and to see the reason for it," Daniel Addison observed, "one must remember that he made public speaking the specialty of his life." Beecher's pulpit in the Plymouth Church, Brooklyn, New York, which he occupied from 1847 to his demise, was intimately associated with him and he with it, and those Americans who were unable to journey to New York City much less to gain access to the crowded church services could attend one of the public lectures that Beecher gave at the apogee of his career from after the Civil War until his death. For the most part, his lecture tours ranged over the entire East coast north of the Mason-Dixon Line and out to the major cities in the Midwest. At his zenith, Beecher was something of the celebrity. Plymouth pilgrims to New York City always caught the Fulton ferry boat from Manhattan to Brooklyn, and soon the ferries became known in the vernacular as "Beecher's Boats." The practice of street car conductors was to call the name of streets at stops, but for Plymouth Church, "Beecher" sufficed. Indeed, Joseph Howard caught something of Beecher's appeal to Victorian Americans: "It became the fashion, among fashionable people, in fashionable churches where fashionable clergymen officiated, to look loftily upon this young man of the people. Well, he rather liked that."[1]

During the time when the United States experienced the industrial revolution, a Civil War, and profound social and intellectual changes, he was a spokesman for a liberal theology that was eminently adjusted to the Victorian era, a pleader for liberal social policies that included woman's suffrage and various reform movements of the mid-nineteenth century, a Christian apologist for Darwinism at a time when conservatives were assured by Anglican Bishop Ussher that the earth was only some six thousand years old, and ardently anti-slavery. Although the difference might be minimal, Beecher was not an abolitionist of the radical kind exemplified by William Lloyd Garrison, nor did Beecher urge disunion with the South that Garrison claimed polluted the Constitution. Nevertheless, Beecher spoke against slavery at a time when most ministers were mute on human bondage.

Such a noteworthy figure has not eluded notice. Beecher's most recent biographer, Clifford E. Clark, Jr., in *Henry Ward Beecher* (Urbana: University of Illinois Press, 1978), has treated Beecher's theological and social contributions to U.S. history and one does not presume to revise significantly his findings. Altina Waller, in *Reverend Beecher and Mrs. Tilton* (Amherst: University of Massachusetts Press, 1982), has explicated the sex scandal of the 1870s that sapped Beecher's emotional strength if not his standing with his congregation and his ethos with his national audience. Concerning whether Beecher had sexual relations with Mrs. Tilton, Waller makes something more than a prima facie case but something less than a compelling case that he did: to borrow a religious reference, one remains an agnostic. And Jane Shaffer Elsmere's *Henry Ward Beecher: The Indiana Years, 1837-47* (Indianapolis: Indiana Historical Society, 1973) remains a standard source for Beecher's early pastorates in Lawrenceburg and Indianapolis, Indiana.

Several authors stand in the first generation of Beecher's biographers. Joseph R. Howard, one of the original founders of the Plymouth Church, produced one of the first biographies entitled *Life of Henry Ward Beecher* (Philadelphia: Hubbard Brothers, 1887). As may be expected, it was fulsome with praise. However, it is a storehouse of information, admittedly anecdotal in nature, about Beecher's oratorical practices. In the same year, Lyman Abbott, who assumed Beecher's pulpit at Plymouth Church after he died, gave a particularly insightful view of Beecher's oratorical practices in *Henry Ward Beecher* (Hartford: American Publishing Company, 1887). William C. Beecher, one of Beecher's sons, and the Rev. Samuel Scoville, Beecher's son-in-law, with the assistance of Mrs. Henry Ward Beecher, produced their tome, *A Biography of Henry Ward Beecher* (New York: Charles Webster and Comapny, 1888). Heavily anecdotal and heartily sympathetic to its subject, the book remains a starting point for research on Beecher's ministry. John Henry Barrows, in *Henry Ward Beecher, Shakespeare of the Pulpit* (New York: Funk and Wagnalls, 1893), has shed some valuable light on Beecher's persuasive practices. Paxton Hibben, in *Henry Ward Beecher: An American Portrait* (New York: George H. Doran Company, 1927), characterized the great minister thusly: "An opportunist he was, certainly. . . a great orator, a great actor–a showman, if one like." Perhaps in reaction to such a portraiture, Lyman Beecher Stowe, son of Charles Edward Stowe and grandson of Harriet Beecher Stowe, subtly defended Beecher in *Saints, Sinners, and Beechers* (Indianapolis: Bobbs-Merrill Company, 1934). His passing comments on Beecher's speaking are used in this study. *The Meaning of Henry Ward Beecher*, written by William G. McLoughlin (New York: Alfred A. Knopf, 1970), places Beecher in the perspective of Protestant thought during the Victorian era; nevertheless, McLoughlin's treatment of Beecher's oratory is worth mining.[2]

With reference to remarks I made in the preface, I think it is worthwhile to make an observation here about the nature of these biographies, particularly the early ones, that I rely upon in this study for Beecher's delivery. Some of the accounts are given by relatively unbiased eyewitnesses, others are from people's memories many years after the fact, and some have probably been manufactured or adjusted to fit the legends that surround Beecher. Nevertheless, there is something to be said for these accounts. They were given by people who experienced Beecher's and other Americans' oratory at first hand. They witnessed a breed of speakers practicing an art that is practically dead in the late twentieth century, and they were equipped to make comparisons with some of the great orators of the nineteenth century, which has rightly been called the golden age of American oratory. To eschew their observations on the ground that they are too effulgent is to miss what Beecher's contemporaries were trying to communicate about the effects of the craft on audiences.

Biographical, historical, and theological perspectives have their rightful places in any discussion of famous preachers, but Beecher was primarily an orator. Lionel Crocker was Beecher's critic in the discipline of the history and criticism of American public address. Yet Crocker's seminal works in professional journals, dating from 1939 to 1962, treated a narrow range of Beecher's speaking activities during the Civil War in articles on Beecher and the English Press of 1863, Beecher's speech at Fort Sumter in 1865, and a comparison of Abraham Lincoln with Beecher. This is not to imply that Crocker's articles are dated or outworn, for his findings are utilized in the study. Rather, the fact is that Beecher had established his public and pulpit personae before the Civil War, and many of his important addresses were delivered after the war on such topics as Reconstruction, political reform, and Darwinism. In a monograph-length study of "Henry Ward Beecher" in *History and Criticism of American Public Address*, edited by William Norwood Brigance (New York: Russell and Russell, 1960), Crocker expanded his focus and treated the full range of Beecher's oratorical activities.

Another problem with Crocker's works on Beecher's public speaking stem from his rhetorical perspective. In *Henry Ward Beecher's Art of Preaching* (Chicago: University of Chicago Press, 1934), which was his doctoral dissertation, Crocker conceived Beecher's rhetoric in the classical mode by treating the rhetorical canons of invention, disposition, and style with a heavy emphasis on the Aristotelian modes of proof: logical, emotional, and ethical. In *Henry Ward Beecher's Speaking Art* (New York: Fleming H. Revell, 1937), Crocker treated at length some of Beecher's famous addresses and reprinted a few of his important speeches.

However, Crocker faced two exigencies that the present study does not. First, this study will also deal, as Crocker did, with the classical canons of rhetoric. The five canons are *inventio*, or the invention of a speech or sermon; *dispositio*, or the arrangement for persuasive effect of the speech; and *elocutio*, the speaker's style or word choice. Unfortunately, Crocker wrote when the discipline of rhetorical criticism did not pay enough attention to *actio*, the speech's delivery, and slighted *memoria*, the devices that would help the orator remember the speech, because these two subjects were somehow unacademic. Only in a book-length study, which is not devoted slavishly to Aristotle's *Rhetoric* and the classical canons, can one gain a complete conception of the ambit of Beecher's rhetorical practices.

Second, when one is constrained by the reigning order of rhetorical criticism to deal with certain topics, such as the classical canons and Aristotelian modes of proof, as was Crocker in his academic mileau, one

4 Henry Ward Beecher

might easily miss other rhetorical factors. Oratory is like a diamond: it has many facets that scintillate under different lighting conditions. (The metaphor of the diamond is appropriate in Beecher's case. He was much given to precious stones, was well known in Tiffany's jewelry store in New York City, and carried around in his pocket a collection of diamonds, rubies, sapphires, and opals. He claimed they calmed his nerves by looking at their flashing colors, and he gazed at the fires of an opal for a half hour back in his hotel room in order to settle himself after his boisterous speech at Liverpool, England, in 1863.) If one is content to examine the diamond from only one perspective, then one runs the risk of overlooking some of its other remarkable facets.[3]

About the Book

The contribution this book makes to the series of "Great American Orators" and to the scholarship on Beecher is threefold. First, it envisages Beecher as an orator and only secondarily as a pastor. Thus conceived, Beecher emerges as a man who used oratory, and the attendant acclaim that surrounded a famous speaker in the nineteenth century, for personal aggrandizement. This does not imply that Beecher was a charlatan, nor that he preached for profit, although he was rewarded handsomely for his stewardship, nor that he was less of a Christian than other untold and unsung ministers of the age. It does hold that Beecher had a bit of the oratorical Barnum and Bailey in him. The same proverbial sucker that was born every minute to attend a circus was also a potential listener at Plymouth or a paying customer on the lecture circuit. As Beecher increasingly allied himself with controversial issues to attract public attention, his stock as a celebrity rose; concomitantly, these causes, which were associated with an increasingly famous person, benefited materially and pyschologically by being identified with one of the leading lights of the age.

Second, this study portrays Beecher as an orator-writer. Always preparing carefully, but never seeming to take his preparation seriously, especially when inspired at the very moment of utterance, Beecher was known for ad-libbing portions of his addresses and sermons. One famous speech at a protest meeting, held in New York, May 30, 1856, to denounce the caning of senator Charles Sumner on the floor of the Senate, propelled him to the forefront of the antislavery movement and seems to have been delivered totally impromptu. Beecher's editing his national journals, the *Independent* and the *Christian Union*, stocked his mind with emotional and logical appeals that he retrieved, whether in a sacred pulpit or on a secular platform, at the moment of address. A corollary of the orator-writer conception is that Beecher realized the powerful effect *actio*, a term the ancients used to denote gestures, voice production, platform deportment, and so forth, had in swaying the audience or congregation. In fact, Beecher's *actio* accounted more for his persuasive successes than has been hitherto realized. The thesis is that Beecher was aware of his *actio*, was at pains to develop a persuasive delivery, and, as a trained speaker, monitored his platform deportment and its effect on the audience. Rhetorical critics should give attention to a variable that the speaker himself understood was efficacious in persuading listeners.

Third, the findings in this study are grounded in original research conducted in the Beecher Family Papers, Yale University Library, New Haven, Connecticut. These primary sources, described fully in the endmatter, are the core materials for the critical chapters, the chronology of speeches and sermons, and the bibliography. The previous research on Beecher in speech communication was not based on the Beecher Family Papers and several new findings are noted where appropriate. The thesis about the role delivery played in Beecher's persuasions will be supported by his observations that attest to the importance he assigned to *actio* in his sermonizing.

About the Chapters

Chapter 1, "The Prelude: Beecher in Indiana," traces the early development of Beecher as a speaker and minister in the smallest state west of the Alleghany Mountains. The fact is that Beecher was called to Plymouth Church, Brooklyn, New York, from Indianapolis, Indiana. His call to the Second Presbyterian Church of Indianapolis was predicated to some degree on his performance for the beginning two years of his ministry at the First Presbyterian Church, Lawrenceburg, Indiana. This chapter will characterize the kind of sermonizing that motivated New Yorkers to summon eastward a man who had no compelling desire to remain a Hoosier. (His wife, an Eastener, detested Indiana, and Beecher was always short of money: Plymouth Church satisfied both exigencies.) Much of Beecher's practice of oratory, perhaps a so-called oratorical theory is too bold a description, was conceived, nurtured, and internalized at Lawrenceburg, 1837-39, and Indianapolis, where he preached from 1839-47. A close scrutiny of Beecher's handwritten sermons from this period, which have not received the attention they deserved from his rhetorical critics, sheds light on his later persuasive practices. A variety of typical sermons from the Indianapolis years, culled from the collection at Yale, is illustrated and criticized in this chapter.

Chapter 2, "Beecher Militant at Plymouth," details the synergism that obtained when a man, a church, and a suburb of New York City united. As the Pilgrim fathers left Great Britain to work out their salvation in the wilderness of New England, so did Beecher leave the woods of Indiana to advance his theology and politics on a metropolitan scale and stage. If the Pilgrims improved their spiritual lives by alighting on Plymouth Rock, Beecher improved his secular standing by stepping into the pulpit of Plymouth Church. The truth to tell, Beecher's romantic religion and rotund rhetoric appealed to the rising gentry in Brooklyn. As he gained fame, his rhetorical religion appealed to the mass audience that read his sermons in the newspapers or in his own publications, and especially to the emerging values of middle class Victorians in the United States. Beecher obliged his listeners' and readers' theological and intellectual needs by appealing to their faith in reason and their belief that spiritual and political values were truly progressing upward. Paxton Hibben accurately observed Beecher's function as an orator in the mid-nineteenth century: "He was not in advance of his day, but precisly abreast of his day. . . . His gift was merely that he was articulate while they [his fellow Americans] were not." This chapter explicates how Beecher changed from a Biblical exegete to a political pulpiteer.[4]

The main focus of chapter 2 is on Beecher's war of words against the peculiar institution. At a time when proper preachers eschewed discussing slavery in the pulpit because the subject was divisive to the Union and thought to be inappropriate to Christian homilies, Beecher carved his reputation by casting himself as one of the foremost ministers in the antislavery drive. He had caused some excitement in Indiana with his series of three sermons on slavery in 1846, but it was at Plymouth Church that the slavers met their match. Because Southern preachers could claim support for the institution of slavery on Biblical grounds, Beecher resorted to logical and pathetical appeals, such as bringing to Plymouth a very young Negro slave girl and auctioning her freedom to the congregation. This rhetorical act, following on the heels of his famous Sumner protest speech, thrust him to the forefront of the antislavery movement. President Lincoln later rewarded Beecher's oratorical efforts on behalf of the Union by inviting the famous preacher to be the principal speaker for the flag-raising ceremony at Fort Sumter, April 14, 1865. The Sumner protest speech is printed in "Collected Sermons and Speeches."

Chapter 3, "Beecher in Britain," examines Beecher at his apotheosis. Beecher's speaking tour of Great Britain in the fall of 1863 was one of the premier rhetorical feats of the nineteenth century, or so Beecher's followers thought at the time, and Beecher was not at pains to dissuade anyone of that perception. Whether Her Majesty's Government would recognize the Confederacy in 1863 was a crucial issue, upon which the outcome of the Civil War seemed to depend. Beecher, conveniently touring the Continent on a vacation subvented by his congregation, was enlisted by British abolitionists to speak at five cities in England and Scotland. Although the British government was more impressed by General Robert E. Lee's military defeat at Gettysburg and the fall of Vicksburg in July, 1863, to General Ulysses S. Grant, than by Beecher's apparent oratorical victories in swaying crowds at his major speaking stops, critics on both sides of the Atlantic, but especially in the United States, inferred that Beecher's oratorical prowess had won the day.

Having stated all the necessary historical caveats, it remains nevertheless to say that Beecher's performance on British soil was a rhetorical gem of the first water. Lesser orators probably could not have risen to the occasion. Against all the forms of harassment the pro-Southern British audience could muster short of physical violence, Beecher countered with all the devices he had mastered over the years to manipulate an audience: humor, sarcasm, *argumentum ad misericordiam*, and turning the tables on opponents. If the British intellectuals did not appreciate Beecher's logical appeals, they at least grudgingly admired his pathetical appeals and his dogged determination not to be shouted down. Copious quotations will be taken from his five speeches in order to illustrate the persuasive problems that he faced and how he attempted to mediate them through oratory.

Chapter 4, "Apologist for Evolution," investigates how Beecher helped make Darwinism respectable in liberal protestant pulpits. He preached a series of six sermons in 1885 on evolution and Christianity. Ostensibly an apologist for science, Beecher actually attacked, and was in the vanguard of famous ministers to do so, the fundamentalists he so abhorred. The debate he began, which was rekindled with great success by the Rev. Harry Emerson Fosdick, who was something of Beecher's successor in the twentieth century, had its denouement at Dayton, Tennessee, at the Scopes' Trial in 1925. Beecher was not a great theologian nor a noted Biblical exegete. So in terms of a lasting contribution to his chosen profession, the sermons on evolution stand as his solid accomplishments. Indeed, it may have been that since Beecher was vindicated on the issue of slavery and was gaining a sympathetic hearing on the other reform issues of his day, that his tremendous prestige with those secular movements was transferred to the sacred question of evolution and Christianity. "The Two Revelations," is printed in Part II, although, as in the case of the British speeches, the other sermons in the series will be discussed as appropriate.

Chapter 5, "The Postlude: Beecher as *Vox Populi*," examines the themes that Beecher espoused until his death. Before the Civil War, he had some success on the lecture circuit and as an author. After the Civil War, which was really his prime time preaching and orating, Beecher addressed the issues of Reconstruction, charmed Chautauqua audiences with his encomia on American virtues, plied his persuasions in ample after-dinner speaking, dabbled in the rhetoric of political reform, and defended himself at the bar in the Tilton seduction case. His talks for the Lyman Beecher Lectures at Yale University also bear investigation because they reveal something of Beecher's rhetorical practices and theory. The purpose of this chapter is to give a sampling, by means of copious quotations, of Beecher's rhetoric in these genres. Although no one persuasion seems to be representative of this period, his speech entitled "Oratory," May 29, 1876, is given because it is really Henry Ward being Beecher on Beecher.

The Conclusion assays Beecher's impact on religion and politics in U.S. history. Although the relevance of an orator who was a thoroughly nineteenth-century figure is not necessarily apparent, the fact is that Beecher was an effective role model for liberal preachers in the early part of the twentieth century, especially for one like the Reverend Harry Emerson Fosdick who forwarded Beecher's work, and also a precursor for the admixture of religion and politics that disturbs some late twentieth-century Americans while delighting others who see Satan, in the form of Communism, liberalism, and humanism, ubiquitous in the nation.

About Beecher's Delivery

The student of Henry Ward Beecher's sermons and speeches must always remember that words on the printed page were first communicated by a living, breathing, gesticulating orator. In terms of the traditional preacher's pulpit, Beecher was an innovator. When given the chance to enact his rhetorical theory concerning platform deportment, he capitalized on the persuasive possibilities in addressing the congregation conversationally. The accepted practice in most churches of the time was to have a large pulpit, sometimes elaborately carved or decorated, that succeeded admirably well in hiding the minister from view, except from the shoulders upward. Thus posted, the pastor was a virtual prisoner in the pulipt. Designed psychologically to separate the minister from the people and to elevate the Word of God above common parlance, the pulpit inadvertently removed any possiblity of the pastor's communicating directly with the congregation as listeners. When Beecher and his congregation needed a larger building in Indianapolis to conduct services, owing to his successfully shepherding the church in three years to the largest Presbyterian church in Indiana, Beecher directed that a speaker's table or desk, rather than a pulpit, be built for him in the new building. He physically broke the distance barrier that separated him from his audience and created the conditions that made his homilies more like addresses than sermons.

Beecher was handed a blessing in disguise when he had been preaching in Brooklyn only two years. When the original Plymouth Church burned in January, 1849, and a new edifice was to be built, Beecher instructed the architects to build the speaker's platform so that it arced into the audience. Contemporary lithographs show that Beecher stood in front of an imposing pipe organ screen. He stationed himself at the side of a speaker's table, but he was not glued to the spot. He ranged over the entire stage, preaching and pleading with his listeners. His characteristic stance was to hold his manuscript notes in his left hand and to gesture with his right hand that was free. Even in the later years, his eyesight was so keen that he did not need to wear glasses in order to see his notes or to read the Scriptural text from the Bible.

Beecher was aware of the psychological impact he made on his listeners with his innovative delivery. In his *Star Papers*, published in 1859, he poked fun, in metaphors that suggest Beecher's command of the language, at contemporary pulpit architecture:

> As to the pulpit, but one thing is usually considered necessary, and that is, that it should be put as far as possible from all sympathetic contact with the people to be influenced by it; that it should be so constructed as to take away from the speaker, as far as it can be done, every chance of exerting any influence upon those whom he addresses. Therefore the pulpit is ribbed up on the sides, set back against the wall, where it looks like a barn-swallow's nest plastered on some beam. In this way the minister is as much as possible kept out of the way of the people, and all that is left is his voice. Posture, free gesture, motion, advance or retreat, and that most effective of all gestures, the full form of an earnest man, from head to foot, right before the people; in short, the whole advantage which the body gives when thrown into argument or persuasion, is lost without any equivalent gain. In this sacred mahogany tub or rectangular box, the man learns every kind of hidden awkwardness. He stands on one leg and crooks the other, like

a slumbering horse at a hitching-post; he leans now on one side of the cushion, or lolls on the other side. And when a man, thoroughly trained by one of these dungeon pulpits to regard his legs and feet as superfluous, except in some awkard and uncouth way to crutch him up to the level of his cushion and paper, is brought out upon an open platform, it is amusing to watch the inconvenience to him of having legs at all, and his various experiments and blushing considerations of what he shall do with them!

Is it any wonder that so little is done by preaching . . . ? Daniel Webster is reported to have said, that no lawyer would risk his reputation before a jury if he had to speak from a pulpit, and that he considered the survival of Christianity in spite of pulpits as one of the evidences of its divinity.

At City Temple, London, July 8, 1886, Beecher encountered a British audience that was accustomed to hearing and seeing a preacher in the pulpit. Typical of the English audience, the cry of "Pulpit! Pulpit!" was exclaimed because Beecher was standing on the chancel level and not in the pulpit. Never one to blush before a British audience, Beecher retorted (note how he used humor to blunt the accusation that he was somehow unministerial):

A great man once said that he considered the continued existence of Christianity *in spite of the* [Beecher's emphasis] pulpits—one proof of its divinity. No my friends—it is not the voice or even the head alone, it is the whole man, informed with his subject, who preaches. I shall not get into the pulpit.

With his remarkable verbal memory, Beecher retrieved at the moment of utterance what he had written over two and one-half decades earlier.[5]

From all accounts, Beecher had a powerful and well modulated voice. The Plymouth Church was a large, acoustic one hundred and five feet long and eighty feet wide. It was a very tall two story building. In addition to seating on the first floor, a balcony completely surrounded the building (except for the large pipe organ behind the pulpit area), and a third floor gallery was tucked under the ceiling in the rear of the church. In all, the church could hold about thirty-two hundred people. How an orator could address such a crowd and be heard without the aid of electronic amplification often baffles the modern mind. The secret was that the audience remained absolutely still. Indeed, Benjamin Franklin observed of George Whitefield, who often addressed thousands of listeners in open fields, that they "observ'd the most exact silence." And, of course, Beecher had a fine voice. *The Bailie* remarked that "In its best days, his voice had something of a trumpet-like quality. It still possesses [1886] a richness of tone, and its notes are clear and distinct." Another eyewitness, a minister from a town in the far West, described Beecher in action:

The great sensation of the season to the rustics who go not out much into the great world has been the advent of Mr. Beecher and the pleasure of hearing him speak. We have seen the lion and heard him roar, and at times he would roar you as "gently as a sucking dove," but would soon assert his lionhood by coming out with his tremendous *basso-profundo*. . . . He is not an imposing presence. There is a good deal of the Little Corporal about him, especially in his power to wield men. But I feel glad and grateful for the privilege of hearing him.

Indeed, Beecher revealed why audiences paid to hear him speak. He liked church and organ music, so he naturally likened his voice to the king of instruments with which he raptured his audiences:

The tongue may be likened to an organ, which, though but one instrument, has within it an array of different pipes and stops, and discourses in innumerable combinations. If one man sits before it not skilled to control its powers, he shall make it but a monstrous jargon. But when one comes who knows its ways, and has control of its powers, then it becomes a mountain of melody, and another might well think he heard the city of God in the hour of its singing. The tongue is the key-board of the soul.

If his tongue was the organ keyboard of his soul, then Beecher selected the stops with his gestures. He evidently preferred the stentorian post horns and bombardes to the soft flutes and dulcianas.[6]

Beecher was something of the showman on the platform and in the pulpit. His enthusiasm for his subject matters and the drama with which he delivered his speeches were well known to an audience. One observer wrote the following description:

One frequent gesture that I noticed in attending his last lecture here he retained through life. It was the habit of raising his right hand high in the air, and after a pause, sometimes prolonged, bringing his arm down sharply to his side. An amusing incident once occured in consequence. At the identical moment that his hand was raised a big, burly fellow, a member of his congregation, aroused from a nap (even his eloquence could not keep every man awake) and seeing the hand uplifted, the sleepy lout thought the benediction was being pronounced. He gathered himself up accordingly and marched toward the door, making a terrible racket with his squeaking boots, to the visible annoyance of the congregation. There was a charming twinkle of fun in the preacher's eye as he gravely said: "If others of the congregation desire to leave I will wait." A laugh went round the audience.

Beecher was extremely adept at reacting in an impromptu fashion to exigencies that arose from the audience. Other examples of his finesse in handling mass audiences are given in Chapter 3, "Beecher in Britain," and Chapter 5, "The Postlude."[7]

Concerning the canon of *memoria*, Beecher was not at pains to memorize his addresses. In fact, the pages of his lecture manuscripts, which were delivered numerous times, are worn on the edges from handling and are soiled from perspiration and dirt; however, his sermonic texts are clean because he usually used them only once. Lyman Abbott, who was intimately associated with Beecher, observed that the only axiom one could state about Beecher's use of a manuscript was there was no rule:

> He sometimes read manuscript; he sometimes spoke without manuscript; he sometimes alternated the two methods in one address; but he could not, or at least he did not, maintain at one and the same time an unbroken connection with the page upon the desk and with auditors in the seat.

Beecher prepared his speeches seriously, but was never bound by his preparation at the moment of utterance. As he warmed to his subject, he was often inspired to stray from his manuscript and to develop some image or to reach a rolling period for which he was famous. *Harper's Weekly* held that "his discourses are generally prepared, but as the tide of feeling rises it overbears the limits of his preparation." John Barrows noted that in his ebullience, Beecher often savaged English grammar: "He poured forth, in the height of his emotion, his rushing sentences with such velocity at times that, not infrequently, he was as careless of grammatical propriety and construction as was the Apostle Paul in the glow and impetuosity of his epistles." As a matter of fact, close observers of Beecher's craft commented that he was most persuasive when not tightly reined by his manuscript. Joseph Howard perceptively noted: "In fact it was often remarked that on 'set occasions' Mr. Beecher was not at his best. His Sunday morning sermons, delivered more especially to the membership of his church, were often the most eloquent, the most impressive, the most touching, the most effective."[8]

In other ancillary matters, Beecher strove to bring the pulpit to the public and the public to the pulpit. He eschewed clerical garb throughout his life. Instead, he wore black suits with the coat cut to the knees as was fashionable in the mid-nineteenth century; thus he achieved a blend of sacred secularism. He wore his hair down to his shoulders and was unbearded at a time when President Abraham Lincoln's beard become the vogue. He wore precious stones set in rings that dangled from his watch fob, and a seal-collared greatcoat in the winter time testified to his worldliness. Contemporary lithographs show him usually gesturing, sometimes with a handkerchief in hand to mop the perspiration. Water stood at the ready to quench his thirst. It all developed a public persona that was, curiously enough, more identified with Mr. Beecher than with the Rev. Beecher.

One assumes that the auditoriums in which Beecher spoke were satisfactory enough. But Beecher was atuned to the acoustics of his halls and on one occasion made a written complaint about one of them. He was on a lecture tour giving the Wastes and Burdens of Society. Unfortunately the place and date are unreadable, but one can read that the "town hall poorly constructed for voice."[9]

Conclusion

Beecher was a stump preacher and a pulpit speaker. The inversion of the terms in the subtitle of this book is purposeful. He brought the range of human emotions that one usually associates with stump political speaking–a vigorous platform presence, copious and expansive gestures, forceful bodily movement that ranged over the platform, an expressive and penetrating voice, and reasonably good eye-contact with the audience rather than with the manuscript–to the pulpit with amazing and documented success.

In comparison to other contemporary secular and sacred figures, he was not as polished as George William Curtis, the famous encomiast and after-dinner speaker, although Beecher was as adept at praise as he was at evoking laughter; not as syllogistically compelling as Charles Grandison Finney, the great revivalist preacher, although Beecher's persuasions marched ineluctably to their conclusions if not always by the shortest route; not a swordsman with words as Wendell Phillips who took delight in impaling his critics with his rapier-like rhetoric, although Beecher could fence verbally with any antagonistic auditor; not as adept at the classical canon of *elocutio* as Robert Green Ingersoll who fashioned elegant sentences with elevated, poetic-like language, although Beecher could entrance audiences with his verbal imagery that ran closer to the ground; nor did audiences sense the divine power and presence in Beecher that innervated Phillips Brooks's preaching at Trinity Church in Boston, although Beecher's forte seemed to be playing to the hilt Henry Ward Beecher. Yet, surpassing Beecher as they did in their particular area of excellence, none of his contemporaries bested Beecher in the amalgamation of individual oratorical attributes. Indeed, *Harper's Weekly* opined in 1858 that Beecher was "the only orator for whom all the halls and all the churches every where are too small."[10]

He stepped to the rostrum with the fervor of the evangelical preacher. He brought sacred Protestantism to secular politics. If his sermons were speeches, his addresses were homilies. The Old Testament oracle who called the chosen people back to God became a nineteenth-century prophet who challenged the citizenery to abandon slavery; the New Testament Gospel became the good news of progress in civic virtue and individual character; St. Paul the preacher became Paul the pleader for Victorian values; Christ crucified became the Union expiated and Beecher exonerated; and the Republican Party, bloated with avarice and graft, became in Beecher's hands lapsed heretics, accused of political apostasy. Indeed, the oratorical epitaph of Beecher's melding the sacred pulpit with the secular rostrum has already been written:

If the test of the oration is its perfection, whether of structure or of expression, other orators have surpassed Mr. Beecher; if the test of oratory is the power of the speaker to impart to his audience his life, to impress on them his conviction, animate them with his purpose, and direct their action to the accomplishment of his end, then Mr. Beecher was the greatest orator I have ever heard; and in my judgment, whether measured by the immediate or by the permament effects of his addresses, takes his place in the rank of the great orators of the world.

The following five chapters have as their avowed purpose the warranting of that effulgent but faithful assessment.[11]

1
The Prelude:
Beecher in Indiana

The Bailie, a British circular, captured something of the essence of the Rev. Henry Ward Beecher just before his death when it opined: "In some sense, as one might say, he has been running a race all his life with the rest of the world, and has backed himself down to his bottom dollar, to come out the winner." If Beecher emerged victorious in his race, and he did, then it is due to his oratorical prowess in the pulpit and to his persuasive accomplishments in secular podiums. Beecher began his race as a yearling at the Lawrenceburg, Indiana, First Presbyterian Church in 1837 and finished in the traces as a seasoned war horse at the Plymouth Church, Brooklyn, New York, at his death in 1887.[1]

BEECHER'S BACKGROUND

Beecher came from fine breeding of Yankee pioneer stock. He was born in Litchfield, Connecticut, on June 24, 1813. He was the eighth child of Lyman and Roxana Beecher. Lyman Beecher was a famous figure in religious circles and a preacher in the Calvinist mold. His profundity in theology was matched by his fecundity in children. Among the more famous were Edward Beecher, a pastor and editor; Charles Beecher, a minister and an accomplished musician and hymnist; George Beecher, a preacher who showed great promise until his fatal accident with a shotgun; and Harriet Beecher Stowe, the author of *Uncle Tom's Cabin*, which was arguably a more persuasive communication against slavery in the North and South than any of Henry's sermons or speeches.

The elder Beecher moved his family to Boston in 1826 to preach at the Hanover Street Church. He then took his famous family to Cincinnati, Ohio, in 1832 to preach in the Second Presbyterian Church and to assume the presidency of Lane Theological Seminary. Lane was a fledgling seminary that ascribed to the theology of the New Presbyterian School, which held that man had some responsibility for his salvation, as opposed to Princeton Theological Seminary, the dowager of Presbyterian seminaries and a stalwart citadel of the old school theology, which was strictly Calvinistic with regard to predestination and the total depravity of man. The clash with the conservatives that motivated Lyman to move west also affected Henry as a young preacher. In his own church at Lawrenceburg, Henry persuaded his congregation to break with the old school, Oxford, Ohio, presbytery and switch to the new school presbytery that was centered in Indianapolis, Indiana. These interminable heresy battles probably filled Henry with disgust and may suggest why, in his adult ministry, he was more concerned with man and his relationship to Jesus than picayune doctrines that contemporary ministers stressed and that Beecher eschewed. Indeed, Daniel Addison observed that these theological disputes tired Beecher: "they also gave him a surfeit of doctrinal controversy, and explain in some measure the absence of dogma from his preaching and teaching."[2]

As an aside that is yet germane to Henry Ward Beecher's career, Lane Seminary witnessed a student debate on slavery that was organized by Theodore Dwight Weld, who was to become an ardent abolitionist. The controversial debate angered the trustees of the seminary, many of whom had Southern sympathies and ties, and after the trustees failed to yield on their ban of abolitionist societies as well as debates on the subject of slavery (against president Lyman Beecher's wishes), Weld and the entire senior class withdrew from Lane and went to Oberlin College, where a department of religion was donated by Arthur Tappan, a wealthy abolitionist from New York City. William Lloyd Garrison, a leader in the abolitionist movement who had also been a sympathetic member of Lyman Beecher's congregation in Boston, panned Lane for its conservatism. The point is that abolitionism, which was certainly not most family's dinner table conversation in the early 1830's, impinged on the Beecher family at an early stage in Henry's youth. He would soon reenact a slavery debate of his own.[3]

ORATORICAL EDUCATION

Serious oratorical training began at Mount Pleasant Collegiate Institute, Amherst, Massachusetts, a preparatory school that Beecher attended from 1827 to 1830. Henry studied elocution under John E. Lovell, whom he credited "for laying the foundations for his success as a preacher and orator." Lovell, in his lectures and book entitled *United States Speaker*, published in 1833, stressed vocal production, delivery, and posture. In 1880, Beecher characterized the kind of training in delivery he received from Lovell:

> His system consisted in drill, or the thorough practice of
> inflexions by the voice, of gesture, posture, and articulation.
> Sometimes I was a whole hour practising my voice on a
> word–like "justice." I would take a posture, frequently at a
> mark chalked on the floor. Then we would go through all the
> gestures, exercising each movement of the arm and the
> throwing open the hand. All gestures except of precision go
> in curves, the arm rising from the side, coming to the front,
> turning to the left or right. I was drilled as to how far the arm
> should come forward, where it should start from, how far go

back, and under what circumstances these movements should be made. It was drill, drill, drill, until the motions almost became a second nature. Now I never know what movements I shall make. My gestures are natural, because this drill made them natural to me. The only method of acquiring an effective education is by practice, of not less than an hour a day, until the student has his voice and himself thoroughly subdued and trained to right exression.

Henry continued courses in public speaking at Amherst College, which he attended from 1830 to 1834. He learned there the classical elements of an oration: invention, disposition, and style. His father, a Yale graduate, reasoned that Henry would have smaller classes and more attention from the professors than at Yale. At Amherst, Henry was particularly active in the Athenian Society, the debating club. A watershed in his college experience was a debate the society sponsored on whether to colonize American slaves back to Africa. Although as president of the debating society Beecher did not participate in the actual debate, he nevertheless credited his preparation for and chairing of the debate with formulating his subsequent stand on the slavery issue: that emancipation was the only viable answer to the peculiar institution.[4]

Upon graduation from Amherst, Henry left the East and returned to Cincinnati where he naturally enrolled in Lane to complete a degree in theology. He finished his prescribed three years of study and graduated in 1834. While at the seminary, he wrote editorials for the *Cincinnati Journal*, an organ of the Presbyterian Church, that proclaimed his antislavery sentiments. Pragmatically, the job gave him forty dollars a month, and Henry always seemed to be in need of money. Having graduated a bachelor of divinity, Beecher cast about for a church in which to preach. He held two pastorates in Indiana, so this chapter is divided into those ministerial positions.

BEECHER AT LAWRENCEBURG, INDIANA

Beecher was called to the First Presbyterian Church of Lawerenceburg, which was about twenty miles downstream from Cincinnati on the Ohio River at the confluence of the Miami River, because of the efforts of a transplanted Yankee. She had heard Beecher preach as a supply minister in Covington, Kentucky, and decided he was to be the minister of her growing church. His first sermon was something of a disaster, but she and the congregation persisted, and he preached two other sermons that were better received. Accepting a call for $250 a year, with the American Home Missionary Society, based in New York City, to contribute another $150, Beecher moved to Lawrenceburg in June, 1837. He quickly married Eunice Bullard, of West Sutton, Massachusetts, whom he had met while at Amherst College. Their first home was two rooms over a livery stable.

At Lawrenceburg, Beecher developed a writing routine for creating his homilies that he used more or less throughout his pastorates. Although it is unclear whether he set aside particular hours or days for writing his sermons, it is clear that he spent considerable time in their composition. The idea was planted, particularly by Beecher's early biographers, and then cultivated by his later critics, that he spoke extemporaneously, which in the nineteenth century meant with little or no preparation from a few hastily assembled notes. He did not disabuse anyone of that perception. But at Lawrenceburg, he tucked his copious notes in a folio-sized Bible that always rested on the pulpit in order to hide from the congregation his practice of writing out his sermons. (These oversize Bibles had large print so that the text could be easily read while standing.)

The Beecher Family Papers contain his sermons, which often run to forty or fifty handwritten pages. His preparation was extensive. He did not write speech outlines or fragmented phrases, but complete sentences in the form of an essay. He often numbered his points, underlined important words and phrases, and also used his own stylized hand-with-a-pointed-finger to mark important thoughts. But these practices should not be construed as an oral outline or a lawyerlike brief because they were not. In addition to clarifying his own thoughts as he composed, the numbering system doubtless helped his congregation to retain something of the logical progression of his thoughts, his underlining cued him to stress orally his language, and his pointed finger probably reminded him to emphasize the thought with a gesture. The handwriting seems to have changed as he developed a sermon, suggesting either that he tired as he wrote at one sitting, or that he returned to the task a number of times throughout the week. Whatever the inference, the fact is that Beecher carefully wrote out his sermons.

Beecher's early handwritten sermons are relatively easy to read. The handwriting was clearly formed and the pages were neatly filled. As Beecher aged, especially from the 1860s until his death, his handwriting became increasingly difficult to decipher. He seemed to dash off sermons and speeches. He increasingly used sentence fragments and catch phrases as the pages waxed. This practice seemed to suffice for the later years in the Plymouth pulpit. But for his major secular addresses, even toward the end as the extant forty-to-fifty page handwritten speech texts attest, he left nothing to chance and wrote out his addresses.

As a rule, Beecher used the classical form of the Puritan sermon, but modified it for his own purposes. Since the time of the Protestant reformation when a premium was again placed on preaching, the sermon was divided by custom into the following sections: the statement of the Biblical text, the doctrine to be derived from the text, the reasons for the doctrine, and finally an application of the doctrine to the congregation. Throughout his life, Beecher based his sermons on a Biblical text. He vastly preferred the New Testament, Matthew, Luke, and Paul's epistles seemed to be his favorite books, to the Old Testament, the Psalms and Isaiah were fruitful books for him. But he was not at pains to burden his congregation with a dry disquisition on ancient history or arcane theology. Rather, he developed doctrines that were applied to contemporary issues or events. Thus, he made the Biblical text and doctrine verify Henry Ward Beecher's views. Hence, the reasons became Beecher's logical and emotional analysis of his thesis. In the section on reasons, he often numbered his points in a debaterlike one, two, and three, and he sometimes carried over this practice to the application.

Beecher's basic Biblical thesis centered on Jesus. Daniel Addison adduced that Beecher "was the exponent of the new theology,—not dogmatic theology, but a life theology. . . the Fatherhood of God and the Brotherhood of man." Holding that Christ was a model for Christians in all eras, Beecher preached Jesus as the good news of God's love for man; as a corollary, he preached that man must love his fellow man. He did not preach so much a contemplative thelogy as a social or active religion. Thus, his stands on antislavery, woman's suffrage, temperance, and political reform were a natural outgrowth of his preaching that God in Jesus wanted men and women to fulfill their Christ-like potential here rather than in the hereafter.[5]

Beecher eschewed practically all of the Calvinist thinking that plagued preachers and parishioners from the sixteenth century well into the nineteenth century. He discarded the doctrine of the total depravity of man, substituting instead man's ability, with God's help, to choose good over evil. Predestination, the notion that an individual was damned or saved from the foundation of the world by an avenging God who, like Jonathan Edward's deity, held man by a slender thread over the pit of hell, was simply discarded in favor of a loving relationship with God in which he invited sinners to repent of their sins of their own volition in order to be saved. Limited atonement, the doctrine that only a few persons would be saved, was expanded to the good news that all could be saved if they believed in God and lived Christ-like lives. Hence, the preacher's role, as conceived by Beecher, was exhortive rather than instructive, persuasive rather than didactic. Whereas Calvinist preachers stressed an intellectual religion that recognized man's utter evil in the sight of God, Beecher preached an emotional religion that emphasized God's love in Jesus. Thus, rather than trying to convince sinners of how base they were and how exalted God was, with an emphasis on what would happen to such persons in a fallen state of grace, Beecher conceived his listeners as basically upright folks. He addressed his audiences with the Gospel that Jesus could improve their lives, allow them to achieve goodness, build their characters, lead them from immorality to morality, and, ultimately, reward them with immortality. In short, hellfire was replaced with the warmth of Christian love, and damnation was displaced with salvation by a loving, not avenging, God. Beecher's theology, as he adjusted it especially after he landed in the Plymouth pulpit, was a clean break with his Calvinistic past and a precursor of modern religion and preaching as it exists, more or less, in the late twentieth century. It is little wonder that people flocked to hear him preach the good news about salvation rather than the bad news about damnation.

The Reverend Beecher was a surefooted writer. To be sure, there exist in the texts of his sermons numerous times when he crossed out sentences, paragraphs, or even entire pages. But on the whole, his sermons flowed remarkably well without many interlinear changes. He made emendations on his drafts, but these seemed to be of the second-thought variety in which he changed words or phrases just written. There are apparently no speeches or sermons that went through more than one draft.

Beecher probably thought aloud or deliberated as he might have spoken, and then wrote down the oral form of what he wanted to say. It is also reasonable to assume that he planned his delivery as he considered the language of his speech or sermon. That this likely occured can be inferred from his "Notebook of Sermons," which will be discussed presently, that he kept for two years at Lawrenceburg.

Beecher's Sunday-to-Sunday sermonic routine might be numbing by contemporary standards. He preached a morning service and an evening service for his first two years at Lawrenceburg, and often conducted prayer services throughout the week. Aside from the serious business of attending to one's soul, there was precious little entertainment, except for saloons that the pious did not frequent anyway, in the Indiana wilderness, so church services existed for more than religious functions. The question arises, "Did he always preach a new sermon?," and a qualified response is "Usually." The proof is in his "Notebook of Sermons." The first sermon he recorded in his journal at Lawrenceburg was one he preached on February 11, 1838. (Beecher numbered this sermon sixty, which implied that he had delivered, and kept a record of, sermons and speeches at Lawrenceburg and perhaps elsewhere. Given that he preached a morning and evening service since June, 1837, he could have spoken close to sixty times; unfortunately, the early pages that would supply these details are lost.) He maintained his journal for two years. He stopped his entries (or subsequent pages of the notebook have been lost) with sermon number one hundred and thirty-five. Thus, out of some seventy-five sermons, he acknowledged that he rewrote two: God's Sovereignty, July 15, 1838, and Righteousness, April 1, 1838. Either he made no attempt to hide the fact or he had a listener with a good memory, for he recorded that a parishioner commented that his revised sermon was better than the first one. From time to time, he also preached sermons in a series. On the one hand, he did not have to prepare a new homily for another Scriptural text, but on the other hand, he had to say considerably more about one passage in two or three consecutive sermons. Sometimes it is easier to achieve shallowness than depth. At Lawrenceburg, he preached a series on the Causes Which Hindered the Spread of Religion in the World Hitherto, April 8 and 22, 1838, and three sermons entitled Perfection, on the evening of May 13, for the morning of May 20, and on Tuesday evening, May 22, 1838. This practice was carried over to Plymouth Church where he preached the Life of Christ Without and Within, October 1 and 8, 1865, and in his series of sermons in the 1880s on evolution. The task of preaching at Lawrenceburg was made easier upon occasion, such as when his brother George preached a sermon or when his father, Lyman Beecher, came down from Cincinnati to officiate in the pulpit. On the other hand, Beecher recorded that on one Sunday he preached a morning and evening service at Lawrenceburg and then another evening service at Elizabethtown, Indiana, about seven horseback miles from Lawrenceburg. Beecher also used sermons that he had prepared for his Indianapolis congregation at Plymouth. He did not do this extensively, but a perusal of the "Chronology of Sermons and Speeches" will indicate that he did it often enough.[6]

Notebook of Sermons

That Beecher monitored his delivery in the pulpit is attested to by his observations in his "Notebook of Sermons." He was a very mature twenty-five-year-old young man. To be sure, he noted all kinds of trivial things in his journal. He observed when it hailed, snowed, or rained, and once claimed surprise when so many members attended church in a downpour. He recorded compliments for his sermonizing, such as "Heard it was liked," "that's a sermon which makes a fellow think," "grand," and "as good as could be." He was especially pleased when the local Methodist pulpit was empty because many Methodists flocked to hear him, which filled the church (May 20, 1838). He also preached a sermon "Aimed at excesses and absurdities during Methodist meeting," June 17, 1838, to counter the effect of an apparently successful revival service. For the evening service of March 4, 1838, he noted there were twenty-two teachers and eighty scholars in the Sunday School, and that he obtained an "excellent contribution $2.79." He occasionally confided some poignant moments in his journal. He preached a sermon entitled Humility, September 30, 1838, because it was "Caused by my own depressed state of feelings in consequences . . . of rumors getting abroad as to my pecuniary matters"; the next Sunday, October 7, 1838, found Beecher in no better straits: "As on Sunday before subject drawn from the need of it," and his sermon, On Trust in God, seemed to solace him if not the congregation. If Beecher assigned the anecdotal happening to his journal, he also made some telling observations about the effect of the classical canon of *actio*, or delivery, upon his listeners.[7]

Beecher blessed and blamed his deportment in the pulpit with equal fervor. For a sermon entitled Sin, February 18, 1838, he acknowledged "subject good, but how unequal delivery–good in spots." Two months later, on April 1, 1838 for Put On Whole Armor of God, he noted "Had liberty of speech, fulness of imagery & word & argument." I take this to mean that he was able to set aside his prepared notes and to speak with some freedom without relying on them verbatim. The following Sunday, April 8, 1830, on Causes Which Hindered Spread of Religion in the World Hitherto, he noted how he combined an effective delivery with persuasive content:

> Felt uncommon liberty of thought and possessed elevated, copious diction, ranged through the subject strongly and unflagging to the last–one of the few times in which I have risen to the last and closed with power. But I feel that probably I had shot over people's heads–But sermon was highly liked, and much spoken of.

For his trilogy of sermons on Perfection, he thought his last one on May 22, 1838, was marked with "great freedom and clearness of thought–good illustrations–best of these I think."

However effective Beecher might have been overall, he acknowledged on May 6, 1838, that he had "great liberty and in places great power, but attention flagged toward end and had to make effort to restore it." This entry testifies to Beecher's awareness of the congregation's needs, and how the orator, through a combination of artisty in language and force in delivery, can command a wavering audience's attention. That a forceful delivery evidently played a prominent role in his ability to move his congregation is warranted by an entry of November 4, 1838, for a sermon entitled Duties of Pastors and Duties of Churches: "I seldom enjoyed greater liberty of *mere speech* [his italics]: the reasoning was not as searching, nor matter as well wrought—but what there was better expressed than usual." Nine years later at Plymouth Church, Beecher also recorded the effect *actio* could have on an audience: "The reception is good; the execution very incomplete but thorough; but *effect* [his italics] by delivery very solemn. This is possible with a sermon extremely faulty in respect to its absolute rhetorical formulation to produce nevertheless strong effect."[8]

Beecher accepted a call to the Second Presbyterian Church in Indianapolis. Instructive of the same practice he repeated when accepting the summons to Plymouth Church, he played hard to get. He refused once, then again, and on the third application deferred to the advice of the Presbyterian synod that advised he take the position at Indianapolis. The pay was greater, Indianapolis was the state capital, and doubtless Eunice would feel more at home in a town of four thousand than in one of two thousand souls that called themselves Lawrenceburg, Indiana. He preached his last sermon at First Presbyterian on July 28, 1839.[9]

BEECHER AT INDIANAPOLIS, INDIANA

"My first recollection of Mr. Beecher," remembered a printer who later set the type for Beecher's *Lectures to Young Men*, to be discussed presently, "was when I was a journeyman printer. A man named King came to me and, with much enthusiasm, declared he had heard the greatest preacher he had ever listened to in his life—a young fellow who was preaching at the Marion County Seminary." Beecher, who was twenty-six years old, made an even greater impact on the state capital where he had a wider ambit.[10]

Beecher on Slavery

The Lawrenceburg, Indiana, and Cincinnati, Ohio, area was heavily influenced by the proximity of Kentucky, a slave state. Many of the early settlers in Indiana also had roots in Virginia. Consequently, one did not bother to mention the slavery question in the pulpit, and Beecher did not. Even when he moved to Indianapolis, there was no pressing reason to address the question, although Indianapolis was considerably less inclined to sympathize with Southern thinking. However, external events happening half a continent away would change all of that. The 1840s produced an exigency to which Beecher would respond rhetorically, but he was more the tortoise than the hare.

Before proceeding any further in this chapter, one must remember that Northerners, if one can conceive Northerners as speaking and believing as one, which clearly they did not, paid lipservice to antislavery arguments in the 1840s. It was downright unhealthy to be an abolitionist, a distinction that was often lost on mobs that did not appreciate the fine line between antislavery and abolitionism. Most whites did not care about black bondage, or if they did, found the institution of slavery repugnant; but that did not mean that they favored social equality with Negroes, nor did they envision political rights for blacks. Indeed, Senator Stephen Douglas exploited white racism effectively in his debates in Illinois with Abraham Lincoln in 1858 by linking the Republican party with black social and political equality, an identification Lincoln and party spokesman were at pains to disabuse at every opportunity.

The first recorded mention that Beecher made of slavery was merely in passing. Critics have overlooked this earliest reference. In preaching Paul as Model for Preaching New Truth on October 29, 1843, he alluded to the slavery question by briefly tracing its history with only these words: "arose the antislavery movement–which I need not say, is now hot enough." So hot in fact, that Beecher passed on without burning his fingers by delving deeper into the subject.[11]

In December of 1845, the republic of Texas became a state. Texas was the last slave state to be admitted to the Union. In the summer of 1846, David Wilmont, a Democratic Congressman from Pennsylvania, added the Wilmont Proviso to an appropriation bill. In the midst of this turmoil, Beecher preached on slavery. Texas, a slave state, was greeted cordially by Southerners who were interested in spreading the peculiar institution into new territories. Some Northerners, sensing the expansion of slavery rather than its eventual demise, advocated its restriction in the territories.

Although Beecher was at pains later in his life to pay himself considerable compliments on his oratorical stands against slavery, he came to his public position by the back door. In 1843, the synod of Indiana framed an open letter to the Presbyterian church, and especially to the brethren in the South, on slavery. This was accomplished, in part, by the help of Lyman Beecher. By 1845, the synod was emboldened enough to instruct all Presbyterian ministers in Indiana to devote a sermon to the evils of slavery; the synod possessed less power in the South, so it petitioned the General Assembly of the Presbyterian Church to "take firm and decided action against slaveholding." It was agitation of this sort that motivated Senator John C. Calhoun of South Carolina, in his swan song before the U.S. Senate on March 4, 1850, to observe the divisiveness of the slavery question:

> The cords that bind the States together are not only many, but various in character. Some are spiritual or ecclesiastical; some political; others social. . . . The strongest of those of a spiritual and ecclesiastical nature, consisted in the unity of the great religious demoninations, all of which originally embraced the Union. . . . [B]ut powerful as they were, they have not been able to resist the explosive effect of slavery agitation. The first of these cords which snapped, under its explosive force, was that of the powerful Methodist Episcopal Church. . . .That of

the Presbyterian is not entirely snapped, but some of its strands have given way.[12]

Beecher finally preached three sermons on slavery in May of 1846. Paxton Hibben, the most faultfinding of Beecher's critics, believed that the minister broached the subject only after forced to do so by the synod and by an unsuccessful exchange with a distiller, who was a member of Beecher's congregation and with whom Beecher came off the loser in a series of accusations and defenses over whether a distiller could be a Christian; the whiskey man won the exchange when he charged that Beecher would rather tilt against alcohol, which was safe, than slavery, which was more controversial.[13]

The first sermon was structured to distinguish the North from the South. According to Beecher, the basic public position in the South was not to talk about slavery; although some Southerners did not favor the institution, they bowed to public pressure not to discuss it, and of course the planters generally favored the peculiar institution. The second sermon attacked the Scriptural basis of slavery upon which the South rested its case. He basically argued that Old Testament slavery differed from Southern slavery because the slave was held in perpetual bondage and that masters mistreated their slaves. Slaves in the South were more akin to Roman slaves than Old Testament slaves who were more like servants. His third sermon was a revision of the New Testament on slavery in which he argued that the whole Bible, but especially the Gospel, argued against human slavery. Indicative of the care with which Beecher approached the problem of slavery in his introduction is how he attempted to spike any negative feedback or reaction from the congregation. Also note how Beecher implied that he was forced to deliver the sermon, rather than its pressing need impelling him to deliver it:

> I approach the subject appointed for discussion today, not with any fear of excitement; for these few words be unworthy of me, as the expectation of it would be of you. If a few, upon either side, allow their feelings to grow something too warm, the body of their discontented men should on that very account be it less excitable. Good feeling and wise judgment have so far regained their sway, that even slavery may be openly discussed, without any prospect of persecution or martyrdom.
>
> But there is yet life in the minds of the community, a sensitivity to the subject which makes it seem, to many, not wise to introduce it into the Pulpit.
>
> In respect to revealed truth, in its imperative forms, I'd not suppose that we have a discretionary time whether to preach or to wait for time's lessons.

The operative rhetorical device that he used in the introduction is apophasis. Apophasis, sometimes called affirmation by denial, is the technique whereby the orator alludes to something while disclaiming any intention to mention it, as in "I will not refer to his sin of drunkenness." Thus, Beecher cleverly announced he did not fear excitement from discussing the question, which would have the effect of calming the congregation, yet gave himself away because he must have thought about the fear in the first place. Along this line, it was a bit dramatic to suggest one could talk about slavery without fear "of persecution or martyrdom," which, again, must have been on his mind as he composed the sermon. And the business about divine truth was a convenient cloak to cover himself from criticism about broaching the subject: after all, God and the synod had demanded that he speak.[14]

Beecher played it safe. He attacked slavery, which most Hoosiers found repulsive, and Southerners, who were not members of his congregation. He wisely curried favor with moderates in his church by maligning the abolitionists, who were also not members of the Second Presbyterian Church. Identifying with the middle road, Beecher scored the Garrisonian abolitionists: "The language of rebuke, of invective, the exaggerated figures of impassioned rhetoric, irony, and above all scorching denunciation, are the very worst possible instruments of affecting a reformation." What did Beecher advocate? Prayer to God to help Southerners solve their problem was the answer.[15]

As problem-solution speeches, these sermons were a safe gambit. Most agreed that slavery was a problem, even reasonable individuals in the South admitted as much, but Beecher had no viable solution. (At least the abolitionists had logic on their side: immediate emancipation, since African colonization was impossible, was the only efficacious solution to the problem.) Clifford Clark kindly evaluated Beecher's rhetoric thusly: "These sermons were well received because they provided Beecher's congregation with a convenient way of rationalizing the guilt that was aroused in those who thought that slavery was wrong, but did not want to have free blacks around"; William McLoughlin less kindly, but nevertheless quite accurately, assayed Beecher's position: "But when one analyzes the solutions Beecher offered for this horrendous crime against man and God, it becomes clear that most of his rhetoric on the score of human rights was mere bombast, the cheapest form of hypocrisy."[16]

Lectures to Young Men

Although slavery was as close as Kentucky, there were other sins readily at hand in Indianapolis that ran closer to the ground. Tilting against all the moral imperfections one could find in a capital city, Beecher carved a strong regional reputation for himself with a series of lectures he delivered in 1842 that were subsequently published in 1843. The lectures warmed to the fires of hell as they progressively descended the poet Dante's path into the inferno:

Lecture I: Industry and Idleness
Lecture II: Twelve Causes of Dishonesty
Lecture III: Six Warnings
Lecture IV: The Portrait Gallery
Lecture V: Gamblers and Gambling

Lecture VI: The Strange Woman
Lecture VII: Popular Amusements

Indeed, in the preface to the second edition, he observed that "within one year past an edition of three thousand copies of these Lectures has been distributed through the West, and it has been generally noticed in the papers, and I have never heard objections from any quarter, that the canvas had been too strongly colored." His stroke and pigmentation for two of the lectures warrants close scrutiny.[17]

The lecture entitled "Six Warnings" was about gaining riches. Beecher was careful. He did not score young men for wanting to attain riches; rather, he gave them some pious cautions about the problems that might accrue if one pursued lucre. Thus, he did not alienate listeners whose parents were well to do or those who individually wished to aspire to wealth, but neither did he praise the attainment of money that could antagonize those who did not have it or were disinclined to seek it.

The lecture contained six doctrines or warnings that were based on Psalms 112:2-3 and Jeremiah 17:11. His first doctrine was, along with Communism, the tried-and-true opiate of the masses: riches do not buy happiness. How comforting it must have been to the poor when Beecher opined: "There is often in the hut more dignity than in the palace; more satisfaction in the poor man's scanty fare than in the rich man's satiety." (Beecher always sought a larger home, owing, in part, to his wife's continual complaints, and finally lived in Brooklyn in a three story house on a corner lot.) Second, he inveighed against the haste with which young men sought wealth, but cleverly not against wealth itself: "Almost every evil which environs the path to wealth, springs from that criminal haste which substitutes adroitness for industry, and trick for toil." Third, he warned "against COVETOUSNESS," holding that it bred misery:

> The sight of houses better than our own, of dress beyond our
> means, of jewels costlier than we may wear, of stately equipage,
> of rare curiosities beyond our reach, these hatch the viper
> brood of covetous thoughts; vexing the poor–who would be rich;
> tormenting the rich–who would be richer.

(At his death, Beecher's estate consisted of a considerable jewel collection, costly books, and an art accumulation of some breadth and depth.) Fourth, he admonished against selfishness. He quoted a Biblical proof text that Archbishop Thomas Cranmer, a Protestant, used at his burning at the stake during the Catholic Counter-Reformation in England under Queen Mary in 1556. Not thrusting his hand that had offended into the fire, as Cranmer did, Beecher safely quoted St. James, 5:2-3: "Your riches are corrupted, and your garments are moth-eaten. Your gold and silver is cankered; and the rust of them shall be a witness against you, and shall eat your flesh as it were fire." Fifth, he cautioned against dishonest men, which, Beecher avowed, "every village has such, and they swarm in cities."[18]

The sixth sin was violent extortion. Beecher bellicosely battled three baleful "BEHEMOTHS." He characterized a slave trader as an "incarnate fiend who navigates the ocean to traffic in human misery and freight with the groans and tears of agony." The second bogy was "sensual habit," which he would fully describe in the next lecture. The third behemoth was a tame beast. Beecher waded into the "smugglers and swindlers" who were Indian traders. "I would rather," Beecher exclaimed, "inherit the bowels of Vesuvius, or make my bed in Etna [notice how his allusion to two volcanoes conjured images of fire and brimstone], than own those estates which have been scalped off from human beings as the hunter strips a beaver of its fur."[19]

The conclusion served as the application. There was solace for the poor but hope for the rich:

> While I do not discourage your search for wealth, I warn you that it is not a cruise upon level seas, and under bland skies. . . . You seek a land pleasant to the sight, but dangerous to the feet. . . . You may be rich and be pure; but it will cost you a struggle. You may be rich and go to heaven; but ten, doubtless, will sink beneath their riches, where one breaks through them to heaven.[20]

If uttering warnings from the pulpit about sanitized sins was accepted practice in the 1840s, talking about "The Strange Woman" was not. The strange woman was a euphemism for the prostitute and the subject was prostitution. Frequenters of bars and bawdyhouses might discuss the oldest profession in the world, but not preachers in the pulpit. It was an manifestation of Beecher's fortitude to broach the subject in church, and a testament to his rhetorical acumen in successfully accomplishing the delicate task.

"The Strange Woman" runs to twenty-six pages. The beginning accounts for four pages, and if one adds four pages that Beecher took to develop his last point in the opening, then the whole introduction comprises eight pages, or almost a third of the entire lecture. This allocation of rhetorical resources was purposeful.

Beecher was at pains to develop four reasons why the preacher should discuss prostitution. Averring that almost every chapter of the Bible alludes to licentiousness, he allowed that "I am entirely aware of the delicacy of introducing this subject into the pulpit." Dealing with the first possible objection that could reside in his listeners minds, that he could contaminate "unaffected purity" by discussing the strange woman, he countercharged: "To any such, who have half-wished that I might not speak, I say:–Nor would I, did I not know that purity will suffer more by the silence of shame, than by the honest voice of truth." Second, preempting the incipient protest that he would use plain language to discuss the subject, he created a false but convincing dichotomy. He thanked God that the English language had "plain words enough to say plain things," and then excoriated "French–the dialect of refined sensualism and of licentious literature." Thus, he played on the audience's native patriotism and dislike for the French, who would "speak by *innuendo*–which is the devil's language." Given the choice between the French or English manner of expression, he was assured of a hearing.[21]

His third objection was masterfully phrased. Putting any accuser on the immediate defensive who would attack him, Beecher inoculated against "vile men . . . when the pulpit disturbs them. . . . How sensitive some men to a church bell! they are high priests of revivals at a horce-race, a theatre, or a liquor-supper; but a religious revival pains their sober minds." Against such detractors, Beecher exclaimed:

> I expect such men's reproaches. I know the reasons of them. I am not to be turned by them, not one hair's breadth, if they rise to double their present volume, until I have hunted home the wolf to his lair, and ripped off his brindled hide in his very den!

Thus cast, anyone who attacked Beecher for delivering this sermon would be identified as indecent, as vile, as reproachful, and no one would run the risk of being perceived in that fashion by the community. Hence, Beecher effectively turned the tables on his opponents before they could utter a reproach. He continued in that vein in his fourth point by allowing that delicacy upon the subject was a false modesty. He then launched into four pages of literary criticism to warrant his claim that "The most dangerous writers in the English language are those whose artful insinuation and mischievous polish reflect upon the mind the image of impurity, without preventing the impurity itself." Paxton Hibben conceived the lecture on the strange woman to be "devoted largely to literary criticism." However, four pages of a twenty-six page lecture is not "devoted largely," and Hibben misanalyzed the rhetorical function of the so-called literary criticism. In reality, it reinforced his fourth introductory point that it was better to discuss things in plain language than artful language that debased, which in turn buttressed his thesis that it was better to discuss prostitution than not at all. Thus assured of the propriety of considering prostitution from the pulpit, Beecher did not disappoint his listeners in lurid descriptions of licentious-ness.[22]

Beecher portrayed the strange woman with five mainheads. Such women forgot the covenant with God; they were an "ensnaring danger of Beauty"; they had "WILES" that were subdivided into those of speech, love, and beguilements; those that consorted with a prostitute were advised "NONE THAT GO UNTO HER RETURN AGAIN"; and fifth, Beecher led the innocent on a tour of the strange woman's house.[23]

"That part of the garden which borders the highway of innocence is carefully planted. There is not a poison-weed, nor thorn, nor thistle there. Ten thousand flowers bloom, and waft a thousand odors" Beecher warned his young audience. He then divided the strange woman's house into five wards: "Pleasure, Satiety, Discovery, Disease, and Death." As for pleasure, he titillated his audience with the interior of a house of ill-repute. "Elastic velvet, glossy silks, burnished satin, crimson drapery, plushy carpets"–one assumes Beecher had this information second-hand–awaited the unsuspecting patron, the reverend assured his audience. But the wages of sin is death, and Beecher outdid himself in a vivid description of death by syphilis and gonorrhea at a time when there was no penicillin:

Here a shuddering wretch is clawing at his breast, to tear away
that worm which gnaws his heart. By him is another, whose
limbs are dropping from his ghastly trunk. . . . Nature, long
trespassed on and abused, at length casts down the wretch;
searches every vein, makes a road of every nerve for the
scorching feet of pain to travel on, pulls at every muscle, breaks
in the breast, builds fires in the brain, eats out the skin, and
casts living coals of torment on the heart. . . . Look upon her
fourth Ward–its vomited blood, its sores and fiery blotches, its
prurient sweat, its dissolving ichor, and rotten bones! Stop,
young man![24]

To make certain the young man heeded his advice, Beecher ended
with an application that was developed in five points. The righteous would
(1) eschew "indulging a morbid imagination"; (2) cease consorting with "evil
companions"; (3) not buy "EVIL BOOKS and EVIL PICTURES"; (4) not
imitate evil in high places; and (5) fight to overcome a "DEPRAVED
HEART." Unlike Jonathan Edwards who offered little hope for the damned,
Beecher preached the good news of Jesus's salvation: "If thou hast sinned,
one look, one touch, shall cleanse thee whilst thou art worshipping, and thou
shalt rise up healed." And now the final liturgical irony, this lecture was
preached on Christmas Eve, 1842.[25]

Conclusion

"The same characteristic of thought and activity are to be seen"
Addison adduced in comparing the Indiana period with the Brooklyn years,
"in the earlier period as in the later one. The preaching was vital and drove
the people to hear him; he dealt with public questions as well as Scriptural
ones."[26]

At age thirty-four, Beecher had achieved some notable oratorical
laurels. He had increased the membership of the First Presbyterian Church
at Lawrenceburg, had gained new members for the Second Presbyterian
Church at Indianapolis, and had overseen the building of a new edifice in
the capital city. This allowed him to speak from a desk on a low platform
in the new church on Market and Circle streets. His successful ministry was
due as much to his dynamism in the pulpit as it was to the theology he
preached. His rhetorical handling of a delicate yet saleable speech on sex
and other assorted sins of the times produced a book of lectures–they were
really homilies–that would precurse his later practice of publishing his
Plymouth sermons. Although coming better late than never to the subject
of slavery in the pulpit, he was liberal enough to satisfy everyone but the
radicals and conservative enough to please everyone but the slavers. Feeling
constrained by the narrow stage in Indianapolis, and no doubt motivated by
his wife who neither accepted the Hoosiers nor was accepted by them
because of her Eastern proclivities, Beecher sought a wider ambit for his
activities and a greater audience for his oratory.[27]

2
Beecher Militant at Plymouth

"His church was crowded," Joseph Howard remembered, "and it was interesting to see hundreds and hundreds of young men, solid rows of young men from New York, strangers from the hotels, clerks from the stores of the great city, regular attendants upon Mr. Beecher's ministrations." On a normal Sunday at Plymouth Church, Beecher delivered sermons to his congregation as other nineteenth-century ministers did, the one exception being that Beecher's house was increasingly filled to capacity, especially toward the later decade of the 1850s. This chapter leaves aside those typical homilies and investigates the atypical but famous rhetoric that invigorated and sustained Beecher's national reputation.[1]

Yet, before doing so, it might be wise to at least sound some of the themes that Beecher preached on the Sabbath. It was, after all, his Sunday-to-Sunday sermonic successes that prepared him for the public platform. Two contemporary views, the one scholarly, the other popular, captured something of Beecher's theology.

The Rev. Newell Dwight Hillis surveyed Beecher's homilies and determined that four theological doctrines informed his sermons. First, Beecher preached that the deity was a "suffering God." Juxtaposed to the Calvinist belief that God was aloof from sinful mankind and would just as soon brush man into hell as not, Beecher preached that it was "impossible for any Christian man to believe that God from his throne in the sky beheld this pilgrim host, with any save emotions of sympathy and sorrow and suffering, and medicinal love." The appeal of that doctrine is immediately apparent to even the most hardened reprobate. Second, Beecher held an unconventional view of Jesus in relationship to the Christian idea of the Trinity. Without delving deeply into a complicated doctrine, Beecher held a Sabellian view of God. That is, Jesus did not have a human intellect or will but was indeed God in the form of a man. Jesus was not so much the Son of God as he was God. While on earth, God experienced human emotions; thus, God could empathize with man. Third, Beecher believed in the sanctity of each individual. As one had, through Jesus Christ, a personal relationship with God, so must one have respect for others of God's creation. Fourth, Beecher preached the immortality of the soul. Implicit in this doctrine was man's ability, through divine help, to affect his own salvation, or, as Hillis observed, "to convince the man of his sin, to convert him from his sin and develop in him the faith of God and the love of Christ, and build up in him a character after Christ's divine pattern."[2]

At the other end of the spectrum at the popular side, *The Practical Christian* assayed the reverend's Gospel in 1886:

> During many years, the sermons of this wonderful man have been read by thousands with eager delight, who have received thereby consolation and comfort, and have found true Salvation for their souls, not in a mysterious and incomprehensible way, but in a way which has brought them closer into communion with God as revealed in our Lord Jesus Christ, in a way which has made them brighter, happier, and more useful workers in daily life, and has given them full assurance of Salvation in the world to come. . . . A great deal of talk has lately been indulged in respecting the orthodoxy of this distinguished American Divine, and some seem to doubt that he is sound and spiritual. If common sense, talk clear and comprehensive arguments, truths plainly described, the removal of cobwebs from the eyes of the people, the condemnation of crotchets and artificial mysteries set us by some puny, narrow chested, dyspeptic, bigoted Pharisee, the exchange of a gloomy religion for a cheerful and natural Christianity, preaching made more simple and natural, if this means that Henry Ward Beecher is unorthodox, then the longer he remains so the better for those who listen to him and follow his teachings.[3]

Beecher on Slavery

The Rev. Beecher's greatness in oratory was grounded in his ability to make sermons speeches and speeches sermons. John Barrows set the stage for Beecher's rhetoric on the peculiar institution when he wrote:

> There is no doubt that the oratorical achievements of Henry Ward Beecher are among the most splendid in the history of the century. His oratorical genius was shown in the pulpit, on the platform, before popular assemblies stirred with political excitement, in the presence of mobs, in the hall of debate, and in familiar conversation.

In his first sermon at Plymouth Church, delivered on October 17, 1847, Beecher outlined the rationale for his rhetorical pulpit. He avowed that the minister should treat topics of trade, morals, and politics.[4]

Sometime in the 1850s, Beecher composed a sermon on slavery that was indicative of his views on the subject. In a kind of classical *partitio*, or division of the speech, he discussed the agitation on slavery. He claimed it was not from business, or a conflict of political ideas, or from religion, nor a social conflict, but it was "*the radical diversity* of the ideas *North and South upon Labor!* [Beecher's emphasis]." Having isolated the problem with Southern slavery, Beecher then discussed three logical consequences. First, he complained about the treatment of slaves in emotional language that stirred the congregation's sympathies. Second, he drew a stark dichotomy between the North and South: "Theory of freedom and slaves are utterly *irreconcilable.* A community cannot long hold both. You cannot believe in despotism in our distinction and in democracy in the other [Beecher's emphasis]." Since this speech is undated, it is difficult to determine a tantalizing possibility. In comparison to Abraham Lincoln's famous "House Divided" speech that he delivered in Springfield, Illinois, June 16, 1858, upon accepting the Republican nomination for the U. S. Senate, both Beecher and Lincoln perceived the same problem–that a house divided against itself could not stand–and that either freedom or slavery must eventually triumph. Whether one orator "borrowed" from the other is unknown. Rather, both orators perceived a Southern conspiracy to make the Union slave, and both urged that the North must react, somehow, to remain free. Third, Beecher used theological language to argue that the South had enacted "moral apostasy." This general approach to the problem was also developed in Beecher's Conflict of Northern and Southern Theories of Man and Society, January 14, 1855.[5]

The Kansas-Nebraska Act, which was supposed to satisfy everyone on both sides of the Mason-Dixon line by admitting Kansas as a slave state and Nebraska as free, was one of the most regrettable acts ever passed by the U. S. Congress. Rather than working as planned by Senator Stephen Douglas, its author and sponsor, it succeeded in accomplishing the exact opposite of his intentions. To distill a complicated story, in order to effect "squatter sovereignty," Southerners rushed to Kansas with their slaves to make it slave, and Northerners rushed to make it free. Bloodshed and violence followed. Northern churches, moving beyond the rhetorical stage, sent immigrants to Kansas armed with Bibles and rifles. Beecher successfully raised enough money at Plymouth Church to send twenty-five rifles and as many Bibles to "Bloody Kansas." Consequently, Plymouth Church was given the sobriquet of the "Church of the Holy Rifles" and the rifles were termed "Beecher's Bibles." But these things rather paled in significance when Beecher crossed the Rubicon in 1856.[6]

The Sumner Protest Speech

Senator Charles Sumner of Massachusetts, a Republican, intending to deliver a philippic against the pro-slavery forces, succeeded all too well in exposing the slave power. He is chiefly remembered today more for the effect of his speech entitled the Crime Against Kansas, May 19-20, 1856, than for the address itself. His speech was noted for the invective that the Athenian orator Isocrates hurled against Philip of Macedonia two millennia earlier. Preston Brooks, a nephew of Senator Andrew Butler of South Carolina, whom Sumner characterized as a Don Quixote who paid vows to his mistress of slavery, was less adept in verbal sparing than Sumner, so he decided to repay Sumner in the only way he knew. On the twenty-second of May, Brooks, a member of the House of Representatives from South Carolina, walked into the Senate chamber and commenced clubbing Sumner at his desk until the senator fell unconscious to the floor. Preston Brooks was expelled from the House but was promptly returned to his seat by the voters of South Carolina. Sumner became a Northern martyr.

Sensing a windfall from the sorry episode, antislavery forces in New York held a protest meeting at the Broadway Tabernacle on May 30, 1856. Taking the Fulton ferry the other way in company with a friend and the friend's young son, Beecher went to Manhattan to listen to the addresses. Several noted speakers took the rostrum and delivered also-ran speeches. The meeting was adjourned when somebody spotted Beecher, the crowd cried for Beecher, and he gave a speech. That much, but no more, can be found in all of the histories on Beecher, save one.

Joseph Howard has given an intriguing account of how Beecher came to deliver the speech. His account, which I find compelling, raises the tantalizing possibility that Beecher was perhaps more an active agent in securing the platform than has been hitherto advanced. And if not, it certainly suggests that public relations people were alive and well in the nineteenth century. Howard recounted how Beecher was called to the platform:

> A moment or two prior to the adjournment Mr. Beecher's young friend whispered to one of the reporters that Beecher was there, and it would be a good idea to call him out. They arranged that the boy should go to the other side of the hall and call "Beecher," which call should be echoed by the reporter, and possibly Mr. Beecher might be compelled to speak.
>
> With considerable difficulty the boy performed his part of the programme, which was duly followed out by the reporter (Edward Underhill). The cry was taken up by several in the audience, and gradually by others, when Mr. Evarts advanced to the front of the platform and said, "It would afford us great pleasure, doubtless, to hear from the reverend gentlemen from Brooklyn, but as he is lecturing in Philadelphia to-night, that pleasure must necessarily be postponed."
>
> At this a shrill voice from the boy aforesaid, on the other side the hall shouted out: "No, he isn't in Philadelphia, either; there he is behind the pillar. Beecher! Beecher!"
>
> That settled it.

That Beecher delivered his speech at the close of the meeting is historical fact. Since none of his biographers or critics gave a reason why or how he was summoned to speak when he was not originally on the program, Howard's account is compelling.[7]

Although there was probably preconcert in enticing Beecher to the platform, the nature of the speech suggests that Beecher was unaware of the behind-the-scenes machinations of his friends, and that the speech was delivered impromptu.   There are certain characteristics of impromptu addresses that are present in Beecher's speech. First, there is no discernible structure in the speech. Called to speak at such short notice, he did not have time to compose an introduction, nor divide the body of the speech into mainheads, nor conclude the speech. Second, impromptu speeches tend to be repetitive. Grasping for thoughts, the speaker often reiterates the same points in the same or similar language.   For instance, in his opening two sentences, Beecher referred to "Divine Providence" or "Providence" three times and used "just this" three times; in his conclusion, which is termed a "conclusion" only because it was the end of the speech, he repeated the word "stealthily" twice in the same sentence, and "stormy" three times in the last sentence.   Although the speech was doubtless impromptu, Beecher nevertheless managed to deliver a short masterpiece.

The speech was epideictic. Aristotle characterized the genre: "The ceremonial oratory of display either praises or censures somebody . . . [is] concerned with the present . . . [and proves] honour or the reverse"; the objects of the genre are "Virtue and Vice, the Noble and the Base." Beecher achieved the desired rhetorical effect in his impromptu address by fusing the disparate elements of epideictic oratory in one address.   When praising Sumner's virtues, he implicitly blamed by juxtaposition Brooks's vices, and when excoriating Brooks's baseness, he subtly lauded by comparison Sumner's noble qualities.[8]

Beecher wasted no words in deploying the dichotomy.   Not yet dignifying Brooks by name, Beecher alluded to him as an "assassin" who did his work in a "cowardly way." On the other hand, Sumner was dignified by name and described as "a scholar by instinct" who did not covet the senatorial office "but accepted it reluctantly." While in office, he was the "purest," "most courteous," and "observed the rules of decorum." The audience could easily infer Brooks possessed none of these praiseworthy attributes.   In fact, Beecher averred "it was because he was so mild that he was struck down by the felon blow," which compounded Brooks's atrocity.

To heighten Brooks's perfidy, Beecher rehearsed communal values that Brooks spurned. No one "so debased" or "so lost to manly instinct," would gainsay the adage that one should not "strike a man when he was down." Since Brooks did exactly that, the reverend asked his audience to affirm that the congressman was debased, unmanly, and violated Northern community norms.

That Brooks breached social rules was further exacerbated by Beecher's portraying Sumner as a hapless victim. Allowing that the senator was nearsighted, Beecher sketched how Sumner was "so bowed over his desk that to strike him would be as mean as to strike a woman." Then Beecher turned the tables on a well known Southern value.   "Oh!" Beecher sarcastically exclaimed, "the chivalry of the man Brooks, of South Carolina!" And what were the blameworthy attributes of that chivalry?   It was the pseudochivalry of one who would creep into the "sleeping room of a woman" and "bludgeon" her; it was the quasi-chivalry of one who would "brain" a "blind man"–so much for Southern chivalry.

Then Beecher stumbled upon one of his inspired verbal images. The language itself hints that the metaphor came to him as he spoke: "There he sat, the scholarly Senator, unarmed, with anything save the pen. Ah! there you have it! The symbol of the North is the pen. The symbol of the South is the bludgeon. [Tremendous applause.]" Fleshing out the metaphor, Beecher allowed that in mythology Hercules had used a club, but that he "never stole upon unarmed men when they had not thought of his approach." "Scripture too," the pastor reminded his secular audience, "has its hero of the club . . . it was Cain. Brooks took his cane and faithfully renewed the wretched deed of his prototype." The audience would have had little difficulty in identifying Senator Sumner as the Biblical Abel, who was slain by his brother Cain.

Having thoroughly juxtaposed the noble to the base, virtue with vice, Beecher took the next logical step in his final words to draw the larger proportion between Brooks and Sumner to the South and the North. Averring that this "outrage is but a pimple on the surface," Beecher claimed the disease "infects the whole body." As Brooks tried to murder Sumner, so the slave conspiracy tried "to murder Kansas," tried to ruin "free Kansas," to which the audience applauded.

As is characteristic of epideictic oratory, Beecher made no direct call for action as one might make in a deliberative setting. But Aristotle did allow that in praising or blaming, one might make "guesses at the future," which Beecher did by paraphrasing the Bible: "Madmen, thus far you have gone, you shall go no farther."[9]

Beecher and the Impending Crisis

The Rev. Beecher was not so much a fomenter of the sectional crisis as a commentator on it. He did not shape events as much as he reacted to them. Although he had nothing to do with the leading of a slave revolt by John Brown, who was captured by federal troops under the command of Robert E. Lee at Harper's Ferry, Virginia (now in West Virginia), Southerners were aghast at Brown's fiasco: it reinforced their fears about slave uprisings that were fomented by Northern abolitionists and allowed the fire-eaters to reply "I told you so." When John Brown was in prison awaiting trial, Beecher delivered a sermon that captured something of Northern sentiment. "Let no man pray," Beecher advised his Plymouth congregation on October 30, 1859, "that Brown be spared. Let Virginia make him a martyr. Now, he has only blundered. His soul was noble; his work miserable. But a chord and a gibbet would redeem all that and round up Brown's failure with a heroic success."[10]

The irony of the Brown affair was that Virginia Governor Henry Wise was advised to commute Brown's death sentence to life imprisonment on the ground that Brown alive would soon be forgotten but Brown dead would be a Northern martyr. Indeed, as he indicated in his sermon, Beecher understood all too well the rhetorical use to which Brown's ignoble actions could be applied. But following the letter of the law, Wise allowed Brown to be executed. After the Civil War began, on the way to the battle front

Union soldiers sang "John Brown's Body Lies A'Moldering in the Grave."

Beecher continued to harp on the institution of slavery. On January 4, 1861, he preached a Plymouth sermon entitled Our Blameworthiness. He used guilt to intensify his rhetoric: "We live on his [the slave's] labor. I confess I see no way to escape a part of the responsibility for slavery. I feel guilty in part for the system." Later he exclaimed: "It is an astounding sin! It is an unparalleled greed!" Realizing that Southern preachers justified slavery on Biblical grounds, Beecher took a sideswipe at them when he contended "Every abomination of earth has been at one time or another justified from the Bible." However, Beecher did not refute the claim that the Bible recognized and condoned slavery, a point Southerners in and out of the pulpit never failed to make.[11]

In the Battle Set in Array, delivered on April 14, 1861, during the siege of Fort Sumter, Beecher told his congregation that the war was justified. "I hold that it is ten thousand times better to have war than to have slavery," the minister assured his listeners. He developed his sermon around five mainheads: the war would "cleanse convictions," thus relieving the guilt of Northerners for cooperating with the South in slavery; it would draw the lines between the two societies; the North should not "measure costs" as it battled the South; there would be a peace on strong foundations of God; and Northerners should not seek "vengeance" or be "savage."[12]

Lest one gain the perception that Beecher was ahead of his times on the racial question, the following excerpts from some of his major sermons during this critical period will correct any misunderstanding. Northerners as a class found the institution of slavery despicable but they did not necessarily like black people. As an unwitting proponent of nineteenth-century white prejudice against blacks, Beecher was at pains to assure his congregation, and the national audience that read his sermons, that slaves were not the social equal of whites. In a sermon entitled Energy of Administration Demanded, delivered in June 1861, against the plodding of the Lincoln administration in bringing the war to a quick and successful close, Beecher assured his congregation that blacks would not flock to the North at the end of the war because the "Climate is against it." In the Churches Duty to Slavery, January 12, 1862, he assured his Plymouth listeners that they did not have to fear political equality with blacks: "Does he demand equality? No. We do not give that to our own white citizens." And in the Beginning of Freedom, delivered on March 9, 1862, after Lincoln announced the preliminary Emancipation Proclamation, Beecher stressed white liberty over black slavery: "Our choice is between republican liberty and slavery. You must have one or the other. You cannot have both. And the North has made up its mind that it is going to have republican liberty."[13]

Beecher and Slave Auctions

However important Beecher's sermons were in preparing and, when the war came, in steeling his listening and reading audiences for the impending crisis, he was more remembered for the pulpit theatrics on a grand scale that only Henry Ward Beecher could enact.

Somehow, Beecher hit upon the scheme of holding a slave auction in Plymouth Church. The idea of bringing flesh-and-blood slaves to Plymouth and conducting a sale, both of which most Northerners had never seen, brought the peculiar institution to Brooklyn's doorstep in an emotionally laden rhetorical situation that words alone could never accomplish. On June 1, 1856, Beecher preached from Luke 10:27 about loving God and your neighbor as yourself. He then stepped forward and announced he would conduct an auction for a slave women, who stepped up to the platform for all to see. Beecher described her thusly: "The white blood of her father might be traced in her regular features and high, thoughtful brow, while her complexion and wavy hair betrayed her slave mother. . . . What will you do now? May she read her liberty in your eyes? Shall she go free? . . . Let the plates be passed and we will see!" "There was hardly a dry eye in the church," an eyewitness recalled, and $783 was raised in the collection plates, enough to purchase freedom for the women and her two-year-old child.[14]

The most newsworthy auction Beecher held was on February 6, 1860, in the Plymouth Church. This time he auctioned off a slave called Pinky. Born in 1851, she was sold in 1858 with her grandmother but was separated from her brother and mother. An abolitionist member of the congregation secured permission from the owner for Pinky to be brought from Alexandria, Virginia, to Brooklyn, New York, in order that her master might be paid. Although the slave owner wanted $900 for Pinky's freedom, Beecher raised over $2000. He remembered that "the rain never fell faster than the tears fell from many." The excess money paid for Pinky's schooling at Howard University in Washington, D.C. As a kind of epitaph, Rose Ward Hart, or Pinky, at age seventy-six, visited the Plymouth Church in 1927.[15]

However spectacular and emotionallycharged these slave auctions were, they nevertheless revealed latent racism in Beecher, his congregation, and the era. Note that in the 1856 speech Beecher used the word "betrayed" to communicate the slave's maternal lineage whereas no derogatory word impugned the white father, who gave his daughter "regular features." Pinky was a mulatto. As a matter of fact, the Beecher Family Papers contain photographs of Pinky and other slaves auctioned off from time to time in Plymouth Church. All of them were decidedly more white than black, a finding that William McLoughlin seconded. The point is that Beecher selected slaves who, for all intents and purposes, were white; he thus obtained considerable identification with his Caucasian congregation. He eschewed Negroid slaves. Moreover, he auctioned slaves who were women or young children—the women had sex appeal over their hapless male counterparts and young children appealed to the audience's pathos more than older slaves.[16]

Beecher was something of a self-appointed critic of the Lincoln administration throughout the war. His evaluations of the president's administration mellowed especially after the Emancipation Proclamation. Representative of this kind of oratory was a lecture entitled A Visit to Washington During the War. Unfortunately, the Beecher Family Papers contain only the dates of this lecture without giving the places, but it was delivered twice in 1861 and in 1863 and once in 1864. Beecher also resurrected this lecture and delivered it fifteen times from 1873 to 1877. Most of the lecture was of the self-congratulatory nature. Since Lincoln did not bother to see Beecher when he visited Washington in 1861, Beecher coyly allowed that he knelt on the grounds of the White House lawn and prayed for the president and the country. Of course, Beecher went to England in the fall of 1863 to deliver a series of speeches on behalf of the Union (see Chapter 3). President Lincoln was not too disappointed with Beecher's criticisms and was especially pleased with Beecher's successes on the British tour. So, when the federal flag was to be raised over Fort Sumter at the conclusion of the Civil War, Lincoln remembered Beecher and invited him to deliver the commemorative address.

Address at Fort Sumter, South Carolina

By the end of the Civil War, Beecher was his own man. He was a nationally and internationally famous preacher, and his rhetorical reputation as a great American orator was renown. Pulpit speaker and stump preacher paraded at Fort Sumter on April 14, 1865. Analyzing the rhetorical situation at Charleston, as well as the needs of the national reading audience, Beecher correctly reasoned that the occasion demanded epideictic oratory. As for the role that praise, which he often intermingled with blame, played in this ceremonial occasion, it has been noted that the speech abounded with "patriotic pablum and orotund oratory." Examples of his purple patches of prose are as follows: "Ruin sits in the cradle of treason. Rebellion has perished. But there flies the same flag that was insulted"; "No more war. No more accursed secession. No more slavery, that spawned them both [applause]"; and "No North, no West, no South, but the United States of America." The speech was so long that Beecher had to ask the military band to play a few pieces in order to break up the speech and to give Beecher some time to rest his voice. Beecher had to relax his vocal chords because he delivered the address in the open air. Contemporary photographs show Beecher surrounded on a festooned speaker's platform with other dignitaries. Listeners were densely packed in front of the platform and the crowd was vast; moreover, there were very few women in the practically all-male audience.[17]

Although the speech suffered from the exuberance of an hackneyed Fourth of July oration of the most pedestrian kind, two rhetorical devices distinguished the address. Doubtless realizing that celebrating a Northern victory would perforce alienate the vanquished South, Beecher sought to reconstitute both sections in this oration. His words of praise and blame were appropriate for the Northern audience, but if his logic was carried to its conclusion, then the North would be justified in riding roughshod over the South. President Lincoln had already made it clear that the South was to be reunited as quickly and smoothly as politically expedient, so Beecher fell into step with the president's plans. To that end, Beecher effectively used the rhetorical techniques of victimization and scapegoat. These strategies, perhaps more appropriate to the pulpit than the platform, were nevertheless designed to appeal to both secular audiences that were to be reunited as one.

The scapegoat, derived from ancient Hebrew thought and practice, functioned by the priest's figuratively placing the sins of the people on the goat and then driving the scapegoat into the wilderness so that the people could be sanctified. Rhetorically, Beecher selected the Southern patricians as the scapegoat, verbally scourged them, and thus cleansed the Southern plebeians so that they could reenter the Union with their treasonous sins purified. This was a wise persuasive strategy. It pleased almost everyone except the patricians. Northerners believed justice was served by making the scapegoat bear the political sins, and Southerners, excepting the patricians, felt relieved that they were not–did not the Reverend Henry Ward Beecher tell them so?–responsible for their transgressions.

The plebeians were not culpable because Beecher applied the healing balm of victimization. Southern patricians had misled the common man in the South. For having duped their fellow Southerners, Beecher metaphorically drove the victimizers into the political wilderness with loathsome lashes:

> an aristocracy as intense, proud, and inflexible as ever existed
> . . . obsequious to the people for the sake of governing them.
> . . [they] ran in the blood of society like a rash not yet come to
> the skin; this political tapeworm, that produced nothing, but lay
> coiled in the body, feeding on its nutriment . . . [so that] slaves
> worked that gentlemen might live at ease.

Beecher's choice of terminology for the leisure class was brilliant. Everyone abhorred rashes and tapeworms, especially at a time when the country was rural and the parasites abounded in humans and animals alike. The audience easily transferred their inherent dislike of these diseases to the Southern aristocrat.[18]

Having identified the guilty class, Beecher then allowed how the blue bloods had victimized the lower classes. Beecher informed Northerner and Southerner alike of the nobility's culpability:

> The war was set on by the ruling class, the aristocratic
> conspirators of the South. They suborned the common people
> with lies, with sophistries, with cruel deceits and slanders. . . .
> I charge the whole guilt of this war upon the ambitious,
> educated, plotting, political leaders of the South. They have
> shed this ocean of blood. They have desolated the South.
> They have poured poverty through all her towns and cities.

Lest the audience miss the point, Beecher communicated his opprobrium for the Southern aristocrats with the anaphora of "They have" three times.

With the scapegoat driven from the body politic, Beecher asked his immediate and reading audiences to reinstate the Southern common man quickly and fully. Thus cleansed, Beecher assured his Northern audience, the Southern people sans patricians could reenter the national temple:

But for the people misled, for the multitudes drafted and driven into this civil war, let not a trace of animosity remain. . . . Recall to them the old days of kindness. Our hearts wait for their redemption. All the resources of a renovated nation shall be applied to rebuild their prosperity, and smooth down the furrows of war.

Although Beecher spoke at Fort Sumter in language that was reminiscent of President Lincoln's Second Inaugural Address in which he pledged "to bind up the nation's wounds," Beecher's address functioned as epideictic rhetoric. As an instance of deliberative rhetoric, which it was not intended to be, it did not quell the political tendencies toward Reconstruction under the radical Republicans that gained headway especially after Lincoln's assassination, which ironically occurred the same day as Beecher's address in Charleston. Nevertheless, the *New York Times* judged Beecher's address a success and noted that it was "delivered in his matchless, eloquent and effective manner."[19]

Conditions of a Restored Union

The heat of Beecher's fervent excoriation of the Southern aristocracy at Fort Sumter had hardly cooled when he abruptly changed rhetorical course. Having helped to fuel some of the retribution against the rebellious South, Beecher realized in the fall of 1865 that perhaps things had gone too far, that for the South to be integrated into the Union as expeditiously as possible, that recriminations and the need to find scapegoats must cease. Accordingly, he stepped to the Plymouth pulpit on October 29, 1865, and abruptly did an about face.

The immediate exigency Beecher addressed was the controversy that arose when General Robert E. Lee consented to an appointment as president of Washington College, now Washington and Lee University, Lexington, Virginia, in the late summer of 1865. Although Southerners looked with approbation upon Lee's appointment, the victorious North viewed Lee's acceptance of the tendered offer with opprobrium. Radical Republicans fumed that the former general would subvert, through his leadership of a college, a generation of Southern youths at a time when repentance, more than reconciliation, was the order of the day. Beecher jumped into the fray.

Never one to mince words, he addressed Lee's case directly. "When his history is impartially written," Beecher acknowledged to his Plymouth congregation and national reading audience, "it can never be covered up that in an hour of great weakness he committed himself wickedly to the cause of rebellion." Not only was Beecher's statement honest, it also served rhetorically to preempt any criticism from the radical Republicans that he was aiding and abetting the enemy. It also subtly suggested that levelheadedness should replace radicalism. Beecher then commenced to build Lee's ethical credibility with the Northern audience. "And when the war ceased, and he laid down his arms," he reminded his audiences, "who could have been more modest, more manly, more true to his own word and honor than he was?" Although Beecher had scored the worst Southern attribute, laziness, in the Fort Sumter speech, he associated the best of Southern chivalry with the defeated general. Beecher continued to press his point with two additional rhetorical questions. First, he artfully played on the Christian concept of the call to the ministry by analogously applying the call to a secular situation: "And when he was called to the presidency of a college, must he not accept it?" An affirmation of Beecher's question was a denial of the radical Republicans' position. Beecher's final question played to the inherent American value of the Protestant work ethic that man must engage in productive employment: "Must he not do something for a living?" Inherent in the radical Republicans' rhetoric was the claim either that Lee should starve or live the old life of lazy luxury. By reducing their position to stark dichotomies that were not reasonable choices, Beecher effectively outflanked the radicals.[20]

Having addressed Lee's specific case, the Reverend Henry Ward Beecher went even further on the subject. In general terms, he argued, it was not Christian charity to castigate all Southern civilian and military leaders. "And I tell you," he affirmed, "we are not making friends, nor helping the cause of a common country, by raising the names of eminent Southern men, one after another, into the place of bitter criticism. It is not generous." But the radical Republicans were not interested in generosity, so Beecher appealed to his congregation with additional argumentation. He utilized the method of residues, a rhetorical application of the disjunctive syllogism, to refute possible objections to his position and to counter his opponents' points. Against those who advocated an immediate adjustment of Southern political attitudes, Beecher played the medical doctor and metaphorically prescribed to his congregation: "Now we are to remember the convalescence is often slower and longer than the run of the disease itself." With respect to those who insinuated against the motives of Southerners who wished to rejoin the Union, Beecher believed it was not "wise or Christian for us to distrust the sentiments of those in the South that profess to be desirous, once again, of concord and union." Conservative Northerners also complained that the South should show a "spirit of humility" toward the victors. Pragmatically, Beecher observed that the South was devastated enough, and then asked should Christians want more than that? Thus, the residue was Beecher's thesis concerning the conditions of a restored Union: the South should be integrated into the status quo ante bellum. That Beecher weighed into the controversy on the part of reconciliation rather than radicalism helped to defuse the Lee episode and the general quietly assumed the presidency of the college. Indeed, the homily was another example of Beecher on the stump in the pulpit: "This sermon demonstrated Beecher's ability to place a pressing political problem in a Christian context wherein religious values could function to solve a secular crisis."[21]

Beecher also took his rhetoric on tour of the victorious Northern cities. To audiences assembled at fifteen cities and villages in the northeast, the reverend rehearsed his contributions to the impending crisis, the vicissitudes of the Civil War, and his suggestions for readmitting the Southern states in a lecture he entitled Reconstruction on Principles National Not

Sectional. This lecture was delivered from December 1865 to late January 1866.

Beecher as Civil War- and Self-Encomiast

Beecher also delivered eulogies for some of the leading lights of the Civil War era. Ostensibly functioning as speeches of praise for such figures as Charles Sumner, Wendell Phillips, and President Ulysses S. Grant, these addresses were as much, or often times more, focused on Beecher's impact on the war as the deceased's importance to the conflict. For instance, in eulogizing Wendell Phillips on February 10, 1884, at Plymouth Church, Beecher introduced his speech with a reference to himself. He erroneously told his congregation that he debated against colonization in the Athenian Society while at college at a time when Wendell Phillips "had just begun his career" (in fact Beecher merely presided at the debate held at Amherst College). Beecher continued to discourse on the history of the sectional conflict and his involvement with it for eighteen pages. When Beecher finally diverted the congregation's attention to Phillips, he allotted only eight pages of a twenty-six page speech. And even then, Beecher was at pains to discourse how he personally caused Plymouth Church to host a public lecture to be delivered by Phillips because he had been refused the Broadway Tabernacle and because the trustees of Graham Institute had withdrawn their auditorium for fear of provoking a mob. But when Beecher finally did address the subject of his epideictic rhetoric, he praised Phillips's mastery in persuasive discourse:

> His eloquence was penetrating and alarming. He did not flow as a mighty gulf stream; he did not dash upon the continent as the ocean does; he was not a mighty rushing river. His eloquence was a flight of arrows, sentence after sentence, polished, and most of them burning. He shot them one after the other, and where they struck they slew; always elegant, always awful.[22]

The Reverend Henry Ward Beecher also delivered a eulogy in Plymouth Church, April 23, 1865, on President Abraham Lincoln. Beecher appropriately chose a text from Deuteronomy that related how Moses was led by God to the top of Mount Pisgah. From there, God allowed Moses to see the Promised Land in the distance but was not permitted to enter it. That passage served as an analogy for the slain sixteenth president. Beecher portrayed the irony of the war that Lincoln was not allowed to witness the great moral and political victory of his presidency to save the Union. Although much of the speech is overly sentimental by today's standards, but must have meet the expectations of the rhetorical situation for Beecher's era when audiences expected maudlin appeals, Beecher did manage a simple sentence that captured Lincoln's essence as a quintessential American: "He was a man from the common people who never forgot his kind."[23]

Conclusion

Henry Ward Beecher was not the first divine to denounce slavery from the pulpit. The Reverend William Ellery Channing, for one, preached against bondage from Federal Street Church in Boston in the 1830s, and the Reverend Theodore Parker, also of Boston, attacked Daniel Webster and the Compromise of 1850 at Faneuil Hall at a time when Beecher was a relatively unknown pastor in Brooklyn. But once Beecher broached the subject, first in Indianapolis and then at Plymouth, although he admittedly approached the exigency in measured installments rather than in burning bridges, he never turned from his course. Granted: (1) the Sumner protest speech helped Beecher's ethos more than it determined public policy toward the peculiar institution; (2) the rhetorical effects of the five speeches he delivered in Great Britain were over estimated; and (3) the quasi-deliberative speeches he delivered immediately after the war on the readmission of the Southern states were unheeded by radical Republicans in their reconstruction of the South. True enough, in addresses he delivered after the Civil War he was guilty of an aggrandizement that would have made a circus barker blush. But the fact remains that in the public's mind, which conception he was often at pains to reinforce and never to debunk, Henry Ward Beecher was the North's *vox populi* on slavery.

3
Beecher in Britain

The lasting impression of Henry Ward Beecher's talking down John Bull in Great Britain in the fall of 1863 evidently stayed with Sir Arthur Conan Doyle. He made Sherlock Holmes analyze Dr. Watson's thoughts about Beecher, whose unframed picture rested on the top of Watson's books, in *The Resident Patient*:

> You were recalling the incidents of Beecher's career. I was well aware that you could not do this without thinking of the mission which he undertook on behalf of the North at the time of the Civil War, for I remember you expressing your passionate indignation at the way in which he was received by the more turbulent of our people. You felt so strongly about it that I knew you could not think of Beecher without thinking of that also.

What Beecher accomplished was not a watershed in adjusting relations between the United States and Great Britain over whether Her Majesty's Government would recognize the Confederate States of America, but it was an oratorical achievement that lighted Beecher's career until his death.[1]

For a good many years after the Civil War, the Fourth of July was not celebrated in the South. The reason was twofold: (1) Confederate forces at Vicksburg, Mississippi, surrendered to General Ulysses S. Grant on July 4, 1863, thus dividing the Confederacy and opening the Mississippi River to Northern navigation; and (2) General Robert E. Lee's troops began their withdrawal from Gettysburg, Pennsylvania, on July 4 after it was clear the Union forces under General George Meade had prevailed. The war was clearly not over, but these two stunning military victories on the battlefield, more than Beecher's rhetorical triumph on the public platform, convinced the British government not to join in an alliance with the French to recognize the Confederacy on January 1, 1864.

The immediate occasion for Beecher's speeches was that his congregation sent him to Europe for a six month period of rest and relaxation. As he had overworked himself to the point that he was sent to Europe in the summer of 1850 by his congregation in order to regain his strength, Beecher had again worn himself out in his preaching at Plymouth and in writing editorials for *The Independent*. All authorities agree that his trip was not a covert cover, nor was it originally sanctioned or intended to be so by the Lincoln administration, for him to speak in behalf of the North or against slavery. He preached his last sermon at Plymouth on May 27, 1863, and left for England and Europe. He refused invitations from his British abolitionist friends to address audiences in Great Britain, and left for the Continent in July and stayed through September. As the time approached for Beecher to return to England, the pressure mounted for him to speak. In September he conferred with Charles Francis Adams, ambassador to the Court of St. James, who suggested a speaking tour might be efficacious for the Union. The timing for such rhetoric was propitious.

Beecher faced a persuasive problem of considerable delicacy. He did not perceive it immediately, but his quick and forthright adjustment to it demonstrated anew his persuasive perspicacity in adapting to ever changing speaker-speech-audience exigencies.

Part of the problem he faced was the war aims of the Lincoln administration. Although Beecher's editorials in *The Independent* had continually scored the president for not moving faster on freeing the slaves, and other leading abolitionists, such as Wendell Phillips and William Lloyd Garrison, had mounted their own campaigns with no better success than Beecher had, Lincoln remained adamant. In a widely published letter, August 22, 1862, the president had sent to Horace Greeley, the editor of the New York *Tribune*, who wrote an editorial entitled "The Prayer of Twenty Millions" that urged Lincoln to free immediately all slaves in the South, Lincoln replied in his now-famous defense of the federal government:

> I would save the Union. . . . My paramount object in this struggle *is* to save the Union, and is *not* either to save or destroy slavery. If I could save the Union without freeing *any* slave I would do it, and if I could save it by freeing *all* the slaves I would do it; and if I could save it by freeing some and leaving others alone I would also do that.

To the antislavery and abolitionist forces, Lincoln's reply was not responsive. With regard to the British audience, the high moral ground the abolitionists held was not inhabited by their president; hence, if one appealed to British antislavery sympathies, one could easily be accused of being politically naive or disingenuous.[2]

Responding to many pressures on several fronts, President Abraham Lincoln issued the Emancipation Proclamation on January 1, 1863. It was a publicity stroke of the highest order. Unfortunately, it did not free any slaves under federal control or in slave states, such as Missouri, Maryland, and newly formed West Virginia, which remained in the Union, and only freed slaves in the rebelling states. Thus, although it allowed Lincoln and the North to seize the high moral ground, the proclamation was operative only if the North won the war. Astute Britishers could perceive the president's rhetorical legerdemain.

Thus, the first exigency Beecher faced in Great Britain was to equate the Union with antislavery, or to be more precise with abolitionism, because Southern sympathizers in England had a political point on their side. Although British pro-Southerners were not pro-slavery, they had natural sympathies with the ideals of Southern aristocracy, they felt the economic pinch of the Northern blockade that practically stopped shipments of cotton to British mills, and they had no great love for Northern democracy. Obviously, most Southern supporters were from the established social, political, and business classes, whereas the common man sympathized more with Northern values and aims. The second exigency was dependent upon the first. If he could succeed in equating the North with abolitionism, the converse of the argument would cast British pro-Southerners as pro-slavery, an identification that would be fatal to British sympathizers with the Confederacy. But given that the North was fighting for Union more than for the abolition of slavery, the reality of political fact militated moral platitudes.

Speech in Manchester

Approximately six thousand listeners jammed the Free Trade Hall in Manchester, England, on October 9, 1863, to hear the Rev. Henry Ward Beecher. Manchester, a center of British manufacturing interests and decidedly working class in nature, fielded an audience that was on the whole sympathetic to Beecher and his position. Yet, Beecher was aware that his speech would be reported to the entire nation, so he adjusted to two audiences. Judging from the audience's responses that were interpolated into the text, Beecher faced a partisan assembly. However, he took advantage of the occasional interruption to polarize the meeting. He played his majority against the small but vocal minority. Thus, he let the wider audience that the newspapers served infer that he was being harassed by the pro-South element. This tactic functioned effectively as *argumentum ad misericordiam*, or pity poor me.

Beecher was introduced by J. H. Estcourt who gave him a favorable introduction. Estcourt informed the audience that Beecher represented those "who were now fighting for constitutional government, and free speech, and personal, civil, social, political, and religious freedom." Estcourt did not imply that Beecher was speaking, nor the North fighting, against slavery.[3]

In order to argue his general thesis that the Union equalled freedom, with the audience left to infer that a Northern victory would mean the abolition of slavery, Beecher used several interesting rhetorical techniques to persuade his listeners.

Identification

Beecher built effectively upon Estcourt's introduction about free speech. When there was an interruption shortly after he began to address the crowd, Beecher retorted: "I have not come to England to be surprised that those men whose cause cannot bear the light are afraid of free speech [Cheers.]. . . . Little by little, I doubt not, I shall be permitted to speak to-night. [Hear.]" He then launched into an encomium on British values and political institutions. Seeking consubstantiation with the Manchester audience, he employed striking metaphors such as: "The same blood is in us. [Cheers.] We are your children, or the children of your fathers and ancestors"; in comparing American polity with English institutions, he said: "we beheld that the very foundation stones were taken from the quarry of your history"; and he evoked loud cheers when he allowed that "your own beloved Queen" commands "our simple, unpretentious, and unaffected respect."[4]

After warming the British audience by paying sufficient compliments and praise to preempt criticism from everyone but the most hardened Southern sympathizer, Beecher broached his thesis. "We now only ask," ambassador Beecher beseeched his audience, "of the government strict neutrality and of the liberty-loving people of England moral sympathy. Nothing more! We ask no help, and no hindrance. [Resumed cheers.] . . . All that we say is, let France keep away, let England keep hands off; if we cannot manage the rebellion by ourselves, then let it be not managed at all. [Cheers.]."[5]

Begging the Question

Carefully monitoring his language, Beecher cast the Civil War in terms of saving the Union. He let the audience assume a victorious North would abolish slavery, although he never proved that contention. Indeed, he had to argue obliquely that way because of the announced war aim of the Lincoln administration. But he cleverly implied that saving the Union would be beneficial to democracy: "liberty of speech" would be practiced throughout the Gulf States, there would be liberty of the press, there would be common schools for everyone, and the land would "not be parceled into gigantic plantations, in the hands of a few rich oligarchs–[loud cheers]; but shall be divided to honest farmers, every man own his little–[renewed cheers]." The working class audience responded handsomely to Beecher's side-swipe at the rich. A little later in his speech, he returned to the theme of Union and liberty, but he did not exactly say the Union stood for the abolition of slavery, but strongly implied it:

> It is none the less a contest for liberty and against slavery, because it is primarily a conflict for the Union. It is by that Union, vivid with liberty, that we have to scourge oppression and establish liberty. Union, in the future, means justice, liberty, popular rights. Only slavery has hitherto prevented Union from bearing such fruit."[6]

Humor

He often used levity to make a telling point. He reminded the audience the effect of the cotton gin on Southern slavery. When Beecher finished with the slavers in the following excerpt, they were craven scoundrels:

> Slaves that before had been worth from three to four hundred dollars began to be worth six hundred dollars. That knocked away one-third of adherence to moral law. They then became worth seven hundred dollars, and half the law went [cheers and laughter]; then eight or nine hundred dollars, and then there was no such thing as moral law [cheers and laughter]; then one thousand or twelve hundred dollars, and slavery became one of the beatitudes [cheers and laughter].

When arguing that Great Britain had "thrown her arms of love around the Southerners and turns from the Northerners," to which some in the audience responded "No," Beecher replied: "I have only to say that she has been caught in very suspicious circumstances [laughter]."[7]

Turning the Tables

In terms of refuting the opposition's arguments, Beecher handily dispatched pro-Southern rhetoric by turning the tables. In comparing the U.S. Constitution to those of the slave states, Beecher starkly contrasted the language used to denote black people. Under the Constitution, Negroes were "*persons* (not chattels) held to *service* (not servitude)." But in South Carolina, Mississippi, and Louisiana, slaves were a "thing."[8]

In rebuting Lord Wharncliffe, the president of the Society for Southern Independence, who held that the South did not support the existence of slavery and that pro-Northerners were imputing base motives to his organization, Beecher had a field day. While endeavoring sarcastically to overcome errors of perception concerning the Society, Beecher averred that it should also try "to do away with four million slaves in the South"; and then he administered the rhetorical coup de grace. He reminded the audience that the South had enacted a new constitution that "for the first time introduces and legalizes slavery as a national institution, and makes it unconstitutional ever to do it away." He also quoted from Confederate Vice President Alexander Stephens's speech that "to trample on the manhood of an inferior race is the only proper way to maintain the liberty of a superior [race]."[9]

Beecher also played the role of an American history professor lecturing the British undergraduates. He traced the practice of slavery from colonial times to the present. But the most interesting argument he adduced was one that twentieth-century historians have validated. Beecher accurately observed that before the Civil War the South had a majority of justices, who held slaves, on the bench of the Supreme Court; had presidents who were either slave-owners themselves or "licked the feet of slave-owners"; and had control of the U.S. Senate. Thus, the slave power conspiracy that Beecher thundered against in the 1850s had probative value once the Civil War exposed the lengths to which Southerners would go to maintain slavery.[10]

Speech in Glasgow

On October 13, 1863, Beecher took the podium in City Hall. Glasgow was a center for shipbuilding and workers there had constructed blockade runners for the South. Like Manchester, Glasgow was working class, and, judging by the decreased numbers of interpolated interruptions, hisses, and jeers in the speech text, Beecher had an even more favorable audience. However partisan his audience was initially, his rhetorical strategy was brilliant in audience adaptation.

To be sure, he began his speech in Glasgow as he had at Manchester. Substantial measures of praise, references to free speech and liberty, and *argumentum ad misericordiam* softened the audience. He played the role of professor by dividing the slave states into farming and plantation states, which set the stage for introducing his thesis.

Beecher forced the audience to take sides by making an equation based on a dichotomy. The North equalled free work, which supported the dignity of the common working man; the South equalled slave work, which supported the cupidity of the aristocracy. Beecher identified with his working class audience by skillfully playing on class antagonisms that were as inherent in Great Britain as in the United States. "Throughout the South," he claimed for Southern white men, "there is the most marked public disesteem of honest homey industry." Things were different in the North: "But even in the most favored portions of the South, manual labor is but barely redeemed from the taint of being a slave's business, and nowhere it is honored as it is in the great and free North." To clinch the argument, he quoted Governor James Hammond of South Carolina who called Northern laborers "the mudsill of society." Having informed his audience of what Southern aristocrats really thought of Northern workers, and by implication Glasgow workers, Beecher practically guaranteed assent:

> I have a right to demand of the workmen of Glasgow that they should refuse their sympathy to the South, and should give their hearty sympathy to those who are like themselves, seeking to make work honorable, and to give to the working man his true place in society. Disguise it as they will, distract your attention from it as they may, it cannot be concealed, that the American question is the *working man's question*, all over the world! The slave master's doctrine is that *capital should own labor*–that the employers should own the employed. This is Southern doctrine and Southern practice. Northern doctrine and Northern practice is that the laborer should be free. . . . It is monstrous that British workmen should help Southern slaveholders to degrade labor [Beecher's emphasis].[11]

Beecher also reminded his audience that if anyone supported the South, then that person favored slavery. He extended the argument to another distasteful step. Given its chance, the South would nationalize slavery. Then in the final application of the rhetorical technique of *argumentum ad absurdum*, reducing the argument or position to absurdity, he stated flatly: "every freeman in Great Britain that goes for the South, really goes for the opening of that trade [the slave trade]. [Cheers and hisses.] . . . *You* do not mean the slave-trade, but *they do*; and all that they ask of you is–"Be blind." [Laughter and applause.] [Beecher's emphasis].[12]

The appearance of a classical *refutatio*, or section of the speech wherein one rebuts the opposition, suggests that Beecher realized he should address certain questions that were on the minds of many listeners in the audience and readers of the newspapers. If the refutation did not change any opponents' minds, it could nevertheless function to reinforce partisans' beliefs in their pro-North stand. The first objection was why not just let the South go? He countered that slavery was a removable evil (note that he did not say the Union once victorious would remove it): "The nature of our institutions is against it. The laws of nature are against it. The conscience of the nation, the public sentiment of Christendom, are against it." By mentioning the "sentiment of Christendom," he employed the bandwagon effect, and he used epistrophe effectively by ending successive sentences with "against it." If that were not proof enough, then he used the tried-and-true technique of answering a question with a question: "Be pleased to tell me what part of the British Islands you are willing to let go from under the crown when its inhabitants secede and set up for independence?"[13]

He dispatched a second objection that the war had nothing to do with slavery. He never stated that the North was fighting against slavery, but cleverly avowed that the South went to war to save slavery. He wisely argued a point on which he could make a compelling case, but never mind that his argument did not directly refute the real objection. Examples of his reasoning are as follows: "Slavery [was] adopted as the central principle of Southern political economy;" "all her quarrels with the North [have] been about slavery"; and "all her principal statesman [have] made interferences with slavery *wrongs* at the hands of the North . . . the very reason of rebellion. [Beecher's emphasis.]"[14]

Third, he clarified the real reason for the Southern rebellion. Again quoting Vice President Alexander Stephens of the Confederacy, Beecher reminded the audience that the "only foundation of our liberty is to own the laborer and to oppress the slave."[15]

In his conclusion, he brought the pulpit to the podium. In balanced cadences, he intoned:

> I say that the man that gives his aid to the Slave Power is allied to it, and is making his money by building up tyranny. [Hear and cheers.] Every man that strikes a blow on the iron that is put into those ships for the South, is striking a blow and forging a manacle for the hand of the slave. [Applause and hisses.]

Every free laborer in old Glasgow who is laboring to rear up
iron ships for the South, is laboring to establish on sea and on
land the doctrine that capital has a right to own "labor."
[Cheers and hisses.] . . . You strike God in the face when you
work for slaveholders. . . . I charge you to come out from
among them, to have nothing to do with the unclean and filthy
lucre made by pandering to slavery.[16]

Speech at Edinburgh

If anything, the audience at Free Church Assembly Hall, Edinburgh,
Scotland, on October 14 was more favorable to Beecher and his speech.
Adapting to a university city, Beecher eschewed appeals to class antagonisms
and focused instead on an intellectual discussion of the Union with respect
to the South's insistence on slavery. Although there were occasional hisses,
these were always overshadowed by cheers, hears, and applause. There were
relatively few rhetorical pyrotechnics in the speech, but some of Beecher's
appeals nevertheless warrant examination.

He continued to argue, as he had in the two previous speeches, that
public and political opinion in the South had evolved from an apologetic
stance on slavery to one of slavery as a positive good. Beginning with
Senator John C. Calhoun of South Carolina in the 1830s, Beecher claimed
there was "a retrogression in morals–an apostasy":

Men no longer apologized for slavery; they learned to defend
it; to teach that it was the normal condition of an inferior race;
that the seeds and history of it were in the Word of God; that
the only condition in which a republic can be prosperous, is,
where an aristocracy *owns the labor* of the community. That
was the doctrine of the South, and with that doctrine there
began to be ambitious designs, not only for the maintenance
but the propagation of slavery [Beecher's emphasis].

The collision, according to Beecher, came when the North, and especially
the Republican party, decided that slavery could not be national, that it must
be contained, that it could not spread. Although Lincoln and the Republican
party never intended to touch slavery in states where it already existed, they
did claim the federal government could legislate for the territories:

Then came the last act of this revolution of feeling in the
North–the election of Mr. Lincoln. [Loud and protracted
cheering.] The principle that was laid down as a distinct
feature of the platform on which Mr. Lincoln was elected, was,
that there should be no more slave Territories–in other words,
the breathing hole was stopped up, and slavery had no air; it
was only a question of time how long it would last before it
would be suffocated. [Laughter and cheers.][17]

Toward the latter part of his address, Beecher turned to refute additional objections that had arisen in the conservative newspapers concerning the war aims of the Lincoln administration. A serious threat to the logic of Beecher's speeches was the allegation that the North was fighting to keep an unwilling South in the Union, which, on the face of it, seemed to be unconstitutional. As a precursor of the famous "neighbor's garden hose" analogy that President Franklin D. Roosevelt used to refute objections to his policy of Lend-Lease before World War II, Beecher employed the analogy of the fire fighter. When a fire breaks out, Beecher said, the initial reaction is to try to contain the blaze. But when the conflagration begins to spread, houses are destroyed in order to create a gap so that the fire will not expand. By analogy, he asserted that Lincoln did not in the beginning of the Civil War think so many lives would have to be sacrificed. In fact, Beecher confessed: "Long he paused, I know; for I assisted in bombarding him. [Laughter and cheers.]" But at last, Lincoln moved to save the Union and the Constitution, even at a tremendous cost to the North and South.[18]

Against those who decried that the war was too long, he chided the British for aiding the South, which prolonged the conflict. He asked the audience to takes sides and not to straddle the fence: "If you want to sympathize with us, do so; and if you must assist the rebels, do so; but do not attempt both things at once. [Hear, hear; and applause.]"[19]

British Southern sympathizers invented a telling argument. Realizing that Northerners were just as bigoted about blacks as Southerners were, the pro-South newspapers alleged that blacks were just as badly off in the North as in the South, and would be no better off under a victorious North. Curiously, it never dawned on Beecher to argue that even if that proposition were true, and it probably was, one difference obtained: at least in the North Negroes were not slaves. Although the audience was receptive to Beecher's answer, it was disingenuous to argue the way he did:

> At one time I admit that there was a prejudice against the black man, arising out of the political condition of things; but I can bear witness that this prejudice has almost entirely passed away, in so far as the native population is concerned. [Cheers.] I shall not say who are the bitterest enemies of the black men, because you would hiss me if I did so. [Loud cries of "Speak out," and a voice, "The Irishmen"–another voice, "The Irish Roman Catholics."]

Beecher effectively engaged the audience in two ways. First, he subtly invited them to supply the scapegoat–notice he said "native population"–that, second, rested on the inherent British dislike for the Irish and Roman Catholics. After the audience swallowed the bait, Beecher reeled in the catch: "There is no doubt that the Irish have a strong prejudice against the negroes . . . [because] were the slaves freed, they would dispute the field of labor with them." Not to worry, Beecher piously comforted his audience, for "were they freed, the Northern negroes would flock to the South, leaving the North for Northern laborers."[20]

As another instance of white racism in the nineteenth century, Beecher tried to counter the charge that "the Americans are seeking to destroy the Anglo-Saxons for the sake of a few million negroes." When Beecher claimed the North was fighting "for the good of all mankind–black, white, and yellow," he drew derisive laughter from the audience.[21]

Beecher was on firmer ground when he stated that President Lincoln was sincere in the Emancipation Proclamation. He assured his audience: "The President was very loath to take the steps he did; but, though slow, Abraham Lincoln was sure. A thousand men could not make him plant his foot before he was ready; ten thousand men could not make him move it after he had put it down."[22]

Approximately twenty-five hundred people heard Beecher's address at Edinburgh. At the conclusion of the meeting, a resolution was made and seconded that the house protested American slavery and encouraged the sympathy of the abolitionists. It passed with three dissenting votes.[23]

Speech at Liverpool

This is what Beecher faced at Liverpool, England, on October 16, 1863:

> It was a grand spectacle–in St. George's hall, Liverpool–when he struggled two livelong hours against that raging sea of insult, taunt, irony, impertinent questioning, blackguardism, curses, hisses, cat-calls, stampings, hootings, yellings. . . . There has not been a more heroic achievement on any of our fields of battle than the successful delivery of that speech against the odds which opposed it.

Liverpool was the center of British pro-Southern sentiments. The pro-South people placed placards over the city that invited listeners to disrupt the meeting. They did. It was the ruffians' reaction to this speech that so troubled Dr. Watson.[24]

Approximately twenty-five hundred persons packed into Philharmonic Hall to listen to Beecher. Although most of the audience was pro-North, the pro-Southern block managed to enlist enough protesters to do an effective job. In addition to disturbances of varying degrees that occurred almost continually, Beecher was interrupted four times with demonstrations that ran from four to five minutes in length, while the chairman strove to regain order. On two occasions, demonstrators were physically removed from the hall by the police. J. M. Buckley, an American eyewitness to the scene, observed that shills had been placed "in different parts expressly to act in concert; and after a while I was able to identify two or three who were obviously leaders." Since Beecher repeated the same general themes at Liverpool as he had in his previous speaking engagements, there is little utility in rehearsing those arguments again. Rather, it is worthwhile to note how Beecher dealt with an exceedingly rowdy crowd.[25]

Humor

Whenever he could, Beecher tried to use laughter to disarm his critics and to reinforce his adherents. He played the majority against the agitators. He deployed this strategy throughout the speech. The following examples are illustrative of his technique.

Subtly appealing to pity, Beecher cast his detractors as the villains:

> Those of you who are kind enough to wish to favor my speaking–and you will observe that my voice is slightly husky, from having spoken almost every night in succession for some time past–those who wish to hear me will do me the kindness simply to sit still and to keep still; and I and my friends the Secessionists will make all the noise.   [Laughter.]

After a prolonged interruption, Beecher regained some control over the audience by using humor at his opponent's expense:

> Well, you have had your turn; now let me have mine again. [Loud applause and laughter.] It is a little inconvenient to talk against the wind; but after all, if you will just keep good natured–I am not going to lose my temper; will you watch yours? [Applause.] Besides all that,–it rests me, and gives me a chance, you know, to get my breath. [Applause and hisses.] And I think that the bark of those men is worse than their bite. They do not mean any harm–they just don't know any better. [Loud laughter, applause, hisses and continued uproar.]

And Beecher poked fun at an interrupter:

> Excuse me, sir, I am the speaker, not you; and it is for me to determine what to say. [Hear, hear.] . . . however, as to this logic of cat-calls, it is slavery logic,–I am used to it. [Applause, hisses, and cheers.][26]

Turning the Tables

Beecher was particularly adept at turning objections from the audience back on the objectors. It was an indication of his skill in the art of public speaking that he could react on the spot in such a telling fashion. This often gained him persuasive points from the audience. Against shouts that the North was not fighting for Union, which ensured emancipation, Beecher retorted:

> Because we shall never forget the testimony of our enemies. They have gone off declaring that the Union in the hands of the North was fatal to slavery. [Loud applause.]   There is

>testimony in court for you! [A voice: "See that," and laughter.]
>. . . Because the South believed that the Union was against
>slavery, they left it. [Renewed interruption.]. Yes. [Applause,
>and "no, no."]

He maligned another vocal intruder with the allegation that that person
sought to suppress information harmful to the Southern cause: "you will get
a word at a time; to-morrow will let folks see what it is you don't want to
hear." In the same vein, he later taunted his detractors: "If the pro-slavery
interrupters think they will tire me out, they will do more than eight millions
in America could."[27]

Fortunately for posterity, J. M. Buckley recorded something of
Beecher's deportment on the podium at Liverpool. He noted that Beecher
"paced the platform like a lion about to spring upon the assembly."
Concerning his voice, Buckley wrote:

>Mr. Beecher's voice, when he was excited and spoke very loud,
>had a roaring sound. They [the interrupters] would pitch their
>voices upon the same key, so that when he ended a paragraph
>in a clarion tone, taking the same pitch, they would bellow like
>a score of infuriated bulls, and continue sometimes for five
>minutes at a stretch.

Speaking at length in such a volume eventually took its toll on Beecher's
voice, as the *Liverpool Chronicle* noted:

>Mr. Beecher had a cold, and in straining his voice occasionally
>to fill the vast area, it sometimes degenerated into a falsetto.
>The malcontents availed themselves of this defect to mimic his
>manner, which caused, of course, a good deal of laughter,
>without for a moment impairing the temper of the speaker.

Indeed, Beecher was probably buoyed by some sympathetic listeners who
cried "Shame" and "Turn him out" against the detractors.[28]

Beecher's speech lasted approximately two hours. How long he
actually spoke was probably considerably less than that because of the
interruptions. Not counting cheers, hears, and applause that Beecher
doubtless welcomed, he was interrupted from the floor at least sixty-five
times. Toward the latter part of his speech, his voice gave out, but he was
able to rest it while the crowd was out of control; when order was finally
restored, he was able to regain his voice.

Two evaluations of Beecher's rhetoric may close the Liverpool speech,
one from an opponent, the other from a partisan. The one deprecated his
logic, but both commented on his *actio*:

>What Mr. Beecher said he said with the noble fervor
>and enthusiasm that distinguish him; but fervor cannot alter
>the Constitution, nor can enthusiasm reconcile contradictions.

For physical power, self-control, diversified forms of public speaking, indomitable will without the loss of the power to respond to the changing moods of the audience, and affability essential to persuasion, I have never seen its equal and cannot imagine its superior.[29]

Speech in London

The speech in Exeter Hall, London, on October 20, 1863, before an audience of three thousand persons, was the apotheosis of Beecher's rhetoric. He had survived the treacherous shoals at Liverpool and was at last in safe harbor. Although there were a few hisses from the floor, the overwhelming response from the audience was quite positive. There were no disturbances, uproars, or shouting matches.

As in the previous speeches, Beecher rehearsed his general arguments. He recapitulated his themes of liberty, Union, and free labor, but these were played like a Bach organ fugue. He varied the key signatures, changed the rhythms, and introduced new turns and trills to enliven the melodic discourse. But amazingly, Beecher did not repeat himself in any of the five speeches.

If one rhetorical canon can epitomize the persuasiveness of this speech, it was surely Beecher's mastery in style. At ease with a friendly audience, he was able to employ the kind of rotund rhetoric that made him famous at Plymouth. Except for a few notable asides concerning other facets of Beecher's rhetoric, the main foci in this section are Beecher's *elocutio*, or style, and how he marshalled his arguments in a classical *refutatio*, or the section of the speech devoted to rebutting objections.

Benjamin Scott, the Chamberlain of London, gave Beecher a warm introduction. Setting the stage for the reverend's speech, Scott indulged in some rhetorical flights of fancy that delighted the crowd:

He took his stand, not on the shifting sands of expediency, but on the immovable rock of principle. [Cheers.] He had put his hand to the plough, and would never turn back. Some people had allowed their ears to be stuffed with cotton [laughter and cheers], some were blinded by gold dust, and some had allowed the gag of expediency to be put in their mouths to quiet them. [Cheers.]

With that, and amid a standing ovation as he advanced to the front of the platform, Beecher sallied forth.[30]

Beecher began his address by recalling the speeches he had delivered in the cities before London. He drew a round of applause when he facetiously allowed that "In Liverpool I labored, under difficulties [laughter and cheers]." He then introduced a device that he had not used hitherto. He asked the audience to be the judge at the bar, to sympathize with the accused, and then to render a verdict—it was a master rhetorical stroke: "I merely ask you to put yourselves in our track for one hour, and look at the objects as we look at them [cheers]—after that, form your judgment as you please. [Cheers.]"[31]

The interesting feature of this speech is how quickly Beecher moved to a classical refutation. Particularly at Liverpool, he was at pains to actually refute opponent's objections. But, since the London audience was so friendly, why would they object to his positions? Of course, they would not. What Beecher really used the *refutatio* for was an application of the rhetorical device of the straw issue. By appearing to demolish pro-Southern arguments, which the London audience had previously rejected, Beecher reinforced values and attitudes already held by his partisans. By reiterating arguments to which he knew they would give assent, he easily dispatched those positions the audience had already rejected.

For instance, he raised the straw issue of why the North could not contend against slavery in the South. Based on the doctrine of state's rights, he claimed the North would violate the Constitution. He used a homey analogy to make the point clear. If Englishmen could not fathom the intricacies of the federal government, they could understand that the City of London had certain rights that Parliament could not violate, but that in all other political areas London was subservient to Parliament.[32]

Another objection he dismissed with a metaphor was the charge that Lincoln had issued the Emancipation Proclamation for political reasons. Beecher avowed of course it was political, but asserted Lincoln's disposition was personal. To establish the point, he used the example of a surgeon who desired to help a young boy by operating on a cancerous leg, but that the doctor could not act professionally until called to do so by the boy's father. Having paved the way with that example, Beecher then completed the argument:

> At first the President could not touch slavery, because in time of peace it was a legal institution. How then can he do it now? Because in time of war it has stepped beyond its former sphere, and is no longer a local institution, but a national and public enemy. [Applause.] Now I promised to make that clear: have I done it? [Hear, hear, and applause.][33]

He used *argumentum ad absurdum* to answer another straw issue. Why not let the South go, he asked. His answer was one of political principle. He used the technique that Senators Daniel Webster and Henry Clay had employed in their speeches for the Compromise of 1850–that the logical conclusion of secession was anarchy:

> If every treaty may be overthrown by which States have been settled into a Nation, what form of political union may not on like grounds be severed? There is the same force in the doctrine of Secession in the application to counties as in the application to States; and if it be right for a State or a county to secede, it is equally right for a town and a city. [Cheers.] This doctrine of Secession is a huge revolving millstone that grinds the national life into powder. [Cheers.]

Lest the audience miss the point, Beecher used the technique of apostrophe. He turned to the pro-Southerners who were not present in the hall and asked "those English gentlemen who hold that it is right for a State to secede when it pleases, how they would like it, if the county of Kent should try the experiment. [Hear, hear.]"[34]

He also used apophasis. "I will not mention names," he coyly declared, "but I will say this, that there have been important organs in Great Britain that have deliberately and knowingly spoken what is not true." The enthusiastic audience supplied the responses of "The *Times*!" and "Three groans for the *Times*." So successful was his scapegoating the *Times* that he returned to the theme later in his speech: "I don't believe in the *Times*. [Groans for the *Times*; groans for the *Telegraph*.]"[35]

Sometimes the eddies of a river are more teeming than the main current, and the following example affirms the point. One of the most interesting arguments Beecher made on why there should not be two nations in place of one Union was that "we do not want to become a military people." (That was one of the unforeseen consequences of the Civil War: the United States emerged as a world naval power with an army that followed closely behind.) Whereas the North American continent had militated a large army, if the South were victorious, both the North and South would have to maintain standing armies. In language that presaged President Dwight Eisenhower's famous military-industrial complex speech in 1960, Beecher used a compelling frontier image: "And if America, by this ill-advised disruption, is forced to have a standing army, like a boy with a knife, she will always want to whittle with it. [Laughter and cheers.]"[36]

The Reverend Henry Ward Beecher's conclusion demonstrated that he knew as much about the stage as he did the pulpit:

I thank you for your long patience with me. ["Go on!"] Ah! when I was a boy they used to tell me never to eat enough, but always to get up being a little hungry. I would rather you go away wishing I had spoken longer than go away saying, "What a tedious fellow he was!" [A laugh.] And therefore if you will not permit me to close and go, I beg you to recollect that this is the fifth speech of more than two hours' length that I have spoken, on some occasion *under difficulties*, within seven or eight days, and I am so exhausted that I ask you to permit me to stop. [Great cheering.] [Beecher's emphasis.][37]

Conclusion

One steps on hazardous rhetorical ground in attempting to assay the effect of Beecher's speeches in Great Britain.

Beecher's contemporaries believed that he had scored a major rhetorical victory. In addition to his early biographers who naturally assigned favorable results to his five speeches, the following sources were relatively unbiased but fulsome in their assessments. The *New York Times* opined upon

Beecher's return: "It is no exaggeration to affirm that the five speeches he has delivered . . . each pursuing its own line of argument and appeal, have done more for our cause in England and Scotland than all that has been before said or written." Oliver Wendell Holmes, writing in the *Atlantic Monthly*, characterized Beecher's tour thusly: "it has been to lift him from the position of one of the most popular preachers and lecturers, to one of the most popular men in the country."[38]

Later critics assigned less efficacy to Beecher's persuasive prowess. Hibben, after carefully sounding historians' analyses of Beecher's speeches, concluded they were "after all, of no great political value to his country." Although granting that "It took considerable courage to speak to the hostile English audiences," Clark concluded that Beecher "did little to change English attitudes toward the conflict."[39]

Lionel Crocker, of all Beecher's critics, delved the deepest into the newspapers' reactions to Beecher's speeches. Without deprecating Crocker's excellent work, what his findings really illustrate is that owners and publishers of newspapers are, and in Beecher's case were, more often conservative than liberal. Thus, the critic's trying to assay the worth of an orator's efforts on the basis of newspaper reaction can be instructive but of limited utility. Of the twenty-four major metropolitan newspapers Crocker surveyed, he determined that six favored Beecher and eighteen were unfriendly. Yet, as Franklin D. Roosevelt demonstrated in 1936 when he won a landslide election even though the so-called Tory press was against him, the conservative British newspapers reflected little more than their own prejudices. Neither Lord John Russell nor Parliament nor Prime Minister Palmerston were turned from their pro-Northern path. Allan Nevins, in a few cogently argued pages, gave the non-rhetorical reasons, which were primarily military, why official British posture became decidedly cooler to the South and considerably warmer to the North during the critical year of 1863, and these factors had little to do with Beecher or the British press.[40]

Yet, all of Beecher's critics have failed to criticize his practice of the art of rhetoric. On the one hand, if one may borrow the hackneyed religious metaphor, Beecher preached to the choir at four of the five cities. But it must be stated in his favor that success or failure was inherent in each of the four speeches. His ability to adapt to different audiences, however favorably disposed they might have been at the beginning, certainly contributed to his carrying them with him to the end. Appeals to free speech, liberty, shared historical values, and the particular adaptation to the labor audience at Glasgow, the academic audience at Edinburgh, and the cosmopolitan audience in London, were rhetorical adaptations of the first rank. Second, the unfavorable newspapers, which Crocker surveyed, were more adept at printing *argumentum ad personam* epithets (pejoratively known as "if you have no case, then abuse your opponent") against Beecher than they were in disproving his basic propositions. The editors did not defend the South, or slavery, or deny Beecher's equation that the Union equalled liberty. Rather, they quibbled with details. Beecher's ability to constrain the newspapers' responses to his themes was doubtless due to his framing of the argumentative battle. He took the high moral ground by drawing stark dichotomies between the North and South with regard to labor versus leisure, freedom versus slavery, and democracy versus aristocracy.   Except for editorial potshots, his position was impregnable, unless one frontally attacked it.   To do so, the conservative owners and publishers would have had to avow slavery, aristocracy, and the leisure class, while disavowing freedom, democracy, and work, a task too distasteful even to them and their readers.

Liverpool was another story.   If the other four cities had been inviting parlors, then Liverpool was a dangerous lion's den.   Beecher still had a majority for him in the audience, but the increased size of the minority made it an intense oratorical encounter.   Yet, Beecher prevailed:

> Mr. Beecher possesses the faculty, beyond any living American, of combining close, rapid, powerful, *practical* reasoning with intense passion. . . . whereby he adapts himself completely to the exigency of the instant, gives him a rare command over a common audience.   Even those who hate, can't help admiring, and those most steeled with prejudice, have to wince in spite of themselves. . . . Mr. Beecher, in doing this, while at the same time vindicating our National cause with unflinching spirit, has entitled himself to the gratitude of every right-hearted American. [Emphasis in original.][41]

4
Apologist for Evolution

There are a great many men," Beecher assured an audience at the Central Music Hall in Chicago on February 7, 1883, "who think it is unworthy of the dignity, of the glory, of man to have come down from a monkey; and so they make a little pile of mud and call that the beginning of man–created out of dust. Which is the worst, a living monkey or a pile of mud? [Laughter and applause.]"[1]

The Reverend Henry Ward Beecher, perhaps more so than any other contemporary preacher, was responsible for adjusting Charles Darwin's theory of evolution to Christianity and Christians to Darwin's theory. For in truth, Beecher had an interrelated persuasive exigency. He needed to assuage late nineteenth-century believers that Darwin's thesis did not disturb the basic religious tenets of the Bible, and concomitantly to assure them that believing Christians could also be thinking Christians. In the late spring and early summer of 1885, as if to symbolize by the seasons that Christianity was still in full bloom notwithstanding evolutionary tendencies in the flora and fauna, he preached a series of eight sermons that were also telegraphed to leading newspapers so that readers, as well as Plymouth listeners, could benefit from his liberal exegesis. But as was the case with the issue of slavery, Beecher did not come to the sermons on evolution at Plymouth Church without first stating his ideas in other forums. The first major attack against fundamentalism and for evolution was not a speech but a major essay in the *North American Review* in 1882 that was entitled "Progress of Thought in the Church." The motivation to speak out on the subject was prompted in part by the success of the article, which was a marked success, and by the invitation to deliver an after-dinner speech. Beecher delivered his first spoken broadside at a farewell dinner in honor of Herbert Spencer, an English social philosopher who favored a kind of Darwinian survival of the fittest in weeding out poor people from the body politic. The dinner was held at Delmonico's restaurant in New York City at the end of Spencer's lecture tour of the United States in late 1882. Building on those successes, in 1883 Beecher delivered a series of national lectures entitled "Evolution and Revolution." (Unfortunately, the Beecher Family Papers do not contain detailed information about places or dates for this tour, except that he delivered a lecture in Chicago on February 7, 1883, and in Denver, Colorado, on September 17, 1883.) In order to understand the series of sermons that are the focus of this chapter, the essay, the Spencer address, and the lectures need to be explicated as a prolegomena to Beecher's persuasions in the pulpit.[2]

Evolving Rhetoric on Evolution

The Reverend Beecher made many points in "Progress of Thought in the Church," but two of them are particularly germane for this chapter. First, Beecher burned his bridges with regard to the literal inspiration of the Bible. He granted that the Holy Scriptures contained precious truth. "But," Beecher believed, "they claim no such mechanical perfection as has been claimed for them." This was in direct contravention to the conservatives who held that the Bible was divinely inspired down to the last jot. If the Bible were not *the* truth, then one could reasonably look elsewhere for it, and Beecher turned to evolution as a scientific source for revealed truths. Beecher understood intellectually that the doctrine of the divine inspiration of the Bible was diametrically opposed to the tenets of evolution. The conservatives also understood that Beecher cut out the core of their beliefs, which leads to Beecher second point.[3]

Beecher did not reject the Bible as much as he rejected what fundamentalists said the Bible said. Beecher dismissed their theology as so much humbug: "Our age is not in rebellion against clear, intellectual statements of religious truth. But there is rebellion against the tyranny of mediaeval creeds." Beecher realized that evolution stepped not on the toes of the Bible but on the toes of pastors and priests who had a vested interest in maintaining the theological status quo: "To admit the truth of evolution is to yield up the reigning theology." Then Beecher dethroned the king, John Calvin. In a series of objections that utilized *reductio ad absurdum*, Beecher demonstrated the modern problem with Calvinism, which was based on Augustinian doctrines derived in the fourth century A.D. The following example demonstrates how Beecher deprecated the Calvinistic doctrines of predestination and the depravity of man by running them to their logical but absurd conclusions: "It appears then, that the earth was a vast machine for the manufacture of corruption; that God himself planned that corruption . . . ."[4]

In the conclusion of his essay, Beecher waxed eloquent on the Victorian notion of progress as applied to Christianity. The following passage also suggests his mastery in metaphor:

> The future is not in danger from the revelation of science. . . .
> Changes must come and old things must pass away, but no tree
> sheds its leaf until it has rolled up a bud at its axil for the next
> summer. Navigation does not cease when correct charts
> supersede faulty ones . . . Our time is one of transition. We
> are refusing the theology of Absolute Monarchy–of Divine

Despotism, and framing a theology consistent with the life and teachings of Jesus Christ.

As the "Progress of Thought in the Church" was for the reading intelligentsia, so was the Herbert Spencer speech for sophisticated New Yorkers.[5]

Close to midnight on the evening of November 9, 1882, Henry Ward Beecher rose to give the last after-dinner speech to honor Herbert Spencer. Lyman Abbott, an eyewitness to the event, captured the mood of the audience:

> The room was filled with tobacco-smoke. The auditors were weary and ready to go home. Not a vibrating note had been struck throughout the evening. It seemed to me as Mr. Beecher rose that all he could do was to apologize for not speaking at that late hour and dismiss his audience. By some jest he won a laugh; caught the momentary attention of his audience; seemed about to lose it; caught it again; again saw it escaping, and again captured it. In five minutes the more distant auditors had moved their chairs forward, the French waiters, who had paid no attention to any one else, straightened themselves up against the walls to listen. . . .[6]

The reason the tired audience listened was because Beecher cast his speech in humorous dichotomies. Humor always disarms an audience and dichotomies are easy on the mind, especially late at night.   In the introduction of his speech, Beecher arrested his audience by juxtaposition: "The old New England churches used to have two ministers; one was considered as a doctor of theology, and the other a revivalist and pastor. The doctor has had his day, and you now have the revivalist. [Laughter.] . . . I cannot for the life of me reconcile his [Spencer's] notions with those of St. Augustine. I can't get along with Calvin and Spencer both. [Laughter.]" Having established his ethos as the pastor versus the theologian, the warm humanist versus John Calvin, the cold logician who held that most sinners were going to Hell, Beecher praised evolution and Spencer, but he was at pains to leaven his speech with levity. For instance, Beecher found it was efficacious to poke fun at the fundamentalists by applying in a good-natured manner the theory of evolution, not as it was actually taught, but as the fundamentalists asserted the theory must be applied.   Tongue-in-cheek, Beecher told his audience: "It is a hypothesis that we are but the prolongation of an inferior tribe, and there are many evidences among men that it is so. [Laughter.] . . . I would just have lief have descended from a monkey as from anything else if I had descended far enough. [Laughter.]"[7]

Another argument that Beecher developed in the Spencer speech, and which would find its way into subsequent addresses on evolution, was the idea that science and religion were two compatible, not antagonistic, ways of understanding God. For instance, Beecher claimed that science and religion both revealed God's creation:

There is a record in geology that is as much a record of God as the record on paper in human language. [Applause.] They are both true–where they are true. [Laughter.] The record of matter very often is misinterpreted, and the record of the letter is often misinterpreted, and you are to enlighten yourselves by knowing both of them and interpreting them one by the other.

And in the final words of his conclusion, he again allowed how science would improve the old Calvinist theology: "[Evolution would] emancipate that life from superstition, from fears, and from thralls, and make me a citizen of the universe. [Applause.]"[8]

The effect of the Spencer speech, much like the Sumner protest rally speech, was to cement the public's identification of Beecher with evolution. At the end of the speech, which Beecher concluded with a prayer, Abbott recalled that "the whole audience rose by a common impulse to their feet, as if to make the prayer their own, cheering, clapping their hands, and waving their handkerchiefs." The address also attracted media attention. The *New York Times* noted that "The Rev. Henry Ward Beecher made a characteristic and witty speech" and observed "Mr Beecher's remarks were cheered at their conclusion."[9]

In his lecture on "Evolution and Revolution," Beecher continued the themes he had broached in the Spencer address. Beecher's handwritten notes for this lecture exist in outline form in the Beecher Family Papers. He wrote some complete sentences, some sentence fragments, and often one or two words sufficed to remind him of his thoughts for the lecture. Nevertheless, enough verbiage exists to indicate Beecher's general train of thought. The dichotomies he developed in the Spencer speech were present in the lectures. For instance, he juxtaposed evolution to the old time religion in the following ways. With relation to "Inspiration" and "Theology," Beecher claimed the "Basic idea of *old* is *Fear & Conscience* [Beecher's emphasis]" whereas the thrust of the new is "*Love, Hope, Humanity* [Beecher's emphasis]." Evolution was a revolution because, as Beecher believed, "This will involve change in sermonizing in all the ways of influencing human mind."[10]

In an extended passage, Beecher indicated to the popular audience how evolution would revolutionize their religious beliefs. The theme was the Victorian notion of progress, and Beecher applied it to the spiritual world:

The unbelief of to-day is the faith of tommorrow. Scepticism unveils truth. The theology that is rising upon the horizon will continue to rise. Each succeeding generation will find new beams. You young men and maidens are living in a morning which thousands of noble natures desired to see, but they died without the sight. . . . We ought to have expected this change, for the voice of the whole Testament is the voice of one who looks forward hopefully.

The effect of the Reverend Beecher's lectures on the populace is hard to gauge, but Clifford Clark graded them "an immense success." Daniel Addison noted that listeners and readers reacted favorably to Beecher's ideas: "That they were read by the people as much as by the students was an additional reason why they may be considered as having played an important part in the reconstruction of American religious ideas."[11]

The Sermons on Evolution

As in Beecher's triumphal tour of Great Britain in 1863 where the Liverpool address came to symbolize his rhetorical prowess, so did one of his sermons on evolution emerge as a first among equals. Delivered on May 31, 1885, Beecher's "Two Revelations" stands enshrined as his major sermon on the subject. The other homilies he delivered were "The Sign of the Times," May 17, 1885; "Evolution in Human Consciousness of the Idea of God," May 24, 1885; "The Two Revelations," May 31, 1885; "The Inspiration of the Bible," June 7, 1885; "The Sinfulness of Man," June 14, 1885; "The New Birth," June 21, 1885; "Divine Providence and Design," June 28, 1885; and "Evolution and the Church," July 5, 1885. What has not been realized hitherto about "The Two Revelations," and this also applies to the rest of the sermons, is how Beecher, the ostensible apologist for Darwinism, in fact enacted the role of accuser against the fundamentalist bigotry of the times. Beecher realized that often the best defense is a strong offense, and he accused the anti-Darwinists with an aggressive attack that placed them on the defense.   That the fundamentalists eventually developed a reactionary conservatism that did not appeal to mainline Christians in the late nineteenth and twentieth centuries is not ascribable totally to Beecher's speeches. But it may certainly be stated that he opened the attack, which progressive ministers, such as the Reverend Harry Emerson Fosdick in the twentieth century, carried forward, and he helped alter the argumentative presumption of the status quo in favor of Darwinism and against fundamentalism.

This sermon was one of Beecher's better reasoned discourses, and it also excelled in organizational strategies that helped the listener or reader grasp his persuasive argument. All too often Beecher's sermons and speeches seemed to meander over the countryside, proving that in garrulous speech the shortest distance between two points is not a straight line. But in this sermon Beecher marshalled his language so that it marched ineluctably to do battle with the fundamentalists. The sermon's title, "The Two Revelations," stated the interconnected crux of his exegesis: the Bible and the earth were both God's revelations, each revealed different aspects of his will, both could be believed without contradicting each other, and both reinforced one another.

Beecher took as his text John 1:3: "All things were made by Him, and without Him was not anything made that was made." Beecher, unlike the fundamentalists, understood that the Bible described God as the creator of the universe, but Beecher claimed "how he made them—whether by the direct force of a creative will or indirectly through a long series of gradual changes—the Scriptures do not declare."[12]

Beecher then employed an interesting argumentative strategy. Since the time of Korax in ancient Greece and Cicero in Rome, the orator was advised to develop a *confirmatio* in which the arguments and reasoning for the speaker's thesis were presented, and then to invent a *refutatio* in which the orator rebutted opposing arguments. In the "Two Revelations," Beecher adapted the pattern to his persuasive goal by slightly changing the prescribed arrangement. In organizing his speech, he devised a *confirmatio*, then a *refutatio*, then another long argument section. This was a wise persuasive posture for two reasons. First, many of the members of Beecher's liberal congregation already believed to some degree in evolution, so he did not so much persuade them as he reinforced their ideas; therefore, he first confirmed their beliefs, then attacked fundamentalist holdings, which most of his congregation already deprecated, and then adduced additional argumentation for his and their beliefs. Second, for those who were undecided, and this probably pertained more to the newspaper audience than the Plymouth listeners, his skillful one-two-one rhetorical punch targeted those who, still wavering, would rather choose wisdom (Beecher's stance) than ignorance (the conservative's stance).

First *Confirmatio*

Beecher held that the Bible disclosed two revelations of God's interactions with his creation. One was the relationship of God to man and the other was God to physical matter: "So we have two revelations: God's thought in the evolution of matter, and God's thought in the evolution of mind; and these are the Old Testament and the New–not in the usual sense of those terms, but in the appropriate scientific use of them." Thus, the Old Testament recorded "God's thought in regard to the globe as a habitation for man." However, that record was incomplete. According to Beecher, the faithful could turn to science as another source to understand God:

> [W]hen I reflect that the silent stones and the buried strata contain the record of God's working, and that the globe itself is a sublime history of God as an engineer, and architect and as a masterbuilder, I cannot but marvel at the indifference with which good men have regarded this stupendous revelation of the ages past, and especially at the assault made by Christian men upon scientific men who are bringing to light the long-hidden record of God's revelation in the material world. . . .
>
> Science is but the deciphering of God's thought as revealed in the structure of this world; it is a mere translation of God's primitive revelation. If to reject God's revelation of the Book is infidelity, what is it to reject God's revelation of himself in the structure of the whole globe?

Beecher was able to argue the way he did because he did not believe in the literal interpretation of the Bible. He spoke of "the poetical Eden," which represented man's early history, but argued that the earth was actually prepared by God for man with convulsions, storms, and grinding ice. For Beecher, the Bible was the Word of God, but not *the* Word of God. Thus, the Bible and science illuminated one another because neither was final truth. This theme was argued in the essay, the Spencer speech, and the lecture tour.

Beecher summarized the first part of his arguments section with a telling juxtaposition. On the one hand, he praised the "noble body of investigators who are deciphering the hieroglyphics of God inscribed upon this temple of the earth [who] are to be honored and encouraged." He then turned on the fundamentalists with invective and *argumentum ad personam* that deprecated them and demarcated them from wise believers:

> As it is now, vaguely bigoted theologists, ignorant pietists, jealous churchmen, unintelligent men, whose very existence seems like a sarcasm upon creative wisdom, with leaden wit and stinging irony swarm about the adventurous surveyors who are searching God's handiwork and who have added to the realm of the knowledge of God the grandest treasures. Men pretending to be ministers of God, with all manner of grimace and shallow ridicule and witless criticism and unproductive wisdom, enact the very feats of the monkey in the attempt to prove the monkey was not their ancestor.

The monkey argument was also in the Herbert Spencer speech and the lecture. Anybody in the congregation or reading audience who still believed in the fundamentalist position found themselves, or so Beecher asserted, in company with the simians they so detested; and those who sided with Beecher against the conservatives could chortle with their preacher against apish antics. Having polarized the issue, Beecher then rebutted positions held by the conservatives, and this was made all the easier by initially using humor to debunk their stands.

The *Refutatio*

Giving the conservatives their due, Beecher allowed "It is objected to all assertions of the validity of God's great record in matter, that science is uncertain and unripe." In one of the homey metaphors in which Beecher excelled, he refuted the conservative's argument with a telling warrant: "The whole Christian world for two thousand years, since the completion of the canons, has been divided up like the end of a broom into infinite splinters, quarreling with each other as to what the book did say, and what it did mean." He also quoted the Reverend Dr. Hopkins who noted that "No less than nineteen different varieties of Christianity are at present trying to convert the Japanese. . . . Now, if Christians with eighteen centuries of accumulated tradition cannot agree, how can we expect the heathen to solve the great riddle?" The inference Beecher invited his congregation to make was involved but compelling: if the Bible were divinely inspired to the point of inerrancy, then there should be little debate over its interpretation; since not even the conservatives could agree on what the Bible said, then it must not be inerrant nor be literally interpreted; therefore, science is at least as believable as the Bible, if not more so, and should be admitted as another way to understand God's creation of and purpose for the world.

The second tenet Beecher dispatched was the belief that "a layman should not meddle with that which can be judged by only scientific experts." Beecher acknowledged that the scientific method might not be in the ken of many believers, but held that "there comes an important duty" for parents, teachers, and clergymen to understand and evaluate scientific findings.

A third point he dismissed was "A vague notion exists with multitudes that science is infidel." Beecher wisely used the word "multitudes" because members of the Plymouth Church would not conceive themselves to be the *hoi polloi*. No member of the Brooklyn church would characterize himself as Beecher did the conservatives: "Men of such views often say, 'I know that religion is true. I do not wish to hear anything that threatens to unsettle my faith.'" In effect, the fundamentalists asked their believers to behave as ostriches. Not so with Beecher, for he counterattacked such ostrichlike mental crutches: "But faith that can be unsettled by the access of light and knowledge had better be unsettled." He summarized his *refutatio* with an appeal to values that were believed in Victorian times. Of progress and the moral perfectability of man, Beecher assured his audiences: "Of one thing I am certain, that whatever may have been the origin, it does not change either the destiny or the moral grandeur of man as he stands in the full light of civilization to-day."

The Second *Confirmatio*

The Reverend Beecher gave his listening and reading audiences seven arguments on the validity of evolution. For the purposes at hand, only two of those arguments are interesting rhetorically. But before turning to those arguments, it might be wise to sketch the nature of the other five arguments.

First, he claimed that the theory of evolution eschewed the chronology of the earth being created in six twenty-four hour days, but that "the divine method occupied ages and ages of immense duration." Thus, Beecher did not exclude God from his own creation, nor did evolution demand that he be excluded. Next, he observed that evolution was the method by which the world was created, and subtly applied the band wagon effect by allowing that "ninety-nine per cent" of the scientists in the world believed that way. Third, he extended the band wagon effect by demonstrating that evolution was the "working theory" of scientists throughout the world. Fourth, he allowed how evolution was taught in academies, colleges, and universities. He then cleverly argued a compelling inference. Recounting that Galileo and Newton encountered ecclesiastical reactions to their theories of heliocentrism and gravitation, Beecher countered: "The whole Church fought them; yet they stand, conquerors." Listeners and readers could easily reason that evolution, which was right, would also conquer conservative churchmen, who were wrong. His fifth argument was a rhetorical application of *argumentum ad vercundiam*, sometimes pejoratively known as the Honorable Chinese Ancestors argument. He listed nine leading theologians and educators–persons who lived in the United States, Scotland, and England, one of whom was even a duke, all of whom were representatives of either the Catholic church, the Anglican church, or the major American Protestant churches (and Beecher even mentioned a spiritualist for good measure)–who believed in evolution.

His sixth argument was rhetorically and theologically important. Beecher claimed that, in a spiritual sense, theology and religion were at loggerheads with one another. Evolution would invigorate religion and improve theology:

> Simple religion is the unfolding of the best nature of man towards God, and man has been hindered and embittered by the outrageous complexity of unbearable systems of theology that have existed. If you can change theology, you will emancipate religion; yet men are continually confounding the two terms, religion and theology. They are not alike. Religion is the condition of a man's nature as toward God and toward his fellow-men. . . . Theology is the philosophy of God, of divine government, and of human nature. The philosophy of these may be one thing; the reality of them may be another and totally different one. Though intimately connected, they are not all the same.

Beecher did not draw this distinction lightly. His dichotomy, for instance, explained why the Christian world had been divided into the splinters of a broom because men differed on the fine points of theology, a theology, after all, that theologians had constructed a millennia earlier, and that fundamentalists in the late nineteenth century had inadvertently let cloud the true message of the Bible. Yet, Jesus had not come to teach men theology but the love of God and the love of their fellow man, which was Beecher's conception of religion. Thus, Beecher claimed, evolution might undermine or overturn some man-made tenets of theology, but not to worry: evolution could never sever the vital and living link between man-to-man and man-to-God. In fact, the reverend held that evolution would clear the cobwebs of arcane pedantry:

> Evolution will multiply the motives and facilities of righteousness, which was and is the design of the whole Bible. . . . Not only will those great truths be unharmed, by which men work zealously for the reformation of their fellow-men, but they will be developed to a breadth and certainty not possible in the present philosophical condition. At present the sword of the spirit is in the sheath of a false theology. Evolution, applied to religion, will influence it only as the hidden temples are restored, by removing the sands which have drifted in from the arid deserts of scholastic and medieval theologies. It will change theology, but only to bring out the simple temple of God in clearer and more beautiful lines and proportions.

The metaphors that Beecher selected were excellent examples of adaptations to the listening and reading audiences. The "sword of the spirit," which was religion, was marvelously portrayed in "the sheath" of theology. The implication was very clear: one had only to withdraw religion from theology's sheath in order to experience the true meaning and message of the Bible. The conservatives evidently preferred to keep religion encased in a backward theology. In the other extended image, Beecher effectively eschewed discussing pedantic medieval theologies by dismissing them as the "sands" that drifted in from "arid deserts"; and as archeologists cleared ancient temples and ruins, which surely appealed to the imagination of Victorian Americans who were witnessing the rediscovery of the ancient world, the imagery of God's temple being brought out in "more beautiful lines and proportions" would have been rhetorically compelling.

Beecher continued in his seventh point with the dichotomy he had established in his previous point. He held that evolution would "obliterate the distinction between natural and revealed religion, both of which are the testimony of God." As theology had divided instead of united man-to-man and man-to-God, so had the distinction between Biblical religion and spiritual religion cleaved Christians. At stake was an issue that Martin Luther raised during the Reformation, but in truth the problem inhered in Christianity almost from its foundation.

Arguing that good works could not justify or save one in the sight of God, Luther advanced that one could only be saved by faith alone. In protesting against the ascendance of good works over faith in the practice of Catholicism in the sixteenth century, Luther inadvertently assured the reverse of what he decried: the new status quo stressed faith to the detriment of good works. Many Protestant Christians placed so much emphasis upon faith and correct doctrines (theology) that they lost sight of good works, moral actions, and spirituality (religion). The Reverend Beecher actually revitalized the nexus between faith and good works, between theology and religion. Beecher held that evolution would restore a much needed balance in Protestant Christianity:

> What is called morality will be no longer dissevered from religion. Morals bear to spirituality the same relation which the root bears to the blossom and the fruit. Hitherto, a false and imperfect theology has set them in two different provinces. We have been taught that morality will not avail us, and that spirituality is the only saving element; whereas, there is no spirituality itself without morality; all true spirituality is an outgrowth, it is the blossom and fruit on the stem of morality.

In truth, Beecher confronted the age-old problem of the irony of the unchurched versus the churched. Why do some people, who do not attend services or believe in theology, seem good; whereas others, who hold correct doctrines and attend church regularly, do not appear to be Christ-like individuals? Beecher had the answer. He told his congregation and reading audience that evolution would rectify this religious anamoly: "It is time that these distinctions were obliterated, as they will be, by the progress and application of the doctrine of Evolution."

Having developed seven arguments in the second *confirmatio*, which he nicely enumerated for a clear comprehension of his points, Beecher then concluded his sermon by again attacking the conservatives.   He first challenged his audiences to assume their duties in squaring evolution with their religious beliefs, "to hail the rising light." Then he turned to the targets of his verbal barbs and fired one last rhetorical fusillade against the fundamentalists:

> And above all, those zealots of the pulpit—who make faces at
> a science which they do not understand, and who reason from
> prejudice to ignorance, who not only will not lead their people,
> but hold up to scorn those who strive to take off the burden
> of ignorance from their shoulders—these men are bound to
> open their eyes and see God's sun shining in the heavens.

Thus, Beecher's conclusion was marked by a subtle use of the light-dark metaphor, another carryover from the Spencer speech and the lectures. The advocates of evolution enjoyed "rising light," "wholesome beams," and "God's sun shining in the heavens"; by implication, the conservatives faced darkness, saw only unwholesome light, and were unable to see God's sun because their vision was so clouded by false theologies.

Continuing in that vein, Beecher used the imagery of Christ's cleansing the temple of the money changers to imply that Beecher was clearing away false doctrines. He stated that men "pick and choose" portions of the Bible in which to believe and "reject portions constantly." By stressing a religion that was open to reason, Beecher claimed he could help deter nineteenth-century Christians from rejecting altogether the Bible.

Reminiscent of his eulogy on Abraham Lincoln with the reference to Mount Pisgah, Beecher then closed his sermon with the observation that "We of this age have come to the mountain top; yet we can only see the promised land of the future." Then, in a very personalized peroration, Beecher claimed he was neither "infidel, nor an agnostic, nor an athiest." Rather, he dedicated the last years of his life to expounding God's revelation of the globe and the human mind.

Conclusion

The irony of this sermon is that Beecher used dichotomies to achieve his rhetorical purpose while concomitantly scoring such dichotomies in theology versus religion, in spiritualism versus morality. Persuasively, the dichotomies functioned to polarize the believers or evolutionists from the unbelievers or antievolutionists by starkly contrasting the two camps. A receptor of the reverend's rhetoric, unless a committed conservative, would have found it difficult to identify with the antievolutionists, who possessed the unacceptable intellectual traits of intolerance and ignorance. Beecher surely realized that such language would alienate the fundamentalists, but they were not his target audience for persuasion. Rather, he sought to reinforce partisans and to appeal to neutrals. Thus, any listener or reader, who was tolerant and intelligent, would believe in evolution. Since most people prefer light to darkness, Beecher wisely assured assent from reasonable individuals.

But concerning the sixth and seventh points in his sermon, Beecher scored the compartmentalized thinking he had used so successfully to gain assent for evolution in his first five points. As a matter of fact, he committed the logical fallacy of *petitio principii*, or begging the question, when he claimed that evolution would moot the dichotomy between theology and religion, between spiritualism and morality. How or why evolution would "multiply the motives and facilities of righteousness" he never proved.

To further compound the irony, Beecher enacted the very roles of St. Augustine and John Calvin that he so detested. By elevating evolution, in which Christians must now believe, he inadvertently introduced a new doctrine, as Augustine had with predestination and Calvin with the depravity of man. But these dogmas were hardly germane to the perennial preaching problem in Christianity, the relationship of belief to action, of faith to good works, of theology to religion. Beecher assured that Christians who believed in evolution might be more intelligent, but he paradoxically added another splinter to the broom that exacerbates the problem of intolerance that divided Christians then, and divides them now.

5
The Postlude:
Beecher as *Vox Populi*

In 1858, the Reverend Henry Ward Beecher was characterized as a "most popular and effective preacher. . . . He has the largest Protestant congregation in America. . . . He is the most popular of American lecturers." Whereas the other chapters have focused on Beecher as a preacher and as an advocate for the Union, this chapter is about Beecher as a public speaker. To be sure, Beecher's ethos was probably never disassociated in the public mind with Plymouth Church, but the focus here is on secular topics. Concerning the role of public orator, John Henry Barrows opined: "Although, perhaps, not the greatest, he was yet the most successful of American lecturers, addressing larger audiences with greater pecuniary rewards than any other speaker."[1]

This chapter is divided into three sections that correspond to Beecher's miscellaneous speeches. The first section will detail his lectures in general. Subsequent sections are keyed to the "Collected Sermons and Speeches" and will treat his views on oratory and woman suffrage.

Beecher as Public Lecturer

If Henry Ward Beecher was a stump speaker who stumbled into the pulpit, he was equally adept at stepping from the pulpit into the public platform. His lectures, mainly epideictic in nature, are as informative about nineteenth century interests and tastes as they are about public speaking on the circuit.

The lectures were really public entertainment. The talking season for Beecher ran from late October to early March. This was not happen chance. Fall harvesting was completed and spring planting had not begun. The fall and winter also offered relief from the heat that plagued public auditoriums in the summer. Since Beecher was constrained to preach at Plymouth on Sunday, he delivered most of his lectures during the week. This schedule was also facilitated by the fact that most of his major lectures were delivered in upstate New York along the route of the New York Central Railroad, in the cities of eastern Pennsylvania that were serviced by the Pennsylvania

Railroad, in the towns and villages around Boston, and in the nearby states of New Jersey, Connecticut, Rhode Island, and New Hampshire. These locations could be sandwiched easily into his busy preaching schedule. Thus, when Beecher claimed in his series of speeches in Great Britain that he could not speak in the South, he mislead a bit. He was really a regional speaker who addressed audiences primarily in New England and along the northern East coast.

When Beecher delivered lectures further west, he usually allotted a week or so and was thus away from Plymouth for a Sunday. For instance, he delivered "Dangers to Be Guarded Against" in the 1855-56 season. He journeyed directly to Chicago, where he spoke on October 10; then to Milwaukee on the thirteenth; Rockford, Illinois, on the fifteenth; Bloomington, Illinois, on the seventeenth; Indianapolis, Indiana, on the twentieth; and Cleveland, Ohio, on the twenty-fourth. In the main, Beecher did not address bucolic audiences in out-of-the-way hamlets. He chose to speak in larger towns and cities, which could provide sizeable audiences and a handsome recompense, and which were on major rail lines.

The one exception to the general rule seems to be Beecher's "The Reign of the Common People," for which lecture he travelled in the upper Midwest and mountain states. Beecher was a gregarious person, and he maintained a diary of the trip in which he indicated how he sought to identify with local audiences. He noted in his diary that he liked to sit on the top of the stagecoach and talk to the driver, who was a wealth of information about the area. For instance, he jotted down homey facts such as that from Minneapolis, Minnesota, 30,000 barrels are shipped daily; that in Winnipeg, Manitoba, there were only two houses ten years ago but now the town had 25,000 inhabitants; and that the "Dacotah" [sic] produced great amounts of wheat. These homey references to local interests were then incorporated into his addresses. Perhaps the reverend remembered the following joke from a stage driver when Beecher addressed an audience in the Northwest. Concerning the temperature there in the winter time, Beecher wryly told an audience "it would have been much colder if the thermometer had been longer."[2]

Beecher gave seven major lecture tours. On these tours he gave approximately 140 known speeches. The real number is much greater than this because so many of the places and/or dates, which are noted in Beecher's handwriting, are indecipherable. This figure does not count lectures that he delivered only a few times in the environs of New York City. His war horse was "Patriotism," given at least twenty-nine times, in the 1854-55 season. This was followed by the "Waves and Cycles of National Life and Thought," 1875-76, at twenty-five speeches; the "Burdens of Society" with twenty-three addresses in 1858-59; and "Wastes and Burdens of Society" with twenty-two performances in 1877-78. These four lectures comprised approximately 70 per cent of Beecher's stock-in-trade speeches. The other major lectures were: "Reconstruction on Principles National Not Sectional," delivered at least fifteen times in the 1865-66 season; "Dangers to Be Guarded Against," eight times in the 1855-56; and "Gradations of Personal Social Power," seven times in 1856-57.

As might be imagined, Beecher made considerable money on his tours. Although it is impossible to suggest the equivalent amounts in today's dollar, the figures alone are impressive and one would do well to remember that the United States was on the gold standard in the nineteenth century. According to John Howard, Beecher was paid around $550,000 for forty years of preaching at Plymouth Church (Beecher was among the best paid preachers in the country). During the same time, Beecher made approximately $465,000 from his lectures. For those who are interested, Barrows estimated that Beecher earned approximately $1,500,000 total from his salary, lectures, books, and other royalties.[3]

"Woman Suffrage Man's Right"

Probably under the auspices of the Women's National Loyal League, whose president was Susan B. Anthony, Henry Ward Beecher delivered at Cooper Institute, New York City, February 2, 1860, a lecture on woman's right to vote. Clifford Clark characterized this address as a "major speech on women's suffrage." However, Clark did not reveal the rhetorical techniques that Beecher employed in the speech nor did he examine the reverend's argumentative strategies on the suffrage question.[4]

The major organizational pattern of the speech was topical. But how Beecher treated the topics within his address was related to the nature of the audience. Realizing that many committed followers would attend the speech, Beecher created materials that would reinforce partisan beliefs. Cognizant that neutrals and opponents would probably be in attendance, he needed to assuage their reservations. The rhetorical strategy he employed was to argue by negation–the speech was in reality an extended classical *refutatio*. That is, he took the reservations and objections that would reasonably reside in his opponent's minds and openly refuted them. Concomitantly, this confutation would augment adherent's allegiance to the cause. Beecher accomplished his persuasive goal by rebutting eight arguments advanced by men and women who opposed woman suffrage.

"Woman suffrage," Beecher announced to his audience, "will bring civilization into our primary meetings and decency into our secondary ones." Decrying the "heathenism" that infested New York City, Beecher doubtless induced the audience to laughter when he allowed that New Yorkers kept "specimens of everything this side of perdition, and some, I think, of things the other side." With the audience in a good mood, Beecher stated his thesis: "Woman's influence, if introduced into public affairs, would work in the same direction there that it has worked, and is working, in social life, in literature, and in religious assemblies." He supported his argument, not so much by proving it, as by disproving positions to the contrary.[5]

His transition to the first refutation was "But let us attend to some of the objections that are made." If women voted, opponents argued, then they would be subjected "to rudeness and to an exposure painful to delicacy." Beecher handily turned the tables by warranting that that very rudeness was "the result of woman's absence" from polling places, which were in "vile precincts and in pest-holes." As for delicacy, Beecher countered that in mailing letters at a post office women were "made more public" and "fully as indelicate as in depositing her vote." Having dispatched those scurrilous objections, Beecher claimed that giving the vote to women would carry into national life "a power almost like the right hand of the Almighty."

The second major objection Beecher confuted was the argument that women should stay at home and have an influence there through their male relatives. He used humor to debunk that position. Allowing that males praised "the sweetening home affections" of women in the home, Beecher found it ironical that when women did attempt to influence men, the men "turn with lordly authority" and announce that the woman's role is in "the nursery and kitchen." Indeed, Beecher held that there was "a large infusion of vulgar arrogance even in good men" who held that God made woman "as nurse, cook, and plaything." He then used *reductio ad absurdum* to demolish the opposition. Using the examples of female school teachers, artists, and writers, who had general acceptance in Victorian America, Beecher asked why did not those who opposed woman suffrage also argue that women should eschew these jobs as well and instead stay at home and work through their male relatives to effect change. Beecher efficiently explicated the absurdity of his opponent's position.

The third objection was: "If women were to vote, then, of course, she would be eligible for public offices." Never one to mince words, Beecher followed his own logic and proclaimed, "Well why not?" He again argued by example. Utilizing homey instances of a farmer, merchant, editor, and schoolmaster, with which listeners could easily identify, Beecher observed that no one objected to wives taking the place of dead husbands to carry on the work. He then asserted the idea of natural law for women's rights:

> I hold that it should be recognized her rights to engage in
> everything for which she is fitted, public affairs not excepted.
> . . . Wherever there are gifts, there should be liberty of exercise.
> Faculty always demands function. Every human being has a
> natural right to do whatever he or she can do well.

Although Beecher's logic was compellingly sound, not all listeners are convinced with systematic logic.

"But it is objected that," as Beecher stated his fourth point, "by mingling in public affairs, women would soon extinguish that delicacy that now gives them both grace and influence." In reality, this was a recapitulation of his first point, but Beecher refuted it differently. He constructed a compelling argument for a Victorian audience. Starting with the premise that "womanly qualities are God's gift," to which most Americans would give assent, Beecher then concluded that God's gifts could not be subverted. By elevating women above men on a moral level, but beneath men on a political plane, the opponents of women's rights inadvertently invited Beecher, who was a clever debater, to beat them at their own game. The reverend easily turned the tables on his opponents: "it is not probable that the exercise of large public duty will efface the marks of her original constitution, and that an active patriotism will tarnish her purity, and that zeal for public justice will demoralize her nature."

His fifth refutation concerned what would happen when one's wife and daughter were subjected to "brutal rowdies" in public places. Beecher contended that he could take his wife and children any place in the United States. He then allowed that most men respect a woman's presence. Only "now and then" did Beecher see men smoking as they walked with women on the public streets, and "only once in a while" did men smoke when a woman was on an omnibus, the precursor of streetcars and the modern bus. Thus, Beecher concluded that civilized men would treat women in public affairs as they treat "her in the sanctuary and in these halls."

The sixth topic dealt with the woman's sphere argument. Opponents charged that if women became active in politics, then they would abandon the home, their true calling. Again, Beecher constructed a telling argument, based on example, that turned the tables on his opponents and reduced their argument to absurdity. He did not reject the woman's sphere argument, but merely held there was room in that sphere for political action. In reality, his chain of argumentation was built on the man's sphere argument. Observing that men attend to the duties of citizenship and yet still operate banks and stores, Beecher concluded "It would not take any more of woman's time than it does of man's." As a matter of fact, he opined, women would benefit men:

> And if men were morally elevated, they would strike for rectitude without all those struggles and tergiversations which now impede their progress. Attention to public affairs, then, would not draw woman from her appropriate sphere one whit more than it draws man from his.

The Reverend Beecher's seventh argument was a recapitulation of the delicacy argument that he developed in his first point. But the supporting examples were different. Beecher observed that men did not object to women singing in public. He reminded the audience that the English operatic singer Jenny Lind, who toured the United States in the early 1850s, was widely praised and well received, and that Madame Sontag, another vocalist, sang before the assembled clergy of New York City and Brooklyn. However, no one commented about her "exposure, about her being unsexed, or about her being out of her sphere."

To a significant degree, Beecher's eighth and last refutation against woman suffrage was brilliantly conceived. When he delivered this speech, Queen Victoria reigned on the British throne. He used this fact to support his contention that women could serve a public function. But Beecher turned the idea of class distinction, upon which the aristocracy ruled, to his rhetorical advantage. He argued that males in the United States should trust their democratic women as much or more than British males trusted their aristocratic women. He thus played on inherent democratic values that he juxtaposed to European monarchical practices. Observing that societies "have been obliged to pass through the contention of the democratic and the aristocratic elements," he stated that women through the ages had been given power and public trust if they would "accept them in aristocratic form" as an "abbess, a countess, a queen." However, women "lower down in the social scale" were hindered by being female. On the one hand, Beecher used Queen Victoria as a model for the positive potentiality of female power:

> To-day, the proudest throne on the globe is honored by a woman. No person is shocked that she is at the head of empire. Every reason urged against a larger liberty for woman is illustriously confuted by the dignity, purity, and womanly propriety with which Victoria stands before her empire, and before the world.

On the other hand, he appealed to democratic values by arguing that Americans should eschew aristocratic attitudes toward women:

> It is only woman *without a title* [Beecher's emphasis] that must have no privileges. Woman, in her own simple self, with nothing more but what God gave her, plain, democratic woman, is not deemed worthy of honor and publicity. With a crown on her head, she may enter parliaments, and govern empires. With only her own simple personal virtues, she may not lift up her hand to cast a vote.

To complete the irony, Beecher invoked the subtle dislike that democratic American held against British royal titles: "That which is good enough for a queen is not too good for my wife. That which is noble in a duchess is honorable in my daughter." If one did not agree with Beecher's conclusion, then one was left in the unenviable and undemocratic position of holding that British aristocratic women were better off politically than their democratic counterparts in the United States.

Beecher used a smooth transition to close his address: "This, then, is the sum of what I wished to say to you to-night." In keeping with the nature of his speech, which was epideictic, Beecher targeted his conclusion more toward contemplation than action. In one of his homey metaphors, he urged reflection rather than immediate endeavor: "I have said it more in the expectation that it will work in you as a leaven than that it will bear immediate fruits. But, as the farmer sows seed in October that he does not expect to reap till July, so we must sow, and wait patiently for the harvest." He allowed that he did not expect to see female suffrage in his lifetime, but expected that his children might see it because "thoughts move faster than they used to."

He then finished his speech with a metaphor that expressed the Victorian value of progress. Given that biologists believed that plants grew in three stages, Beecher held that the root, which takes the longest to develop, grew until the advent of Christ; the stem, which grows faster, had been growing from Christ's time to the present; and "that in the period in which we stand it is growing by the blossom and the fruit." (It evidently never dawned on Beecher to complete the metaphor: that the blossom and fruit wither and die in a relatively short time; therefore, progress would have to start all over again.) In his final words to the audience, Beecher asserted that women should have the vote because he advocated "*man's rights*" [Beecher's emphasis].

Although Beecher supported his thesis for woman suffrage by negation, and did so compellingly well, he suffered one major logical flaw in his speech. He never did prove how or why woman suffrage was a man's right. Neither did he prove it was a man's right by disproving the opponent's arguments against the female vote. The title of the speech, "Woman Suffrage Man's Right," was certainly a catchy come-on to attract listeners, but the real persuasion was accomplished by applying a classical *refutatio* in order to demolish the sham arguments with which nineteenth-century males barred women from voting.

"Oratory"

The Reverend Henry Ward Beecher was invited to give the commencement address for the third graduation exercises of the National School of Elocution and Oratory, Philadelphia, Pennsylvania, on May 29, 1876. The school was founded in 1873 by J. W. Shoemaker for the purposes of educating its students in oratorical endeavors. Once underway, the school usually had about two hundred students and a faculty of ten. The school endured until 1943 when it was forced to close by the exigencies of World War II.[6]

Beecher adapted his remarks well to the audience of parents and students who were interested in oratory as training for a public career. But the focus here is not so much on how Beecher identified with his audience as it is on Beecher's conception of the art of oratory. The speech also illustrates Beecher's penchant for argumentation by negation. He had a particular flair for refuting reservations in the minds of his listeners. He must have realized that the persuasive power of the orator can appear to be greater when demolishing the positions of others than in sustaining ones own arguments. Adversative address, with its combative stance, is more exciting to listen to than expository persuasion.

"Training in this department [oratory] is the great want of our day," Beecher assured his audience in his thesis statement given early in his address, "for we are living in a land whose genius, whose history, whose institutions, whose people, eminently demand oratory." Well trained students doubtless would have appreciated how Beecher constructed his proposition with the anaphora of "whose." The reason for the need, according to the reverend, was because people misunderstood its methods and ends:

> I think that oratory, with the exception of here and there an
> instance which is supposed to be natural, is looked upon, if not
> with contempt, at least with discredit, as a thing artificial; as a
> mere science of ornamentation; as a method fit for actors who
> are not supposed to express their own sentiments, but unfit for
> a living man who has earnestness and sincerity and purpose.

In the remainder of his address, Beecher would set his audience straight.[7]

Tilting against the common prejudice that "oratory is an artificial thing," Beecher asked his audience to consider the delivery of speakers in three important professions. Of preachers, Beecher held they were "grotesque," "awkward," and "dull"; lawyers fared no better because of their "everlasting monotone and seesaw"; and politicians were scored for their "bellowing" and "shouting." Little wonder that Beecher exclaimed: "How much squandering there is of the voice!"

Having decried unpracticed and uncultured speakers, Beecher defined oratory. It was a definition that stressed results that were obtained by the synergism of man, method, and truth: "I define oratory to be *the art of influencing conduct with the truth set home by all the resources of the living man* [Beecher's emphasis]." First, Beecher required that a man know and speak the truth. "Let no man who is a sneak try to be an orator," he cautioned; rather, the man "must have something to say. He must have something that in his very soul he feels to be worth saying." Thus, Beecher closely mirrored Plato's famous definition of oratory that it is "the function of speech to influence souls."[8]

Second, Beecher told his audience that the living man had to deliver the speech. To Beecher, some orators appeared to be dead. Plying the audience with some humor, Beecher wryly observed that some orators appear to "have well-nigh crucified the body. If they have, why are they lingering here below, where they are not useful and where they are not needed?" The lively body on the platform, held Beecher, was, in twentieth-century parlance, a nonverbal statement: "At times there are no gestures that are comparable to the simple stature of the man himself." To illustrate his point, Beecher portrayed in words–perhaps he acted the scene for his audience?–a minister, "bent over a desk, like a weary horse crooked over a hitching block, and preaching first on one leg, and then on the other."

If posture made a statement, so did gestures. Beecher did not conceive gestures to be an overlay or veneer that one applied to words. Rather, he conceived the body to be at one or in unison with language:

> How many things the body can tongue when the tongue itself
> cannot well utter the thing desired! The tongue and the person
> are to co-operate; and having been trained to work together,
> the result is spontaneous, unthought of, unarranged for.

The last factor in delivering the speech was the voice. When Beecher asked "How many men are there that can speak from day to day one hour, two hours, three hours, without exhaustion, and without hoarseness?" he must have had himself in mind as one of the few who could. Again, training was the key to a voice that was "not artificial, not prearranged in the man's thought, but by the assiduous training made to be his second nature. Such a voice answers to the soul, and it is its beating."

Beecher then turned to refute objections that critics made of the study and practice of public speaking. "It is said that if a man knows what he wants to say, he can say it." Beecher cleverly overcome that argument with humor:

> The very man who will not train his own voice to preach, to

lecture, to discourse, whether in the field or in the legislative hall, or in the church, will pay large dues through weary quarters to drill his daughter's voice to sing hymns, and canzonets, and other music.

In a similar vein, to the objection that "does not the voice come by nature?" Beecher retorted with common sense: "Is a man, because he has learned a trade, and was not born with it, thought to be less a man?"

Beecher spent consider time refuting the objection that speech training was "artificial . . . mere posturing . . . simple ornamentation." Cleverly turning the tables, he exclaimed: "Ah! that is not because there has been so much of it, but because there has been so little of it." Beecher claimed that only training would obviate a delivery that draws attention to itself:

> When the thing which a man does is so completely mastered as that there is an absence of volition, and he does it without knowing it, he does it easily; but when the volition is not subdued, and when, therefore, he does not act spontaneously, he is conscious of what he does, and the consciousness prevents his doing it easily. Unconsciousness is indispensable to the doing a thing easily and well.

Turning to his own profession, Beecher phrased his rebuttal: "Say men, 'The truth is before you; there is your Bible; go preach the Word of God.'" The reverend had an excellent response: "Well, if you were not to meddle with what God has provided for, why was not the Bible sent instead of you? You were sent because the very object of a preacher was to give the truth a living form, and not have it lie in the dead letter." Perhaps that was the secret of Beecher's success as an orator and preacher: through his practiced delivery he gave his words a polished impact.

His next refutation concerned the contention that "Our greatest orators have not been trained." Although Beecher admitted that Patrick Henry did not have extensive training, he was also quick to add that "only one or two of his [Henry's] efforts" remained. As a better illustration, Beecher held that Daniel Webster "was so studious of everything he did, even to the buttons on his coat." Beecher referred to the brass buttons that Webster wore on his dark blue waistcoats. As for Henry Clay, who was unschooled, Beecher claimed that Clay taught himself "through culture." Beecher was correct when he warranted that mastery over the arts, of which public speaking is one, has been attained only through study and hard work:

> You shall not find one great sculptor, nor one great architect, nor one great painter, nor one eminent man in any department of art, nor one great scholar, nor one great statesman, nor one divine of universal gifts, whose greatness, if you inquire, you will not find to be the fruit of study, and of the evolution that comes from study.

One imagines that it was rhetorical study that enabled Beecher to cast one sentence in the form of anaphora–"nor one . . ."–that warranted his conclusion with the technique known as argument by accumulation–wherein the orator adduces so many examples that it overwhelms the opponent.

A man of his times, Beecher realized the power of the print media. Indeed, the print media enabled his sermons and speeches to reach national and international audiences. Against the opinion that "books, and especially newspapers, are to take the place of the living voice," Beecher replied "Never! never!"; rather, he held that the office of the newspapers was to "convey information":

> They cannot plant it [information]. They cannot open the soil and put it into the furrow. They can not enforce it. It is given only to the living man, standing before men with the seed of knowledge in his hand, to open the furrows in the living souls of men, and sow the seed, and cover the furrows again.

Although Beecher used an impelling farm imagery to suggest that newspapers would not prevail, his was a naive view, even in the 1870s, of newspapers' power over public opinion.

Beecher ended his speech rather quickly. Maybe the audience was relieved. At any rate, the conclusion was not so much a summary of the address as it was a personal epitaph about Henry Ward Beecher's career as a peripatetic preacher:

> To make men patriots, to make men Christians, to make men the sons of God, let all the doors of heaven be opened . . . . Whatever there is that can make men wiser and better–let it descend upon the head of him who has consecrated himself to the work of mankind, and who has made himself an orator for man's sake and for God's sake.

Conclusion

"But the moment you tell me that a thing that should be done is unpopular," John Howard recounted Beecher's saying, "I am right there, every time. I fed on the privilege of making men hear things because I was a public speaker." The scope of the Reverend Henry Ward Beecher's rhetoric ranged over most of the issues that confronted the United States from the 1840s to the 1870s, and he brought a liberalism to the pulpit that lighted later generations in their efforts to make the Christian religion a nineteenth-century, and then a twentieth-century, religion rather than a sixteenth-century one. These goals were obtained by an almost matchless record of public persuasions and significant sermons.[1]

Secular speeches, if anything, gained Beecher a place in the pantheon of great American orators. Although Beecher's critics have charged him with coming late to the pulpit on the slavery issue, and they are correct with regard to timing, when Beecher finally committed himself to the cause of black bondage, he expiated his sins of omission. No other figure, save William Lloyd Garrison, who was really known more for his attacks against the peculiar institution in his newspaper *The Liberator* than in his oratory, attracted such national attention on the slavery issue, and no other preacher excoriated slavery from such a prestigious pulpit as Plymouth Church. Other abolitionists might have successfully faced the crowds in Great Britain in the fall of 1863, but the fact remains that Beecher did and with overwhelming success. If any complaint is to be made concerning Beecher's handling of the slavery issue, surely a better case could be made about how he played to the hilt his antislavery role and his speeches on behalf of the Union to a degree that was not warranted by the rhetorical record. Nor was Beecher any better than other contemporary figures whose arms would have quickly tired of waving the bloody shirt after the Civil War but whose voices seemed to be inexhaustible on the genre. But still, such petty carpings should not besmirch Beecher's addressing so effectively the issue of his age in which he was surely a first among equals.

Although Beecher's great orations, which hang like battle trophies in the oratorical temple, gained him entrance, it was truly his preaching that propelled him to the temple door. If Beecher's sermons were less spectacular than his speeches, save the series on evolution, his homilies were a vast Milky Way in which the occasional secular super nova seemed less stellar. A fact that the speech chronology attests to is that however often Beecher left the pulpit to give an important speech, or to deliver one of his many lectures, if his itinerary permitted it, he was back in the pulpit on a Sunday. As close as can be calculated, Beecher delivered approximately eighty-four sermons at Lawrenceburg, Indiana.   At Indianapolis, seventy-eight known sermons survive.   These figures could easily be revised upward because not all morning and evening homilies for these two periods are accounted for. During the Plymouth pulpit years, Beecher preached at least 850 known sermons. This number is only the tip of the iceberg. Assuming that Beecher preached thirty-six morning sermons and thirty-six evening sermons a year, which generously allows for his usual two-to-three month vacations in Maine or New Hampshire, it is not unreasonable to assert that he easily could have delivered at least seventy sermons a year. (This does not take into account homilies at funerals, prayer meetings, and talks for religious and national observances that did not fall on a Sunday; morever, although the chronology was constructed with the best available evidence, it is necessarily deficient because the books that contained Beecher's collected sermons usually only printed a morning or evening one whereas Beecher gave two sermons every Sunday.) With seventy sermons a year given during the forty year pastorate at Plymouth, it is safe to venture that Beecher probably delivered well over 2500 sermons.

Continuing in the statistical vein, the number of his lectures pales in comparison to his known sermons and become insignificant when juxtaposed to the number of homilies he probably preached. In all, Beecher delivered approximately 132 lectures.

Overall, then, the chronology lists about 1150 known sermons and speeches. Realistically and conservatively, Beecher probably delivered twice that number in his adult ministry.

That Beecher was something of a stump speaker who stumbled into the pulpit elucidates the role of religious rhetoric in the United States. From Puritan times to the present, great preachers, if not great divines, have tested the secular doctrine of separation of church and state. Perhaps the role of the church and its preachers in nineteenth-century United States history is taken for granted, but it is interesting to note that neither Beecher's contemporary critics nor his twentieth-century ones cavilled at a man of the cloth being such a noted nonpolitical politician. Indeed, it may have been to Beecher's advantage in terms of his persuasive *ethos*, or ethical appeal, that as a disinterested Republican he could criticize the Republican party when it had grown rich from graft, and could turn to Grover Cleveland to clean up the mess in Washington. No one thought it curious that a minister should address the raising of the flag at Fort Sumter, or the excesses of radical Republicanism.   And except for Southerners, who rather wished he had remained silent, and timid clergymen in the North, who could not brace themselves to the task, Beecher's pounding at slavery from the Plymouth pulpit provided a breath of fresh air to a church that had remained too long silent on the pressing moral question of the age.   Nor did Beecher's contemporaries think it odd to pay dollars then backed by gold to hear a sacred talk on secular themes on the Lyceum circuit.   The discussion converges on the following point.

Beecher enacted a rhetorical role that has not been realized by his previous critics. In a real sense, he was the precursor, if not the prototype, of the preacher militant that has marched into American's hearts and minds first over the radio and then over the television. As a matter of fact, Beecher exploited the technology of his times to reach as many listeners and readers as he could. The railroad allowed him to traverse substantial distances to speak to great audiences in out-of-the-way places that were unheard of by the Lawrenceburg and Indianapolis, Indiana, congregations in the 1830s. He used his newspapers to reach even larger audiences than could be addressed at Plymouth Church, and the deluge of his printed sermons reached more eyes than ears who heard him in Brooklyn. Beecher also had a kind of a press secretary. Shortly before the Civil War in 1858, a man by the name of T. Ellinwood became Beecher's stenographer. As a part of the small publicity apparatus that promoted Beecher, Ellinwood was later responsible for publishing his collected sermons. Major James B. Pond handled Beecher's advance notices and arranged the stops for his lectures. In 1886, Beecher last visited Great Britain with his manager and returned almost $12,000 richer due to the good offices of the portly Pond.[2]

In the twentieth century, Father Charles Coughlin and the Reverend Dr. Harry Emerson Fosdick took to the airwaves to reach the mass audience. Coughlin was more interested in social justice and needling the Franklin Roosevelt administration, and Fosdick tilted against the fundamentalists and headed the peace movement of the 1920s and 30s. Regardless of these two famous preachers' theological or political perspectives, the point is that men of the cloth reached large and receptive audiences, and that Americans of the 1930s, at least the ones who tuned to their broadcasts, read their sermons, and in the case of Coughlin, sent him Depression-era dollars, thought the padre's and the preacher's roles to be appropriate in American polity.

In the late twentieth century, the video vicars arose. Whether one agrees with their assorted views, which range from extreme fundamentalism to right-wing patriotism, the point is that they stand in a long line of black-robed preachers who have enacted the ancient role of prophet and preacher in a secular society.   Henry Ward Beecher's legacy to American public address is that he made straight paths for the preacher to adjust Americans to God and God to Americans.

Notes

Introduction

1. Daniel Dulany Addison, *The Clergy in American Life and Letters* (London: The Macmillan Company, 1900), p. 309; Halford R. Ryan, "Henry Ward Beecher" in *American Orators Before 1900: Critical Studies and Sources*, edited by Bernard K. Duffy and Halford R. Ryan (Westport: Greenwood Press, 1987), p. 36; Joseph R. Howard, *Life of Henry Ward Beecher* (Philadelphia: Hubbard Brothers, 1887), p. 236.

2. Paxton Hibben, *Henry Ward Beecher: An American Portrait* (New York: George H. Doran Company, 1927), p. viii.

3. For a discussion of Beecher's preoccupation with precious stones, see William C. Beecher and Rev. Samuel Scoville, assisted by Mrs. Henry Ward Beecher, *A Biography of Rev. Henry Ward Beecher* (New York: Charles L. Webster Company, 1888), pp. 649-51.

4. Hibben, *Henry Ward Beecher: An American Portrait*, p. viii.

5. Henry Ward Beecher, "Churches and Organs," in *Star Papers* (New York: Derby and Jackson, 1859), pp. 260-61; The Beecher Family Papers, Series II, Box 55, Folder 251, Manuscripts and Archives, Sterling Memorial Library, Yale University, New Haven, Connecticut. Hereafter, citations to the Beecher Family Papers will be given as BFP. Hereafter, second citations to books authored by Henry Ward Beecher will be given as HWB.

6. Quoted in Eugene E. White, "George Whitefield," in *American Orators Before 1900: Critical Studies and Sources*, p. 428; *The Bailie*, September 1, 1886, p. 1; John Henry Barrows, *Henry Ward Beecher: The Shakespeare of the Pulpit* (New York: Funk and Wagnalls, 1893), pp. 479-80; HWB, "A Rhapsody of the Pen upon the Tongue," in *Star Papers*, p. 77.

7. Beecher and Scoville, *A Biography of Henry Ward Beecher*, p. 186.

8. Lyman Abbott, *Henry Ward Beecher* (Hartford: American Publishing Company, 1887), p. 398; *Harper's Weekly*, July 17, 1858; Barrows, *Henry Ward Beecher*, p. 481; Howard, *Life of Henry Ward Beecher*, p. 236.

9. BFP, Series II, Box 55, Folder 251.

10. *Harper's Weekly*, July 17, 1858, p. 1.

11. Abbott, *Henry Ward Beecher*, p. 403.

Chapter 1: Beecher in Indiana

1. *The Bailie*, September 1, 1886, p.1.

2. Daniel Dulany Addison, *The Clergy in American Life and Letters* (London: The Macmillan Company, 1900), p. 313.

3. Lyman Beecher Stowe, *Saints, Sinners, and Beechers* (Indianapolis: Bobbs Merrill Company, 1934), pp. 58-59.

4. Ibid., p. 248; William C. Beecher and the Rev. Samuel Scoville, assisted by Mrs. Henry Ward Beecher, *A Biography of Rev. Henry Ward Beecher* (New York: Charles L. Webster & Company, 1888), p. 95; for how Beecher often gilded the truth, in this case concerning the abolitionist debate, see Paxton Hibben, *Henry Ward Beecher: An American Portrait* (New York: George H. Doran Company, 1927), p. 63.

5. Addison, *The Clergy in American Life*, p. 313.

6. BFP, "Notebook of Sermons," Series III, Box 71, Folder 15.

7. Ibid.

8. Ibid.; February 5, 1848, BFP, Series II, Box 55, Folder 256.

9. Beecher and Scoville, *A Biography of Henry Ward Beecher*, p. 180.

10. Ibid., pp. 181-82.

11. Paul as Model for Preaching New Truth, Indianapolis, Indiana, October 29, 1843, BFP, Series II, Box 72, Folder 70.

12. Quoted in Hibben, *Henry Ward Beecher*, p. 118; John C. Calhoun, "Constitution and the Union," in *American Public Address: 1740-1952*, edited by A. Craig Baird (New York: McGraw-Hill Book Company, 1956), p. 81.

13.   Hibben, *Henry Ward Beecher*, pp. 118-19.

14.   Slavery, Indianapolis, Indiana, May 1, 1846, BFP, Series II, Box 52, Folder 77.

15.   Ibid.

16.   Clifford E. Clark, Jr., *Henry Ward Beecher: Spokesman for a Middle-Class America* (Urbana: University of Illinois Press, 1978), p. 68; William G. McLoughlin, *The Meaning of Henry Ward Beecher: An Essay on the Shifting Values of Mid-Victorian America, 1840-1870* (New York: Alfred A. Knopf, 1970), pp. 189-90.

17.   Henry Ward Beecher, *Lectures to Young Men on Various Important Subjects* (New York: John B. Alden, Publisher, 1890), p. iv.

18.   Ibid., pp. 49-55.

19.   Ibid., pp. 56-58.

20.   Ibid., p. 59.

21.   Ibid., pp. 101-02.

22.   Ibid., pp. 103-04; Hibben, *Henry Ward Beecher*, p. 113.

23.   HWB, *Lectures to Young Men*, pp. 110-116.

24.   Ibid., pp. 117, 120-22.

25.   Ibid., pp. 123-26.

26.   Addison, *The Clergy in American Life and Letters*, p. 307.

27.   Beecher and Scoville, *A Biography of Henry Ward Beecher*, p. 183.

Chapter 2: Beecher Militant

1.   Joseph R. Howard, *Life of Henry Ward Beecher* (Philadelphia: Hubbard Brothers, 1887), p. 236.

2.   Newell Dwight Hillis, "The Ruling Ideas of Henry Ward Beecher's Sermons," *The Congregationalist and Christian World*, January 2, 1904, pp. 11-12.

3.   "Rev. Henry Ward Beecher," *The Practical Christian and Life Illustrated*,

August, 1886, p. 1.

4. John Henry Barrows, *Henry Ward Beecher: The Shakespeare of the Pulpit* (New York: Funk and Wagnalls, 1893), p. 478; William C. Beecher and the Rev. Samuel Scoville with the assistance of Mrs. Henry Ward Beecher, *Autobiography of Henry Ward Beecher* (New York: Charles R. Webster and Company, 1888), p. 221.

5. Henry Ward Beecher, Sectional Conflict speech, 1850s, BFP, Series II, Box 55, Folder 256; Halford R. Ryan, "Henry Ward Beecher," in *American Orators Before 1900: Critical Studies and Sources*, edited by Bernard K. Duffy and Halford R. Ryan (Westport: Greenwood Press, 1987), p. 37.

6. Beecher and Scoville, *Autobiography of Henry Ward Beecher*, p. 283; Paxton Hibben, *Henry Ward Beecher: An American Portrait* (New York: George H. Doran Company, 1927), p. 159.

7. Howard, *Life of Henry Ward Beecher*, pp. 248-9.

8. The text of Beecher's speech is given in "Collected Sermons and Speeches" and may also be found in "Rev. H. W. Beecher's Speech," *New York Times*, May 31, 1856, p. 1; Aristotle, *Rhetoric*, trans. by W. Rhys Roberts (New York: The Modern Library, 1954), 1358_b15-30, 1366_a25.

9. Ibid., 1358_b20.

10. Henry Ward Beecher, "The Nation's Duty to Slavery," in *Freedom and War Discourses* (Boston: Ticknor and Fields, 1863), p. 7.

11. HWB, "Our Blameworthiness," in *Freedom and War Discourses*, pp. 71, 76, 79.

12. HWB, "Battle Set in Array," in *Freedom and War Discourses*, pp. 95, 103.

13. HWB, "Energy of Administration Demanded," "Churches Duty to Slavery," and "Beginning of Freedom," in *Freedom and War Discourses*, pp. 170, 221, 235.

14. Beecher and Scoville, *A Biography of Henry Ward Beecher*, pp. 298-99.

15. Ibid., pp. 294-97; "'Sold' by Beecher in '60, Slave Girl Revisits Church," *New York Herald Tribune*, January 8, 1927, p. 13.

16. William G. McLoughlin, *The Meaning of Henry Ward Beecher: An Essay on the Shifting Values of Mid-Victorian America, 1840-1870* (New York: Alfred A. Knopf, 1970), p. 200; Photographic File, BFP, Series V, Box 88, Folder 26.

17. Ryan, "Henry Ward Beecher," p. 38; Henry Ward Beecher, "Fort

Sumter," *New York Times*, April 18, 1865, p. 8; see also Photographic File, BFP, Series V, Box 88, Folder 31.

18.   HWB, "Fort Sumter," p. 8.

19.   HWB, "Fort Sumter," p. 8.

20.   Henry Ward Beecher, "Conditions of a Restored Union," *Patriotic Addresses* (New York: Fords, Howard and Hulbert, 1887), p. 720.

21.   HWB, "Conditions of a Restored Union," pp. 721, 714-18; Ryan, "Henry Ward Beecher," p. 40.

22.   Henry Ward Beecher, "Wendell Phillips," *Lectures and Orations by Henry Ward Beecher*, edited by Newell Dwight Hillis (New York: Fleming H. Revell Comapny, 1913), pp. 209, 230.

23.   Henry Ward Beecher, "Abraham Lincoln," *Lectures and Orations by Henry Ward Beecher*, p. 273.

Chapter 3: Beecher in Britain

1.   Arthur Conon Doyle, *The Resident Patient*, in *Memoirs of Sherlock Holmes* (2 vols.; Garden City: Doubleday and Company, 1930), I: 424.

2.   Abraham Lincoln, "My Paramount Object," in *The Political Thought of Abraham Lincoln*, edited by Richard N. Current (Indianapolis: The Bobbs-Merrill Company, Inc., 1967), p. 215.

3.   Henry Ward Beecher, "Speech in Manchester," in *American Rebellion: Report of the Speeches of the Rev. Henry Ward Beecher* (London: Sampson Low and Son, 1864), p. 438. Information supplied in brackets was supplied by original observers to the speeches.

4.   Ibid., pp. 439, 441-2.

5.   Ibid., p. 443.

6.   Ibid., pp. 444-5.

7.   Ibid., pp. 449, 450-1.

8.   Ibid., pp. 448.

9.   Ibid., pp. 458.

10.   Ibid., p. 453.

11. Ibid., pp. 472-3, 473-5.

12. Ibid., pp. 479-80.

13. Ibid., p. 483.

14. Ibid., p. 485.

15. Ibid., p. 490.

16. Ibid., p. 492.

17. Ibid., pp. 500, 505.

18. Ibid., p. 508.

19. Ibid., p. 509.

20. Ibid., p. 512.

21. Ibid.

22. Ibid.

23. Ibid., p. 514.

24. "Mr. Beecher in Great Britain," *New York Times*, November 4, 1863, p. 4.

25. J. M. Buckley, "Beecher at Liverpool," *Century Magazine*, November, 1888, p. 241.

26. HWB, "Speech at Liverpool," in *American Rebellion*, pp. 518, 524, 527.

27. Ibid., pp. 533-35.

28. Buckley, "Beecher at Liverpool," p. 242; quoted in Lionel Crocker, "Henry Ward Beecher and the English Press of 1863," *Speech Monographs* 6 (1939): 28; HWB, "Speech at Liverpool," p. 536.

29. David McRae, "English Trip," BFP, Series IV, Box 77, Folder 21; Buckley, "Beecher at Liverpool," p. 242.

30. HWB, "Speech at London," in *American Rebellion*, pp. 546-47.

31. Ibid., p. 550.

32. Ibid., p. 555.

33. Ibid., p. 559.

34. Ibid., pp. 560-61, 562.

35. Ibid., pp. 567-68.

36. Ibid., p. 563.

37. Ibid., p. 571.

38. "Mr. Beecher in Great Britain," p. 4; Oliver Wendell Holmes, "The Minister Plenipotentiary," *Atlantic Monthly* 13 (1864): 109.

39. Paxton Hibben, *Henry Ward Beecher: An American Portrait* (New York: George H. Doran Company, 1927) p. 191; Clark, *Henry Ward Beecher*, pp. 157-8.

40. Crocker, "Henry Ward Beecher and the English Press of 1863," p. 26; Allan Nevins, *The War for the Union: The Organized War 1863-1864* (New York: Charles Scribners' Sons, 1971), pp. 506-9.

41. "Mr. Beecher in Great Britain," p. 4.

Chapter 4: Apologist for Evolution

1. "Evolution and Revelation," *Chicago Tribune*, February 7, 1883, p. 7.

2. See also "Evolution and Revolution," *The Tribune*, Denver, Colorado, September 18, 1883, p. 2. For an excellent treatment of how Beecher treated evolution when he first entered the controversy with an article entitled "Progress of Thought in the Church" in the *North American Review* in 1882, see Clifford E. Clark, Jr., *Henry Ward Beecher: Spokesman for a Middle-Class America* (Urbana: University of Illinois Press, 1978), pp. 262, 264.

3. HWB, "Progress and Thought in the Church," *North American Review* 135 (August, 1882): 107.

4. Ibid., pp. 110, 113.

5. Ibid., p. 117.

6. Lyman Abbott, *Henry Ward Beecher* (Hartford: American Publishing Company, 1887), p. 404. For the belief that Spencer was absent from the dinner "because of ill health," see Clark, *Henry Ward Beecher*, p. 263; however, the *New York Times* printed a text of Spencer's speech that he delivered, see

"Philosophy at Dinner," *New York Times*, November 10, 1882, p. 5.

7. HWB, "The Herbert Spencer Dinner," in *Lectures and Orations by Henry Ward Beecher*, edited by Newell Dwight Hillis (New York: Fleming H. Revell Company, 1913), pp. 313, 318.

8. Ibid., pp. 322, 324.

9. Abbott, *Henry Ward Beecher*, p. 405; "Philosophy at Dinner," p. 5.

10. Henry Ward Beecher, "Evolution & Revolution," BFP, Series II, Box 56, Folder 302, p. 3. "Evolution and Revolution," *The Chicago Tribune*, p. 7; Clark, *Henry Ward Beecher*, p. 265.

11. "Evolution and Revolution," *The Chicago Tribune*, p. 7; Clark, *Henry Ward Beecher*, p. 265; Daniel Dulany Addison, *The Clergy in American Life and Letters* (London: The Macmillan Company, 1900), p. 317.

12. The text of the speech is given in "Collected Sermons and Speeches." See also Henry Ward Beecher, *Evolution and Religion* (New York: Fords, Howard, & Hulbert, 1885), pp. 44-55.

Chapter 5: Beecher as Vox Populi

1. "Henry Ward Beecher," *Atlantic Monthly*, May, 1858, p. 865; John Henry Barrows, *Henry Ward Beecher: The Shakespeare of the Pulpit* (New York: Funk and Wagnalls, 1893), p. 482.

2. See "Reign of the Common People," [no date given] BFP, Series II, Box 56, Folder 304; Henry Ward Beecher, *A Circle of the Continent* (New York: Fords, Howard, and Hulbert, 1884), p. 6.

3. John Howard, *Henry Ward Beecher: A Study* (New York: Fords, Howard and Hulbert, 1891), pp. 626-7.

4. Clifford E. Clark, Jr., *Henry Ward Beecher: Spokesman for a Middle-Class America* (Urbana: University of Illinois Press, 1978), p. 198.

5. The text of the speech is given in "Collected Sermons and Speeches." See also Henry Ward Beecher, "Woman Suffrage Man's Right," Cooper Institute, New York City, February 2, 1860, BFP, Series II, Box 56, Folder 273.

6. Edyth Renshaw, "Five Private Schools of Speech," in *A History of Speech Education in America*, edited by Karl R. Wallace (New York: Appleton-Century-Crofts, Inc., 1954), pp. 303-4.

7. The text of the speech is given in Collected Sermons and Speeches and is taken from Henry Ward Beecher, *Oratory* (Philadelphia: The National School of Oratory, 1876), pp. 1-48.

8. Plato, *Phaedrus*, translated by H. C. Helmhold (Indianapolis: Bobbs-Merrill Company, Inc., 1956), p. 63.

Conclusion

1. John R. Howard, *Henry Ward Beecher: A Study* (New York: Fords, Howard and Hulbert, 1891), p. 68.

2. Paxton Hibben, *Henry Ward Beecher: An American Portrait* (New York: George H. Doran Company, 1927), p. 350.

II

COLLECTED SERMONS AND SPEECHES

Speech at Sumner Protest Meeting

New York City, May 30, 1856

(Note: As was sometimes the style of reporters who transcribed speeches verbatim in the nineteenth century, they often began a speech in the third person and then subtly changed the speech to the first person. Such was the case with Beecher's address as reported in the *New York Times* on May 31, 1856. Therefore, the speech text that follows is taken verbatim as reported with the exception that third person references have been deleted.)

Nothing more consummately wise could have happened by the ordering of Divine Providence than that just this Senator should be struck down by just this assassin, in just this cowardly way, to arouse free men to the impending danger. It was the ordering of Providence for Providence does sometimes employ infernal instruments to work his will. Mr. Sumner, a lawyer by profession, a scholar by instinct, was caught up by a wave of political feeling and borne into office just as some swelling spring tide might rise and lift a noble ship of George Sumner's matchless moulding, and bear it out to sea. Office sought him and he honored office. I believe I speak what was the sentiment of his heart when I say that he did not covet office, but accepted it reluctantly. I visited him just at the time that the call was made upon him and clergyman that I am, and confessor, perhaps, I may say he confessed to me the secret of his heart. [Laughter.] While he has been at Washington, his course has been the purest, the most courteous, the least calculated to give offence. He everywhere, and at all times, observed the rules of decorum; in fact the only complaint ever heard against him by injudicious friends, I must say was that he was too shrinking and sensitive in his nature, and therefore unfitted to meet the turbulent politics of the day, and it was because he was so mild that he was struck down by the felon blow. I would not ask what man would see him struck down, I would not myself see the raggedest wretch in the street struck down by one stronger than himself without, although I ought to be a man of peace, interfering to protect him at the peril of my life.

Rake the Five Points through, out of the wrecked semblances of men that still crowd that locality, you cannot find one so debased, so lost to manly instinct, that would not resent it as an insult if you ask him whether he "would strike a man when he was down." If you had gone through the assemblage where, day after day, lately the fancy-men of the town held court, and asked them all, from the hero of the ring, principal, second, all, down to the bottom-holder, you could not find one of them but would insist upon that point that "fair play is a jewel."

Senator Sumner had one physical fault which would have excused him from doing military duty–he was very near-sighted; and when engaged in writing must be so bowed over his desk as that to strike him would be as mean as to strike a woman. Oh! the chivalry of the man Brooks, of South Carolina! It was the chivalry of one who would creep into the sleeping room of a woman when she was utterly unconscious of the assassin's approach, and thrusting aside the drapery of her couch, should bludgeon her. It was the chivalry of one who should come upon a blind man sitting cramped in hands and feet, and, seeing no policeman near, should brain him.

There he sat, the scholarly Senator, unarmed, with anything save the pen. Ah! there you have it! The symbol of the North is the pen. The symbol of the South is the bludgeon. [Tremendous applause.] But Brooks is not the only hero of the club. Mythology had her man of the club–her Hercules–but Hercules, though he went about in the dim twilight of the world's improvement, used his club only upon the hydras, Nemean lions, and the like. He never stole upon unarmed men when they had not thought of his approach. Scripture too, has its hero of the club, and he was sacred–it was Cain. Brooks took his cane and faithfully renewed the wretched deed of his prototype.

But, friends, this outrage is but a pimple on the surface. The disease which it indicates lies deeper–it infects the whole body. As Brooks stealthily crept up to murder Sumner, so the President and the Slavery propagandists of the nation have stealthily crept up to murder Kansas. With arms and men the vigor of the Administration has been expended in the inhuman task of ruining free Kansas. [Applause.] It is stormy now, said he, in Kansas; it is stormy now in Washington; and by and by it will be stormy in the whole country, unless we of the North say, "Madmen, thus far you have gone, you shall go no farther."

Woman Suffrage
Man's Right

Cooper Institute, New York City
February, 2, 1860

Woman suffrage will bring civilization into our primary meetings, and decency into our secondary ones; for we have heathenism here as rife as that in any other quarter of the globe. You do not need to go out of New York to see whatever barbarity or truculent heathenism is to be seen anywhere else. We keep specimens of everything this side of perdition, and some, I think, of things the other side.

If it were understood that, in every ward and neighborhood, the adult population–the whole of them, men and women–were to control the primary meetings, there would be no more trouble in these meetings than there is in our households. The restraint, the refining influence of woman, would make that orderly which is now like the tussling of dogs. And that which is true of primary meetings is still more significantly true of legislatures and national assemblies. Woman's influence, if introduced into public affairs, would work in the same direction there that it has worked, and is working, in social life, in literature, and in religious assemblies.

But let us attend to some of the objections that are made to such an introduction of woman's influence into public affairs. It strikes many, before reflection, and none more than women themselves, that a participation in suffrage would subject them to rudeness, and to an exposure painful to delicacy. As if that very rudeness were not the result of woman's absence! As if it were not her very office to carry with her whatever is seemly and decorous!

In the first place, it should be understood that, if women were to vote, there would be an end of indecent voting-places. The polls would no longer be in vile precincts and in pest-holes. If father and mother, husband and wife, brother and sister, man and woman, inspired by the sanctity of patriotism, were to go forth together to vote, do you suppose that our elections would be characterized by the vulgarity and violence which now defile them?

What is there in depositing a vote that would subject a woman to such peculiar exposure? A woman, dropping a letter into the post-office, is made more public, and is fully as indelicate, as in depositing her vote. A vote is the simplest, the neatest, the most unobtrusive thing imaginable. This white slip of paper drops as quietly and gently as a snow-flake on the top of the alps; but, like them, when collected, they descend like avalanches. Woe be to the evil which they strike! Let the man who is the most fastidious, who prides himself most on his refinement, find fault, if he can, with the vote of a woman,–a thing that is so easy, so simple, but that would carry into human affairs a power almost like the right hand of the Almighty.

But why this publicity? Why not remain at home, and exert an influence upon public affairs through husband, father, brother?

Because, while woman is excluded with contempt from political duties, her advice and influence at home must always be at the minimum. If once she began to accept public patriotic duties, she then would exert a tenfold indirect influence at home. But now, men take it for granted that women know nothing of public affairs, and that all their suggestions must, of course, be the result of an ignorant simplicity. A woman is not made a safe adviser by being kept at home in ignorance of all public affairs; and, if she informs herself intelligently, then why should she not act just as much as man? It is amusing to hear men, when pressed upon this point, enlarging upon the silent influence of woman, upon the sweetening home affections, upon their bland and gentle restraints, or excitements, and declaring a woman's home to be the only appropriate sphere of political influence; but the moment she takes him at his word, and endeavors to incline husband or brother to any political conduct, they turn with lordly authority upon her, saying, "My dear, your proper duties are in the nursery and kitchen. What do you understand of public affairs?"

Indeed, there is a large infusion of vulgar arrogance even in good men. They believe that woman was created solely or chiefly for the cradle, the bread-trough and the needle. These complacent gentlemen suppose that God made man for thought, action, heroism, and woman as nurse, cook, and plaything.

But, I ask, why does not this argument in respect to woman's influence hold just as good in everything else as in public affairs? Why do you now say, "A woman ought not to be a school-teacher; if she wishes to teach the race, let her influence her father and brothers and husband, and act through them'? Why not say, "A woman ought not to be an artist, and daub her fingers with paints; let her influence her father and brothers and husband to paint"? or, "A woman ought not to waste her strength in writing; let her influence her father and brothers and husband to write"? Why do you not say; in short, "Woman is a mere silent, interior, reserved force, and man is the universal engine to be set in operation by her"?

There is, undoubtedly, such a thing as indirect influence, as general influence; but I have noticed that men who wish things to remain as they are, are in favor always of general influences, in distinction from directly applied forces. It is open, direct, applied force, that abates evil or promotes good.

Nobody makes out a bank account under the general influence of commerce. Nobody farms on this principle. The general influence of husbandry never drained a swamp. It is the theory of cultivation applied that brings harvests. The general progress of health never cleaned a street; it is sanitary ideas applied that do this work. General influences are nothing but the sum of particular influences. If these men who propose leaving evils to be corrected by general influences were to talk to the clouds, they would say, "Oh, never rain! Leave all things to the general influence of diffused moisture."

It is further objected: "If woman were to vote, then, of course, she would be eligible to public offices." Well, why not? In every respect in which woman is known to have gifts of administration, why ought she not to exercise them? When a farmer dies, if the wife has executive power, she carries on the farm; when a merchant dies, if the wife has tact, she carries on the business; if an editor dies, if the wife is enterprising and able, she carries on the newspaper; if a schoolmaster dies, and the wife is competent, she carries on the school or academy; and nobody supposes but that it is perfectly right. All through society, in a sort of unasserting way, woman goes out of what is considered her sphere, and nobody thinks but that it is perfectly right. But I hold that it should be recognized as her right to engage in everything for which she is fitted, public affairs not excepted. No woman could be elected to the office of a Justice of the Peace unless there was a general conviction that she had peculiar gifts for its duties. This matter is surrounded with such safeguards of popular prejudice that no woman will be called to any office unless it is very apparent that she has a fitness for it. Wherever there are gifts, there should be liberty of exercise. Faculty always demands function. Every human being has a natural right to do whatever he or she can do well.

But it is objected that, by mingling in public affairs, women would soon extinguish that delicacy that now gives them both grace and influence. Are we, then, to believe that womanly qualities are God's gift, or only the result of accident and education? If God made woman with a genius of refinement, tenderness, and moral purity, it is not probable that the exercise of large public duty will efface the marks of her original constitution, and that an active patriotism will tarnish her purity, and that zeal for public justice will demoralize her nature.

We are not to forget that woman's participation in suffrage will at once change the conditions upon which they are to enter. When men ask, "Would it be wise that woman should enter the hurly-burly of the caucus, and mingle with the fanaticism of party fury?" I reply, that her presence would end these evils. Should a man, having an exquisite lamp, burning perfumed oil, refuse to carry it into an unlighted room, lest the darkness should contaminate the flame, all would smile at his ignorance, as if light were not, in its nature, the death of darkness.

And when it is asked, "Would you go among brutal rowdies with your wife and daughter, and subject these to their insults?" I reply, if it were understood to be not an intrusion, nor a violation of constituted law, but a thing in accordance with both custom and law, I would take my wife and daughter, and walk, I care not into what precinct or neighborhood; and there is not, in the United States, a place where they would not be safe. Or, if there were one drunken creature to mistreat them, there would be five and twenty stalwart men to crush the miscreant! For, when it is once the custom for women to mingle in public affairs with men, there will not be found a class of men in our land that will not respect her presence. Now and then I see a man that walks in the street smoking, with a woman on his arm–but only now and then. Once in a while I see a man that rides in an omnibus smoking, when there is a woman in it–but only once in a while. These are exceptions. Men instinctively reverence women. Nor is this the peculiarity of men of cultivation or wealth. Men who toll at the blacksmith's forge, and in the various other departments of manual labor,–men whose hands are so hard that they would almost strike fire from steel,–have under their brawny ribs a heart that loves and reveres the purity of woman. And in whatever sphere her duties might call her, if she were admitted to it by custom or law, men would meet her as now they meet her in the sanctuary and in these halls.

But it is said, "It would draw woman from her appropriate sphere. Home is the place of her life." And I would like to know if public affairs do not draw man from his appropriate sphere just as much? Can any man attend to his duties as a citizen and not give time to them? And yet, does he injuriously abandon his store or his bank? It would not take any more of woman's time than it does of man's. But what is time given for but to be used in duty? Nay, it would save time to men and women, if a higher spirit could be infused into public affairs. It is sordidness and low ambitions that exact so much time and strength of good men in the conduct of affairs. And if men were morally elevated, they would strike for rectitude without all those struggles and tergiversations which now impede their progress. Attention to public affairs, then, would not draw woman from her appropriate sphere one whit more than it draws man from his.

I do not ask that every woman should be a candidate for office, or an officer. There is no danger that she would suddenly become wild and rampant, simply because a high moral duty devolved upon her. Intelligence and real moral power sober the silly passions, restrain vagrancy, give stability and discretion. And woman would be a more discreet stayer at home if she were taught wisely how to act in public duty away from home.

Again, it is said that women lose the charm and delicacy of their sex by mingling in public affairs. No, no; you do not believe any such thing. You do not believe it, who say it; or you say it without thinking. A great many women, having received from God the gift of song, sing in public; and no man ever thought of raising this objection in regard to them. Who ever thought of raising it in regard to Jenny Lind? On the appearance here of Madame Sontag, a kind invitation was sent to the clergymen of New York and Brooklyn to attend a preliminary exhibition of her powers in the old Tripler Hall. You may be sure that we were all there; and she sang as she ought to have sung before the assembled clergy of these two cities. When she had finished, Dr. Cox rose, and, with his inimitable eloquence, expressed our united thanks and admiration to her for what she had done; and blessed God that she had the gift and power exhibited. But not a word did he say about exposure, about her being unsexed, or about her being out of her sphere. It was taken for granted that, since God had given her such song-power, it was her duty not to silence it, but to use it for the good of the greatest number. But what peculiar right is there in Art to enfranchise woman, and make that delicate and proper which custom forbids to religion or public affairs? Is it right to sing and wrong to speak in public? Is it delicate for Jenny Lind to confront five thousand faces standing alone upon a platform, and indelicate upon her husband's arm to go forth to the duty of suffrage?

As the different elements of society have developed in succession, they have been obliged to pass through the contention of the democratic and the aristocratic elements. Woman herself is vibrating between these antagonistic forces. For ages, woman has been advanced to honor, influence, office, and the highest public trusts, if she will accept them in aristocratic forms. Women, as members of the ruling classes, are emancipated from many clogs which yet hinder those lower down in the social scale. If it be as a representative of a noble family, or of a public order, woman is permitted to take her place in public affairs. She may be an abbess, a countess, a queen. To-day, the proudest throne on the globe is honored by a woman. No person is shocked that she is at the head of empire. Every reason urged against a larger liberty for woman is illustriously confuted by the dignity, purity, and womanly propriety with which Victoria stands before her empire, and before the world.

It is only woman *without a title* that must have no privileges. Woman, in her own simple self, with nothing but what God gave her, plain, democratic woman, is not deemed worthy of honor and publicity. With a crown on her brow, she may enter parliaments, and govern empires. With only her own simple personal virtues, she may not lift up her hand to cast a vote. If she represents a power, a state, an art, a class, if she only stand upon an aristocratic base, she is indulged. But woman, in her own nature, and representing her own self, is disowned and rebuffed. Now, as a Christian democrat, I assert for her every right and every privilege that aristocracy accords her. That which is good enough for a queen is not too good for my wife. That which is noble in a duchess is honorable in my daughter.

This, then, is the sum of what I wished to say to you to-night. I have said it more in the expectation that it will work in you as a leaven than that it will bear immediate fruits. But, as the farmer sows seed in October that he does not expect to reap till July, so we must sow, and wait patiently for the harvest. I do not know that I shall see the day when woman will occupy her true position in society. My children may, if I do not; and I think that there will be some approach to it, even in my time; for thoughts move faster than they used to.

It is Guyot who says that plants have three periods of growth. The slowest and longest is that of the root; the next fastest is that of the stem; and the last and quickest is that of the blossom and fruit. I have been wont to think that the world grew by the root till the advent of Christ; that from the advent of Christ to our day, it has been growing by the stem; and that in the period in which we stand it is growing by the blossom and the fruit. Changes that formerly required a hundred years for accomplishment, now require scarcely a score. Things rush to their accomplishment. And I make this plea in behalf of women, not without hope that I may see, in my day, an improvement in her condition.

Men will think about this reform, and talk about it. You will accomplish it by talking first, and thinking before you talk, and remembering that we are advocating this change, not because woman needs it, *but because we need it more.*

I stand, to-night, the advocate of *man's rights.* Because we need it, woman should be eligible to all public trusts, and should have the same liberty of suffrage that man now has.

Oratory

Philadelphia, Pennsylvania
May 29, 1876

I congratulate myself, always, for the privilege of appearing before a Philadelphia audience–intelligent, sympathetic, appreciative; but never more than now, when the audience is assembled both to behold, and to bear witness to, one of the noblest institutions that could be established in your midst; one of the most needed; and one which I have reason to believe has been established under the inspiration of the highest motives, not only of patriotism in education, but of religion itself. This city–eminent in many respects for its institutions, and for its various collections which make civilization so honorable–I congratulate, that now, at last, it has established a school of oratory in this central position, equidistant from the South, from the West, and from the North, as a fitting centre from which should go out influences that shall exalt, if not regenerate, public sentiment on the subject of oratory; for, while progress has been made, and is making, in the training of men for public speaking, I think I may say that, relative to the exertions that are put forth in other departments of education, this subject is behind almost all others. Training is this department is the great want of our day; for we are living in a land whose genius, whose history, whose institutions, whose people, eminently demand oratory. There is nothing that draws men more quickly to any centre than the hope of hearing important subjects wisely discussed with full fervor of manhood; and that is oratory–truth bearing upon conduct, and character set home by the living force of the full man. And nowhere, in the field, in the forum, in the pulpit, or in schools, is there found to be a living voice that informs of beauty, traces rugged truth, and gives force and energy to its utterance, that people do not crowd and throng there.

We have demonstrations enough, fortunately, to show that truth alone is not sufficient; for truth is the arrow, but man is the bow that sends it home. There be many men who are the light of the pulpit, whose thought is profound, whose learning is universal, but whose offices are unspeakably dull. They do make known the truth; but without fervor, without grace, without beauty, without inspiration; and discourse upon discourse would fitly be called *the funeral of important subjects*!

Nowhere else is there to be so large a disclosure of what is possible from man acting upon men, as in oratory. In ancient times, and in other lands, circumstances more or less propitious developed the force of eloquence in special instances, or among particular classes. But consider the nature of our own institutions. Consider that nothing can live in our midst until it has accepted its mission of service to the whole people.

Now and then, men, mistaking good sense, speak contemptuously of popularizing learning, and of popularizing science; but popular intelligence is that atmosphere in which all high scientific truth and research, and all learning, in its amplest extent, are, by advance in civilization, to find their nourishment and stimulation; and throughout our land the people demand to know what are the principles of government, what is the procedure of courts, what is the best thought in regard to national policy, what are the ripening thoughts respecting the reformations of the times, what is social truth, what is civil truth, and what is divine truth. These things are discussed in the cabin, in the field, in the court-house, in the legislative hall, everywhere, throughout forty or fifty millions of people. This is in accordance with the nature of our institutions and our customs; and to the living voice more largely than to any other source are we indebted for the popularization of learning and knowledge, and for motive force, which the printed page can scarcely give in any adequate measure. Yet, though this is in accordance with the necessity of our times, our institutions and our customs, I think that oratory, with the exception of here and there an instance which is supposed to be natural, is looked upon, if not with contempt, at least with discredit, as a thing artificial; as a mere science of ornamentation; as a method fit for actors who are not supposed to express their own sentiments, but unfit for a living man who has earnestness and sincerity and purpose.

Still, on the other hand, I hold that oratory has this test and mark of divine providence, in that God, when He makes things perfect, signifies that He is done by throwing over them the robe of beauty; for beauty is the divine thought of excellence. All things, growing in their earlier stages, are rude. All of them are in vigorous strength, it may be; but not until the blossom comes, and the fruit hangs pendant, has the vine evinced for what it was made. God is a God of beauty; and beauty is everywhere the final process. When things have come to that, they have touched their limit.

Now, a living force that brings to itself all the resources of imagination, all the inspirations of feeling, all that is influential in body, in voice, in eye, in gesture, in posture, in the whole animated man, is in strict analogy with the divine thought and the divine arrangement; and there is no misconstruction more utterly untrue and fatal than this: that oratory is an artificial thing, which deals with baubles and trifles, for the sake of making bubbles of pleasure for transient effect on mercurial audiences. So far from that, it is the consecration of the whole man to the noblest purposes to which one can address himself—the education and inspiration of his fellow-men by all that there is in learning, by all that there is in thought, by all that there is in feeling, by all that there is in all of them, sent home through the channels of taste and of beauty. And so regarded, oratory should take its place among the highest departments of education.

I have said that it is disregarded largely; so it is; and one of the fruits of this disregard is that men fill all the places of power–how? With force misdirected; with energy not half so fruitful as it might be; with sincerity that knows not how to spread its wings and fly. I think that if you were to trace and to analyze the methods which prevail in all the departments of society, you would find in no other such contempt of culture, and in no other such punishment of this contempt.

May I speak of my own profession, from a life-long acquaintance–from now forty years of public life and knowledge and observation? May I say, without being supposed to arrogate anything to my own profession, that I know of no nobler body of men, or more various accomplishments, of more honesty, of more self-sacrifice, and of more sincerity, than the clergymen of America? And yet, with exceptional cases, here and there, I cannot say that the profession represents eminence: I mean eminence, not in eloquence, but in oratory. I bear them witness that they mean well; I bear them witness that in multitudes of cases they are grotesque; that in multitudes of other cases they are awkward; and that in multitudes still greater they are dull. They are living witnesses to show how much can be done by men that are in earnest without offices, and without the adjuvants of imagination and of taste, by training; and they are living witnesses also, I think, of how much is left undone to make truth palatable, and to make men eager to hear it and eager to receive it, by the lack of that very training which they have despised–or neglected, at any rate.

Or, shall I ask you to scrutinize the manner and the methods that prevail in our courts–the everlasting monotone and seesaw? Shall I ask you to look at the intensity that raises itself to the highest pitch in the beginning, and that then, running in a screaming monotone, wearies, if it does not affright, all that hear it?

Or, shall I ask you to consider the wild way in which speaking takes place in our political conflicts throughout the country–the bellowing of one, the shouting of another, the grotesqueness of a third, and the want of any given method, or any emotion, in almost all of them.

How much squandering there is of the voice! How little is there of the advantage that may come from conversational tones! How seldom does a man dare to acquit himself with pathos and fervor! And the men are themselves mechanical and method the bad way, who are most afraid of the artificial training that is given in the schools, and who so often show by the fruit of their labor that the want of oratory is the want of education.

How remarkable is sweetness of voice in the mother, in the father, in the household! The music of no chorded instruments brought together is, for sweetness, like the music of familiar affection when spoken by brother and sister, or by father and mother.

Conversation itself belongs to oratory. Where is there a wider, a more ample field for the impartation of pleasure or knowledge than at a festive dinner? and how often do we find that when men, having well eaten and drunken, arise to speak, they are well qualified to keep silence and utterly disqualified to speak! How rare it is to find felicity of diction on such occasions! How seldom do we see men who are educated to a fine sense of what is fit and proper at gatherings of this kind! How many men there are who are weighty in argument, who have abundant resources, and who are almost boundless in their power at other times and in other places, but who when in company among their kind are exceedingly unapt in their methods. Having none of the secret instruments by which the elements of nature may be touched, having no skill and no power in this direction, they stand as machines before living, sensitive men. A man may be as a master before an instrument; only the instrument is dead; and he has the living hand; and out of that dead instrument what wondrous harmony springs forth at his touch! And if you can electrify an audience by the power of a living man on dead things, how much more should that audience be electrified when the chords are living and the man is alive, and he knows how to touch them with divine inspiration!

I advocate, therefore, in its full extent, and for every reason of humanity, of patriotism, and of religion, a more thorough culture of oratory; and I define oratory to be *the art of influencing conduct with the truth set home by all the resources of the living man.* Its aim is not to please men, but to build them up; and the pleasure which it imparts is one of the methods by which it seeks to do this. It aims to get access to men by allaying their prejudices. A person who, with unwelcome truths, undertakes to carry them to men who do not want them, but who need them, undertakes a task which is like drawing near to a fortress. The times have gone by, but you remember them, when, if I had spoken here on certain themes belonging to patriotism which now are our glory, I should have stood before you as before so many castles locked and barred. How unwelcome was the truth! But if one had the art of making the truth beautiful; if one had the art of coaxing the keeper of the gate to turn the key and let the interloping thought come in; if one could by persuasion control the cerberus of hatred, of anger, of envy, of jealousy, that sits at the gate of men's souls, and watches against unwelcome truths; if one could by eloquence give sops to this monster, and overcome him, would it not be worth while to do it? Are we to go on still cudgeling, and cudgeling, and cudgeling men's ears with coarse processes? Are we to consider it a special providence when any good comes from our preaching or our teaching? Are we never to study how skillfully to pick the lock of curiosity, to unfasten the door of fancy, to throw wide open the halls of emotion, and to kindle the light of inspiration in the souls of men? Is there any reality in oratory? It is all real.

First, in the orator is the man. Let no man who is a sneak try to be an orator. The method is not the substance of oratory. A man who is to be an orator must have something to say. He must have something that in his very soul he feels to be worth saying. He must have in his nature that kindly sympathy which connects him with his fellow-men, and which so makes him a part of the audience which he moves as that his smile is their smile, that his tear is their tear, and that the throb of his heart becomes the throb of the hearts of the whole assembly. A man that is humane, a lover of his kind, full of all earnest and sweet sympathy for their welfare, has in him the original element, the substance of oratory, which is truth; but in this world truth needs nursing and helping; it needs every advantage; for the underflow of life is animal, and the channels of human society have been taken possession of by lower influences beforehand. The devil squatted on human territory before the angel came to dispossess him. Pride and intolerance, arrogance and its cruelty, selfishness and its greed, all the lower appetites and passions, do swarm, and do hold in thrall the under-man that each one of us yet carries–the man of flesh, on which the spirit-man seeks to ride, and by which too often he is thrown and trampled under foot. The truth in its attempt to wean the better from the worse needs every auxiliary and every adjuvant.

Therefore, the man who goes forth to speak the truth, whether men will hear or whether they will forbear, and goes with the determination that they shall hear; the man who carries victory in his hope; the man who has irrefragible courage–it is not enough that he has in his soul this element, which, though it be despised, is the foundation element, and which comes first by birth, thanks to your father and mother, thanks to the providence that gave you such a father and such a mother, and thanks to the God who inspires it and sanctifies it. With this predisposition and this substance of truth which men need, and which is to refashion human life in all its parts, the question arises whether there is need of anything more than gracious culture. Well, so long as men are in the body they need the body. There are some who think they have well-nigh crucified the body. If they have, why are they lingering here below, where they are not useful, and where they are not needed? So long as men touch the ground, and feel their own weight, so long they need the aptitudes and the instrumentalities of the human body; and one of the very first steps in oratory is that which trains the body to be the welcome and glad servant of the soul–which it is not always; for many and many a one who has acres of thought has little bodily culture, and as little grace of manners; and many and many a one who has sweetening inside has cacophony when he speaks. Harsh, rude, hard, bruising, are his words.

The first work, therefore, is to teach a man's body to serve his soul; and in this work the education of the bodily presence is the very first step. We had almost extinguished the power of the human body by our pulpits, which, in early days, were the sources and centres of popular eloquence such as there was; for men followed the Apocalyptic figure of the candlestick, the pulpit in the church representing the candlestick, and the minister being supposed to be the light in it. In those days of symbolization everything had to be symbolized; and when a church was built they made a pulpit that was like the socket of a candlestick, and put a man into it; and thus entubbed he looked down afar upon his congregation to speak unto them! Now, what man could win a coy and proud companion if he were obliged to court at fifty feet distance from her? or, what man, pleading for his life, would plead afar off, as through a speaking trumpet, from the second story, to one down below?

Nay, men have been covered up. The introduction of platforms has been thought, on the whole, to be a somewhat discourteous thing. I will tell you, if you will indulge me, a little reminiscence of my own experience. In the church where I minister there was no pulpit; there was only a platform;

and some of the elect ladies, honorable and precious, waited upon me to know if I would not permit a silk screen to be drawn across the front of my table, so that my legs and feet need not be seen. My reply to them was, "I will, on one condition–that whenever I make a pastoral call at your houses you will have a green silk bag into which I may put my legs."

If the legs and feet are tolerable in a saloon, or in a social room, why are they not tolerable on a platform? It takes the whole man to make a man; and at times there are no gestures that are comparable to the simple stature of the man himself. So it behooves us to train men to use the whole of themselves. Frequently the foot is emphasis, and the posture is oftentimes power, after a word, or accompanying a word; and men learn to perceive the thought coming afar off from the man himself who foreshadows it by his action.

You shall no longer, when men are obliged to stand disclosed before the whole audience, see ministers bent over a desk, like a weary horse crooked over a hitching block, and preaching first on one leg, and then on the other. To be a gentleman in the presence of an audience is one of the first lessons which oratory will teach the young aspiring speaker.

But, beside that, what power there is in posture, or in gesture! By it, how many discriminations are made; how many smooth things are rolled off; how many complex things men are made to comprehend! How many things the body can tongue when the tongue itself cannot well utter the thing desired! The tongue and the person are to co-operate; and having been trained to work together, the result is spontaneous, unthought of, unarranged for.

Now, to the real natural man–and the natural man is the educated man; not the thing from which he sprang–how much is to be added! Many a man will hear the truth for the pleasure of hearing it, who would not hear it for the profit of hearing it; and so there must be something more than its plain statement. Among other things, the voice–perhaps the most important of all, and the least cultured–should not be forgotten. How many men are there that can speak from day to day one hour, two hours, three hours, without exhaustion, and without hoarseness? But it is in the power of the vocal organs, and of the ordinary vocal organs, to do this. What multitudes of men weary themselves out because they put their voice on a hard run at the top of its compass!–and there is no relief to them, and none, unfortunately, to the audience. But the voice is like an orchestra. It ranges high up, and can shriek betimes like the scream of an eagle; or it is low as a lion's tone; and at ever intermediate point is some peculiar quality. It has in it the mother's whisper and the father's command. It has in it warning and alarm. It has in it sweetness. It is full of mirth and full of gayety. It glitters, though it is not seen with all its sparkling fancies. It ranges high, intermediate, or low, in obedience to the will, unconsciously to him who uses it; and men listen through the long hour, wondering that it is so short, and quite unaware that they have been bewitched out of their weariness by the charm of a voice, not artificial, not prearranged in the man's thought, but by assiduous training made to be his second nature. Such a voice answers to the soul, and it is its beating.

Now, against this training manifold objections are made. It is said that it is unworthy of manhood that men should be so trained. The conception of a man is that of blunt earnestness. It is said that if a man knows what he wants to say, he can say it; that if he knows what he wants to have men do, the way is for him to pitch at them. That seems to be about the idea which ordinarily prevails on this subject. Shoot a man, as you would a rocket in war; throw him as you would a hand-grenade; and afterward, if you please, look to see where he hits; and woe be to those who touch the fragments! Such appears to be the notion which many have on this subject. But where else, in what other relation, does a man so reason? Here is the highest function to which any man can address himself–the attempt to vitalize men; to give warmth to frigid natures; to give aspirations to the dull and low-flying; to give purpose to conduct; to train every part of one's self–the thinking power; the perceptive power; the intuitions; the imagination; all the sweet and overflowing emotions. The grace of the body; its emphasis; its discriminations; the power of the eye and of the voice–all these belong to the blessedness of this work.

"No," says the man of the school of the beetle, "buzz, and fight, and hit where you can." Thus men disdain this culture as though it were something effeminate; as though it were a science of ornamentation; as though it were a means of stealing men's convictions, not enforcing them; and as though it lacked calibre and dignity.

But why should not this reasoning be applied to everything else? The very man who will not train his own voice to preach, to lecture, to discourse, whether in the field or in the legislative hall, or in the church, will pay large dues through weary quarters to drill his daughter's voice to sing hymns, and canzonets, and other music. This is not counted to be unworthy of the dignity of womanhood.

"But," it is said, "does not the voice come by nature?" Yes; but is there anything that comes by nature which stays as it comes if it is worthily handled? We receive one talent that we may make it five; and we receive five talents that we may make them ten. There is no one thing in man that he has in perfection till he has it by culture. We know that in respect to everything but the voice. Is not the ear trained to acute hearing? Is not the eye trained in science? Do men not school the eye, and make it quick-seeing by patient use? Is a man, because he has learned a trade, and was not born with it, thought to be less a man? Because we have made discoveries of science and adapted them to manufacture; because we have developed knowledge by training, are we thought to be unmanly? Shall we, because we have unfolded our powers by the use of ourselves for that noblest of purposes, the inspiration and elevation of mankind, be less esteemed? Is the school of human training to be disdained when by it we are rendered more useful to our fellow-man?

But it is said that this culture is artificial; that it is mere posturing; that it is simple ornamentation. Ah! that is not because there has been so much of it, but because there has been so little of it. If a man were to begin, as he should, early; or if, beginning late, he were to addict himself assiduously to it, then the graces of speech, the graces of oratory, would be to him what all learning must be before it is perfect, namely spontaneous. If he were to be trained earlier, then his training would not be called the science of ostentation or of acting.

Never is a man thoroughly taught until he has forgotten how he learned. Do you remember when you tottered from chair to chair? Now you walk without thinking that you learned to walk. Do you remember when your inept hands wandered through the air toward the candle, or toward the mother's bosom? Now how regulated, how true to your wish, how quick, how sharp to the touch are those hands! But it was by learning that they became so far perfected. Their perfection is the fruit of training.

Let one think of what he is doing, and he does it ill. If you go into your parlor, where your wife and children are, you always know what to do with yourself–or almost always! You are not awkward in your postures, nor are you awkward with your hands; but let it be understood that there are a dozen strangers to be present, and you begin to think how to appear well before them; and the result of your thinking about it is that you appear very ill. Where to put your hands, and where to put yourself, you do not know; how to stand or how to sit troubles you; whether to hold up one hand or the other hand, or to hold both down, or both up, is a matter of thought with you.

Let me walk on the narrowest of these boards upon which I stand, and I walk with simplicity and perfect safety, because I scarcely think of walking; but lift that board fifty feet above the ground, and let me walk on it as far as across this building, and let me think of the consequences that would result if I were to fall, and how I would tremble and reel! The moment a man's attention is directed to that which he does, he does it ill. When the thing which a man does is so completely mastered as that there is an absence of volition, and he does it without knowing it, he does it easily; but when the volition is not subdued, and when, therefore, he does not act spontaneously, he is conscious of what he does, and the consciousness prevents his doing it easily. Unconsciousness is indispensable to the doing a thing easily and well.

Now, in regard to the training of the orator, it should begin in boyhood, and should be part and parcel of the lessons of the school. Grace; posture; force of manner; the training of the eye, that it may look at men, and pierce them, and smile upon them, and bring summer to them, and call down storms and winter upon them; the development of the hand, that it many wield the sceptre, or beckon with sweet persuasion–these things do not come artificially; they belong to man. Why, men think that Nature means that which lies back of culture. Then you ought never to have departed from babyhood; for that is the only nature you had to begin with. But is nature the acorn forever? Is not the oak nature? Is not that which comes from the seed the best representation of the divine conception of the seed? And as men we are seeds. Culture is but planting them and training them according to their several natures; and nowhere is training nobler than in preparing the orator for the great work to which he educates himself–the elevation of his kind, through truth, through earnestness, through beauty, through every divine influence.

But it is said that the times are changing, and that we ought not to attempt to meddle with that which God has provided for. Say men, "The truth is before you; there is your Bible; go preach the Word of God." Well, if you are not to meddle with what God has provided for, why was not the Bible sent instead of you? You were sent because the very object of a preacher was to give the truth a living form, and not have it lie in the dead letter. As to its simplicity and as to its beauty, I confute you with your own doctrine; for, as I read the sacred text, it is, "Adorn the doctrine of God our Saviour." We are to make it beautiful. There are times when we cannot do it. There are times for the scalpel, there are times for the sword, and there are times for the battle-axe; but these are exceptional. "Let every one of us please his neighbor for his good to edification" is a standing command; and we are to take the truth, of every kind, and if possible bring it in its summer guise to men.

But it is said, "Our greatest Orators have not been trained." How do you know? It may be that Patrick Henry went crying in the wilderness of poor speakers, without any great training; I will admit that now and then there are gifts so eminent and so impetuous that they break through ordinary necessities; but even Patrick Henry was eloquent only under great pressure; and there remain the results of only one or two of his efforts. Daniel Webster is supposed in many respects to have been the greatest American orator of his time; but there never lived a man who was so studious of everything he did, even to the buttons on his coat, as Daniel Webster. Henry Clay was prominent as an orator, but though he was not a man of the schools, he was a man who schooled himself; and by his own thought and taste and sense of that which was fitting and beautiful, he became, through culture, an accomplished orator.

If you go from our land to other lands; if you go to the land which has been irradiated by parliamentary eloquence; if you go to the people of Great Britain; if you go to the great men in ancient times who lived in the intellect; if you go to the illustrious names that every one recalls–Demosthenes and Cicero–they represent a life of work.

Not until Michael Angelo had been the servant and the slave of matter did he learn to control matter; and not until he had drilled and drilled and drilled himself were his touches free and easy as the breath of summer, and full of color as the summer itself. Not until Raphael had subdued himself by color was he the crowning artist of beauty. You shall not find one great sculptor, nor one great architect, nor one great painter, nor one eminent man in any department of art, nor one great scholar, nor one great statesman, nor one divine of universal gifts, whose greatness, if you inquire, you will not find to be the fruit of study, and of the evolution that comes from study.

It is said, furthermore, that oratory is one of the lost arts. I have heard it said that our struggles brought forth not one prominent orator. This fact reveals a law which has been overlooked–namely, that aristocracy diminishes the number of great men, and makes the few so much greater than the average that they stand up like the pyramids in the deserts of Egypt; whereas, democracy distributes the resources of society, and brings up the whole mass of the people; so that under a democratic government great men never stand so high above the average as they do when society has a level far below them. Let building go up on building around about the tallest spire in this city, and you dwarf the spire, though it stand as high as heaven, because everything by which it is surrounded has risen higher.

Now, throughout our whole land there was more eloquence during our struggles than there was previously; but it was in far more mouths. It was distributed. There was in the mass of men a higher method of speaking, a greater power in addressing their fellow-men; and though single men were not so prominent as they would have been under other circumstances, the reason is one for which we should be grateful. There were more men at a higher average, though there were fewer men at an extreme altitude.

Then it is said that books, and especially newspapers, are to take the place of the living voice. Never! never! The miracle of modern times, in one respect, is the Press; to it is given a wide field and a wonderful work; and when it shall be clothed with all the moral inspirations, with all the ineffable graces, that come from simplicity and honesty and conviction, it will have a work second almost to none other in the land. Like the light, it carries knowledge every day around the globe. What is done at St. Paul's in the morning is known, or ever half the day has run around, in Wall Street, New York. What is done in New York at the rising of the sun, is, before the noontide hour known in California. By the power of the wire, and of the swift-following engine, the papers spread at large vast quantities of information before myriad readers throughout the country; but the office of the papers is simply to convey information. They cannot plant it. They cannot open the soil and put it into the furrow. They cannot enforce it. It is given only to the living man, standing before men with the seed of knowledge in his hand, to open the furrows in the living souls of men, and sow the seed, and cover the furrows again. Not until human nature is other than it is, will the function of the living voice–the greatest force on earth among men–cease. Not until then will the orator be useless, to his aid all that is fervid in feeling; who incarnates in himself the truth; who is for the hour the living reason, as well as the reasoner; who is for the moment the moral sense; who carries in himself the importunity and the urgency of zeal; who brings his influence to bear upon men in various ways; who adapts himself continually to the changing conditions of the men that are before him; who plies them by softness and by hardness, by light and by darkness, by hope and by fear; who stimulates them or represses them at his will. Nor is there, let me say, on God's footstool, anything so crowned and so regal as the sensation of one who faces an audience in a worthy cause, and with amplitude of means, and defies them, fights them, controls them, conquers them.

Great is the advance of civilization; mighty are the engines of force, but man is greater than that which he produces. Vast is that machine which stands in the dark unconsciously lifting, lifting–the only humane slave–the iron slave–the Corliss engine; but he that made the engine is greater than the engine itself. Wonderful is the skill by which that most exquisite mechanism of modern life, the watch, is constructed; but greater is the man that made the watch than the watch that is made. Great is the Press, great are the hundred instrumentalities and institutions and customs of society; but above them all is man. The living force is greater than any of its creations–greater than society, greater than its laws. "The Sabbath was made for man, and not man for the Sabbath," saith the Lord. Man is greater than his own institutions. And this living force is worthy of all culture–of all culture in the power of beauty; of all culture in the direction of persuasion; of all culture in the art of reasoning.

To make men patriots, to make men Christians, to make men the sons of God, let all the doors of heaven be opened, and let God drop down charmed gifts–winged imagination, all-perceiving reason, and all-judging reason. Whatever there is that can make men wiser and better–let it descend upon the head of him who has consecrated himself to the work of mankind, and who has made himself an orator for man's sake and for God's sake.

The Two Revelations

Brooklyn, New York
May 31, 1885

All things were made by Him, and without Him was not anything made that was made. John 1:3

That the whole world and the universe were the creation of God is the testimony of the whole Bible, both Jewish and Christian; but how he made them–whether by the direct force of a creative will or indirectly through a long series of graduate changes–the Scriptures do not declare. The grand truth is that this world was not a chance, a creative fermentation, a self-development, but that it was the product of an Intelligent Being, that the divine will in the continuance of this world manifests itself under the form of what are called natural laws, and that the operations of normal and legitimate laws are the results of divine will.

There are two records of God's creative energy. One is the record of the unfolding of man and of the race under the inspiration of God's nature: this is a mere sketch; of the ancient periods of man there is almost nothing known. The other of these records or revelations–if you choose to call them so–pertains to the physical globe, and reveals the divine thought through the unfolding history of matter; and this is the older. So we have two revelations: God's thought in the evolution of matter, and God's thought in the evolution of mind; and these are the Old Testament and the New–not in the usual sense of those terms, but in an appropriate scientific use of them.

In that great book of the Old there is a record of the progress, order, and result of God's thought in regard to the globe as a habitation for man. Though not every stage, yet the chief stages of preparation of this dwelling for man have been discovered and are now being deciphered and read. The crude, primitive material of the world of matter, the igneous condition, the aqueous stages, the dynamic and chemical periods, the gradual formation of the soil, the mountain-building, the dawn of life, vegetable and animal, the stages of their progress–are not all these things written in the scientific revelation of God's history of creation? When I reflect upon the range of the invisible and the silent God, with the vast and well-nigh incomprehensible stretch of time, and of his compassionate waiting and working through illimitable ages and periods, compared with which a million years as marked by the clock are but seconds; when I reflect that the silent stones and the buried strata contain the record of God's working, and that the globe itself is a sublime history of God as an engineer and architect and as a master-builder, I cannot but marvel at the indifference with which good men have regarded this stupendous revelation of the ages past, and especially at the assaults made by Christian men upon scientific men who are bringing to light the long-hidden record of God's revelation in the material world.

With what eagerness has the world heard of the discovery in Egypt of the tomb that contained the buried kings of the Pharaophnic dynasty! But what are all these mighty kings, wrapped for these thousand years in the shroud of silence, compared with the discovery of God's method and the results of creation millions of centuries ago, retained in the rocks? Were the two tables of stone, written by the finger of God, a memorial to be revered, and their contents to be written in letters of gold in all men's churches, and yet his ministers and priests turn with indifference or with denunciation, even with scorn, sometimes from the literature of the rocks written by the hand of God all over the earth? What were the Ten Commandments but a paragraph out of the book of the divine revelation of nature? Ages before Sinai itself was upheaved in the progress of divine world-building; ages before the human race was enough advanced to have made the Ten Commandments possible, God was slowly moulding the world that was to contain within itself its own history. Science is but the deciphering of God's thought as revealed in the structure of this world; it is a mere translation of God's primitive revelation. If to reject God's revelation of the Book is infidelity, what is it to reject God's revelation of himself in the structure of the whole globe? There is as much infidelity in regard to the great history that science unfolds to-day, as there is in regard to the record of the Book–and more! The primitive prefatory revelation of the structural thought of God in preparing a dwelling for the human race–is that nothing? Man had a cradle represented to antiquity as the poetical Eden; but the globe itself had a different Eden, one of fire, convulsions, clouds and storms, of grinding ice and biting chemistry preparing the soil.

To be sure, the history of man in the Bible is more important than the history of the globe. The globe was created for man as a house is created to serve the family. But both are God's revelations; both are to be received with intelligent reverence; both are to be united and harmonized; both are to be employed in throwing light, the one upon the other. That noble body of investigators who are deciphering the hieroglyphics of God inscribed upon this temple of the earth are to be honored and encouraged. As it is now, vaguely bigoted theologists, ignorant pietists, jealous churchmen, unintelligent men, whose very existence seems like a sarcasm upon creative wisdom, with leaden wit and stinging irony swarm about the adventurous surveyors who are searching God's handiwork and who have added to the realm of the knowledge of God the grandest treasures. Men pretending to be ministers of God, with all manner of grimace and shallow ridicule and witless criticism and unproductive wisdom, enact the very feats of the monkey in the attempt to prove that the monkey was not their ancestor.

It is objected to all assertions of the validity of God's great record in matter, that science is uncertain and unripe; that men are continually changing the lines of science, that it will not do to rest upon the results of scientific investigation. It will be time to consider science when it has ripened into a certainty, say men, but not now. Well, as the case stands, how is the record of the book any more stable and intelligible than the record of the rock? The whole Christian world for two thousand years, since the completion of the canons, has been divided up like the end of a broom into infinite splinters, quarreling with each other as to what the book did say, and what it did mean. Why then should men turn and say that scientific men are unsettled in their notions? At the congress of Christian churches in Hartford recently, the Rev. Dr. Hopkins, a prominent high-churchman, said: "No less than nineteen different varieties of Christianity are at present trying to convert the Japanese. The nineteen do not agree as to what the ministry is, nor as to the word, some including the Apocrypha, and others discarding it altogether; and many differing as to the meaning of the Scriptures. Nor are they agreed as to the Sacraments. So too on doctrine, discipline, and worship. There are all sorts of contradictions of belief. Now, if Christians, with eighteen centuries of accumulated tradition cannot agree, how can we expect the heathen to solve the great riddle?" This is not mine, but I give a hearty Amen to it, and only find fault with it because it is not strong enough. When men, therefore, attempt to pour ridicule upon the legitimate deductions of scientific investigations, that have passed through the periods of trial, discussion, and proof, as if they were less praiseworthy than the declarations of the written revelation, I say to them, "No ground can be less tenable than such a ground as yours if we will look at the way in which the written revelation is misunderstood, and into the infinite splittings and divisions which men have made in attempting to interpret what is said to be the more stable revelation of the truth."

It is said, or thought, that a layman should not meddle with that which can be judged by only scientific experts: that science demands a special training before one can discern correctly its facts, or judge wisely of the force of its conclusions. This is true; it is true both of those who accept and those who deny its results. But, when time and investigation have brought the scientific world to an agreement, and its discoveries pass into the hands of all men, there comes an important duty, which moral teachers, parents, and especially clergymen, are perhaps as well or better fitted to fulfill than mere scientists, viz., to determine what effect the discoveries of science will have upon questions of morality and religion. It is to this aspect that the best minds of the Christian ministry are now addressing themselves.

It may be well before going further to expose some popular errors regarding the Evolutionary philosophy–now so widely accepted by the scientific world–and to point out some of the changes which it will work out in the schools of theology, as a new interpreter of God's two revelations.

A vague notion exists with multitudes that science is infidel, and that

Evolution in particular is revolutionary–that is, revolutionary of the doctrines of the Church. Men of such views often say, "I know that religion is true. I do not wish to hear anything that threatens to unsettle my faith." But faith that can be unsettled by the access of light and knowledge had better be unsettled. The intensity of such men's faith in their own thoughts is deemed to be safer than a larger view of God's thoughts. Others speak of Evolution as a pseudo-science teaching that man descended from monkeys, or ascended as the case may be. They have no conception of it as the history of the divine process in the building of this world. They dismiss it with jest, mostly ancient jests; or, having a smattering of fragmentary knowledge, they address victorious ridicule to audiences as ignorant as they are themselves.

Now the ascent of man from the anthropoid apes is a mere hypothesis. It has not been proved; and in the broader sense of the world "proved," I see certainly no present means of proving it. It stands in the region of hypothesis, pressed forward by a multitude of probabilities. The probabilities are so many, and the light which this hypothesis throws upon human history and human life and phenomena is such that I quite incline to the supposition that it is, in the order of nature, in analogy with all the rest of God's work, and that in the ascending scale there was a time unknown, and methods not yet discovered, in which man left behind his prior relatives, and came upon the spiritual ground which now distinguishes him from the whole brute creation. Of one thing I am certain, that whatever may have been the origin, it does not change either the destiny or the moral grandeur of man as he stands in the full light of civilization to-day. The theory of the evolution of the human race from an inferior race, not proved and yet probable, throws light upon many obscure points of doctrine and of theology that have most sadly needed light and solution.

First, then, what is Evolution, and what does it reveal? The theory of Evolution teaches that the creation of this earth was not accomplished in six days of twenty-four hours; that the divine method occupied ages and ages of immense duration; that nothing, of all the treasures of the globe as they now stand, was created at first in its present perfectness; that everything has grown through the lapse of ages into its present condition; that the whole earth, with their development in it, was, as it were, an egg, a germ, a seed; that the forests, the fields, the shrubs, the vineyards, all grasses and flowers, all insects, fishes, and birds, all mammals of every gradation, have had a long history, and that they have come to the position in which they now stand through ages and ages of gradual change and unfolding. Also that the earth itself went through a period of long preparation, passing from ether by condensation to a visible cloud form with increasing solidity, to such a condition as now prevails in the sun; that it condensed and became solid; that cold congealed its vapor; that by chemical action and by mechanical grinding of its surface by ice a soil was prepared fit for vegetation, long before it was fit for animal life; that plants simple and coarse came first and developed through all stages of complexity to the present conditions of the vegetable kingdom; that aquatic, invertebrate animals were the earliest of animals, according to the testimony of fossils in the earth. Fishes came next in order, then amphibians, then reptiles. "All these tribes were represented by species before the earliest of the mammals appeared. The existence of birds before the earliest mammal is not proved, though believed by some paleontologists upon probable evidence. The early mammals were marsupial, like the opossum and the kangaroo, and lived in the same era called by Agassiz, the reptilian period. True mammals came into geologic history in the tertiary era. Very long after the appearance of the first bird came man, the last and grandest of the series, it is doubtful whether in the tertiary period or immediately sequent. It is not established whether his bones or relics occur as far back as the tertiary era."

This is a very brief statement, not my own, but that of Professor Dana, of renown. No man is more trusted, more careful, more cautious than he, and this brief history of the unfolding series I have taken bodily from his writings.

Second.–As thus set forth, it may be said that Evolution is accepted as the method of creation by the whole scientific world, and that the period of controversy is passed and closed. A few venerable men yet live, with many doubts; but it may be said that ninety-nine per cent.–as has been declared by an eminent physicist–ninety-nine per cent. of scientific men and working scientists of the world are using this theory without any doubt of its validity. While the scientific world is at agreement upon this order of occurrence, it has been much divided as to the causes which have operated to bring about these results. There is a diversity of opinion still, but with every decade scientific men are drawing together in a common ground of belief.

Third.–The theory of Evolution is the working theory of every department of physical science all over the world. Withdraw this theory, and every department of physical research would fall back into heaps of hopelessly dislocated facts, with no more order or reason or philosophical coherence than exists in a basket of marbles, or in the juxtaposition of the multitudinous sands of the seashore. We should go back into chaos if we took out of the laboratories, out of the dissecting-rooms, out of the fields of investigation, this great doctrine of Evolution.

Fourth.–This science of Evolution is taught in all advanced academies, in all colleges and universities, in all medical and surgical schools, and our children are receiving it as they are the elements of astronomy or botany or chemistry. That in another generation Evolution will be regarded as uncontradictable as the Copernican system of astronomy, or the Newtonian doctrine of gravitation, can scarcely be doubted. Each of these passed through the same contradiction by theologians. They were charged by the Church, as is Evolution now, with fostering materialism, infidelity, and atheism. We know what befell Galileo for telling the truth of God's primitive revelation. We know, or do not know, at least, how Newton stood charged with infidelity and with atheism when he announced the doctrine of gravitation. Who doubts the heliocentric theory to-day? Who doubts whether it is the sun which is moving round the earth or the earth round the sun? Who doubts that the law of attraction, as developed by Newton, is God's material law universally. The time is coming when the doctrine of Evolution, or the method of God in the creation of the world, will be just as universally accepted as either of these great physical doctrines. The whole Church fought them; yet they stand, conquerors.

Fifth.–Evolution is substantially held by men of profound Christian faith: by the now venerable and universally honored scientific teacher, Professor Dana of Yale College, a devout Christian and communicant of a Congregational Church; by Professor Le Conte of the University of California, an elder in the Presbyterian Church; by President McCosh of Princeton College, a Presbyterian of the Presbyterians, and a Scotch Presbyterian at that; by Professor Asa Gray of Harvard University, a communicant of the Christian Church; by increasing numbers of Christian preachers in America, by Catholics like Mivart, in England; by Wallace, a Christian not only, but of the spiritualistis school; by the Duke of Argyle of the Scotch Presbyterian Church; by Ground, an ardent admirer of Herbert Spencer and his whole theory, though rejecting his agnosticism–an eminent and leading divine in the Church of England; and finally, among hundreds of other soundly learned and Christian men, by the Bishop of London, Dr. Williams, whose Bampton Lectures for 1884 contain a bold, frank, and judicial estimate of Evolution, and its relations to Christianity.

Sixth.–To the fearful and the timid let me say, that while Evolution is certain to oblige theology to reconstruct its system, it will take nothing away from the grounds of true religion. It will strip off Saul's unmanageable armor from David, to give him greater power of the giant. Simple religion is the unfolding of the best nature of man towards God, and man has been hindered and embittered by the outrageous complexity of unbearable systems of theology that have existed. If you can change theology, you will emancipate religion; yet men are continually confounding the two terms, religion and theology. They are not alike. Religion is the condition of a man's nature as toward God and toward his fellow-men. That is religion–love that breeds truth, love that breeds justice, love that breeds harmonies of intimacy and intercommunication, love that breeds duty, love that breeds conscience, love that carries in its hand the scepter of pain, not to destroy and to torment, but to teach and to save. Religion is that state of mind in which a man is related by his emotions, and through his emotions by his will and conduct, to God and to the proper performance of duty in this world. Theology is the philosophy of God, of divine government, and of human nature. The philosophy of these may be one thing; the reality of them may be another and totally different one. Though intimately connected, they are not all the same. Theology is a science; religion, an art.

Evolution will multiply the motives and facilities of righteousness, which was and is the design of the whole Bible. It will not dull the executive doctrines of religion, that is, the forms of them by which an active and reviving ministry arouses men's consciences, by which they inspire faith, repentance, reformation, spiritual communion with God. Not only will those great truths be unharmed, by which men work zealously for the reformation of their fellow-men, but they will be developed to a breadth and certainty not possible in their present philosophical condition. At present the sword of the spirit is in the sheath of a false theology. Evolution, applied to religion, will influence it only as the hidden temples are restored, by removing the sands which have drifted in from the arid deserts of scholastic and medieval theologies. It will change theology, but only to bring out the simple temple of God in clearer and more beautiful lines and proportions.

Seventh.–In every view of it, I think we are to expect great practical fruit from the application of the truths that flow now from the interpretation of Evolution. It will obliterate the distinction between natural and revealed religion, both of which are the testimony of God; one, God's testimony as to what is best for man in his social and physical relations, and the other, what is best for man in his higher spiritual nature. What is called morality will be no longer dissevered from religion. Morals bear to spirituality the same relation which the root bears to the blossom and the fruit. Hitherto a false and imperfect theology has set them in two different provinces. We have been taught that morality will not avail us, and that spirituality is the only saving element: whereas, there is no spirituality itself without morality; all true spirituality is an outgrowth, it is the blossom and fruit on the stem of morality. It is time that these distinctions were obliterated, as they will be, by the progress of application of the doctrine of Evolution.

In every view, then, it is the duty of the friends of simple and unadulterated Christianity to hail the rising light and to uncover every element of religious teaching to its wholesome beams. Old men may be charitably permitted to die in peace, but young men and men in their prime are by God's providence laid under the most solemn obligation to thus discern the signs of the times, and to make themselves acquainted with the knowledge which science is laying before them. And above all, those zealots of the pulpit–who make faces at a science which they do not understand, and who reason from prejudice to ignorance, who not only will not lead their people, but hold up to scorn those who strive to take off the burden of ignorance from their shoulders–these men are bound to open their eyes and see God's sun shining in the heavens.

That Evolution applied will greatly change the reading and the construction of the earlier periods of the Scripture cannot be doubted. The Bible itself is one of the most remarkable monuments of the truth of the evolutionary process. There has been an immense amount of modern ignorance imported into the Bible. Again the Lord is turning out the money-changers, and those who sell oxen and doves, from the temple. But that operation of old left the temple cleansed and pure for religious uses. With many thoughtful Christian men, large tracts of the Bible lie uncultivated and unused. They do not use the whole; yet if any should take out a single text there would be screams of fear. There is not one Christian man in a hundred, nor in a thousand, that thinks that the whole Bible is necessary to his spiritual development and growth. Men pick and choose, and, in a sort of unconscious way, reject portions constantly. We must save them from throwing it all over. For the growth of knowledge, and of intelligence, will not permit men any longer to hold it as a talisman, an idol; and unless guided by a wise teaching they will reject the Sacred Scriptures not only as false in science, but as a guide to conduct and to character!

We of this age have come to the mountain top; yet we can only see the promised land of the future. Our children shall go over to the land flowing with milk and honey. Great has been the past; the future shall be yet greater. Instead of doubts and dread of ill-omened prophecies, and railings and murmurings, the Church should write upon her banner in this day of the orient, "Rise, shine; Thy light has come. The glory of the Lord is risen upon thee."

The last years of my life I dedicate to this work of religion, to this purpose of God, to this development, on a grander scale, of my Lord and Master Jesus Christ. I believe in God. I believe in immortality. I believe in Jesus Christ as the incarnated representative of the spirit of God. I believe in all the essential truths that go to make up morality and spiritual religion. I am neither infidel, nor an agnostic, nor an atheist; but if I am anything, by the grace of God I am a lover of Jesus Christ, as the manifestation of God under the limitations of space and matter; and in no part of my life has my ministry seemed to me so solemn, so earnest, so fruitful, as this last decade will seem if I shall succeed in uncovering to the faith of this people the great truths of the two revelations–God's building revelation of the material globe, and God's building revelation in the unfolding of the human mind. May God direct me in your instruction!

Chronology of Sermons and Speeches

The Reverend Henry Ward Beecher had no systematic method throughout his ministry that would help the researcher catalog his homilies. His usual practice was to begin writing his sermons and speeches about halfway down on the first page. This allowed him to note at the top when and where he delivered the address. In the case of his lectures, he often did not leave enough room on the page, given that he did not know when and where he might deliver the speech, and he sometimes wrote valuable data into the text of the speech or sermon; consequently, some of the facts are often unreadable. Neither was he consistent with regard to naming his sermons, and this was especially so in the early years of his ministry. Sometimes he gave homilies a title, at other times a title and a Scriptural text, sometimes only a Biblical text, sometimes a date and/or place was given with any of the above variations, and sometimes he supplied none of the information usually preferred in cataloging a homily.

The following chronology of speeches and sermons has been collated from a variety of sources. On the whole, the listed sermons and speeches are contained in the Beecher Family Papers, Manuscripts and Archives, Sterling Library, Yale University, New Haven, Connecticut. The collection ranges from complete texts of sermons and speeches to fragments. Given these constraints, the chronology is divided into the following categories:

    1. Calendar of Scriptural Texts. These are given without dates or places of deliverance and listed in the order the texts appear in the Bible.

    2. Chronology of Sermons, Speeches, and Lectures. These are dated sermons, speeches, or lectures and are given with or without Scriptural text and/or title.

    In the case of secular speeches and lectures, these are inserted chronologically with the sermons according to the first date on which a particular speech or lecture was delivered, and subsequent places and dates follow. Beecher kept fairly good records on when and where he delivered his numerous lectures, but here again, the account is incomplete. To the extent possible, places and dates will be supplied; however, Beecher sometimes did not supply the information or his handwriting was unreadable.

3. Calendar of Sermons and Speeches By Title Only. These are listed without Scriptural text or date or place of deliverance.

Beecher delivered most of his sermons in three churches. Unless otherwise specified, all sermons and speeches were delivered in Plymouth Church, Brooklyn, New York. The other two churches are coded thusly:

First Presbyterian Church, Lawrenceburg, Indiana   LI
Second Presbyterian Church, Indianapolis, Indiana   IND

In his early ministry in Lawrenceburg and Indianapolis, Indiana, Beecher often preached a morning service and an evening service; this practice was carried over to the Plymouth Church, but evidently with less frequency. Occasionally, he also delivered lectures, entitled Lecture Room Talks and so identified in the Chronology, about religious topics on Wednesday or Friday evenings to a variety of Plymouth Church audiences. As appropriate, Beecher's collected sermons and speeches are keyed to the following books (*see* bibliography for complete publication details):

American Rebellion	AR
Evolution and Religion	E&R
Freedom and War Discourses	FWD
Henry Ward Beecher Sermons, 2 vols.	HWBS
Lectures and Orations	LO
Lectures to Young Men	LYM
Original Plymouth Pulpit, 10 vols.	OPP
Plymouth Pulpit Sermons, 4 vols.	PPS

1. Calendar of Scriptural Texts

Genesis 1:1
Genesis 19:20
Exodus 14:15
I Kings 18:21
II Kings 20:1
Psalms 19:2
Psalms 60:4
Psalms 105:1
Psalms 139:21-22
Psalms 147:1
Proverbs 39:1
Ecclesiastes 9:10
Ecclesiastes 12:1
Isaiah 22:8
Isaiah 54:11, 12, 17
Jeremiah 29:11-13
Jeremiah 29:13
Ezekiel 18:20, 24
Ezekiel 36:37

Daniel 9:3-9
Hosea 11:7
Matthew 5
Matthew 5:48
Matthew 6:26-27
Matthew 6:28-30
Matthew 6:33
Matthew 10:22
Matthew 13:19-20
Matthew 18:1
Matthew 18:19
Matthew 23:23
Matthew 24
Matthew 25:14
Mark 4:15-20
Luke 3:3, 7-14
Luke 12:40
Luke 18:7
John 1:10-12
John 1:11
John 1:11-13
John 6:35
John 7:37
John 13:1
Acts 1:9-11
Acts 20:18-27
Acts 24:16
Acts 27:36
Romans 1:28
Romans 3:23
Romans 10:4
Romans 12:1
Romans 14:13-23
Romans 15:1-4
Romans 15:2-3
I Corinthians 2:4-5
I Corinthians 7:17
I Corinthians 8:4
I Corinthians 13:9-10
I Corinthians 15:25
II Corinthians 6:16
II Corinthians 7:10
II Corinthians 9
II Corinthians 12:4-5
Galatians 1:4
Galatians 5:1
Galatians 5:22
Galatians 6:3-4

Galatians 6:9
Philippians 1:29
Philippians 2:14
II Timothy 3:15-17
Hebrews 11:4
Hebrews 11:38
Hebrews 12:17
Hebrews 12:22
I Peter 4:12
I Peter 5:10
Revelation 22:17

2. Chronology of Sermons, Speeches, and Lectures

[no title] Philomen 2:4 , LI, morning, February 11, 1838.
Not for the Kingdom of God, Mark 12:24, LI, evening, February 11, 1838.
Sin, Romans 7:13, LI, morning, February 18, 1838.
Ashamed of Christ, Mark, LI, evening, February 18, 1838.
For That All Have Sinned, Romans 3:25, LI, morning, February 24, 1838.
On Rejecting Christ, John 16:9, LI, evening, February 24, 1838.
Let Your Lights Shine, Matthew 5:1, LI, morning, March 4, 1838.
And Peter Followed Afar Off, Luke 22:54, LI, evening, March 4, 1838.
Not Knowing the Time of Visitation, Luke 19:41-44, LI, evening, March 11, 1838.
Unbelief, Mark 16:14, LI, morning, March 18, 1838.
For or Against, Matthew 12:30, LI, evening, March 18, 1838.
Believing in Christ, John 3:36, LI, morning, March 24, 1838.
Neglect is Sin, James 4:17, LI, evening, March 24, 1838.
Put on Whole Armor of God, Ephesians 6:13-18, LI, morning, April 1, 1838.
Righteousness, I Peter 1:8, LI, evening, April 1, 1838.
Causes Which Hindered Spread of Religion in the World Hitherto, Isaiah 54:11-17 [first of three-part sermon], LI, morning, April 8, 1838.
Persecution, II Timothy 3:12, LI, evening, April 8, 1838.
Examine Ourselves, II Corinthians 13:5, LI, morning, April 15, 1838.
Robbing God, Matthew 3:7-8, LI, evening, April 15, 1838.
Righteousness, I Peter 1:8 [rewritten from sermon of April 1, 1838], LI, evening, April 22, 1838.
Causes Which Hindered Spread of Religion in the Whole World Hitherto, Isaiah. 61:11 [conclusion of sermon begun on April 8, 1838], LI, morning, April 29, 1838.
Sovereignty, I Chronicles 29:11-13, LI, evening, April 29, 1838.
Design of the Church, Psalms 122:65, LI, morning, May 6, 1838.
Prayer of Faith, I James 3:22, evening, LI, May 6, 1838.
Perfection, preached by Beecher's brother, George Beecher, LI, morning, May 13, 1838.

Perfection No. 1, Matthew 5:48, LI, evening, May 13, 1838.
Perfection No. 2, Matthew 5:48, LI, morning, May 20, 1838.
[no title] Leviticus, LI, evening, May 20, 1838.
Perfection No. 3, Matthew 5:48, LI, evening, May 22, 1838.
Repentence, Matthew 4:17, LI, evening, May 22, 1838.
Lord's Supper, I Corinthians 11:27-29, LI, evening, May (?), 1838.
Why Do The Wicked Live? LI, evening, May (?), 1838.
Thy Will Be Done, Matthew 6:10, LI, evening, June 3, 1838.
And He Shall Reign Until Christ, I Corinthians 15:24-28, LI, morning, June
    10, 1838.
Without Holiness, LI, evening, June 10, 1838.
Steadfast, Unmovable, I Corinthians 15:58, LI, morning, June 17, 1838.
Sting of Death in Sin, I Corinthians 15:56-57, LI, evening, June 17, 1838.
Effect of God's Character, II Corinthians 3:18, LI, morning, June 24, 1838.
[no title] Luke 13:23, LI, evening, June 24, 1838.
Christ as Stumbling Block, Romans 9:23, LI, morning, July 1, 1838.
To Him That Overcometh, Revelations 3:12, LI, evening, July 1, 1838.
God's Sovereignty, Psalms 97:1, LI, morning, July 8, 1838.
Living for Christ, Romans 14:7-9, LI, evening, July 8, 1838.
God's Sovereignty, Psalms 97:1, [rewritten from sermon of July 8, 1838], LI,
    morning, July 15, 1838.
[no title] Luke 13:23, [repreached from evening, June 24, 1838] LI, evening,
    July 15, 1838.
[no title] Ephesians 4:30, LI, morning, July 22, 1838.
[no title] Isaiah, 18:20, LI, evening, July 22, 1838.
[no title or text], LI, morning, July 29, 1838.
[no title] Proverbs 1:31, LI, evening, July 29, 1838.
[no title or text], LI, August 5, 1838.
[no title or text], LI, morning, August 12, 1838.
[no title or text], LI, evening, August 12, 1838.
Christ the Author of Salvation, Hebrews 5:9, LI, morning, August 19, 1838.
Repentence, Elizabethtown, Kentucky, evening, August 19, 1838.
Increasing in Knowledge of God, Colassians 1:10, LI, evening, August 19,
    1838.
Probation, Galatians 6:7, LI, morning, August 26, 1838.
[not title or text], LI, evening, August 26, 1838.
Ye Will Not Come Unto Me, John 5:40, LI, morning, September 2, 1838.
Come Unto Me, [no text], LI, evening, September 2, 1838.
[Lyman Beecher, Henry's father, preached], LI, September 9, 1838.
Faith, Hebrews 11:1, LI, morning, September 16, 1838.
Strangers and Pilgrims on Earth, Hebrews 11:13, LI, evening, September 16,
    1838.
Church, Ephesians 1:22-28, LI, morning, September 23, 1838. Beecher
    preached this sermon before the congregational meeting held to
    determine if the Lawrenceburg church should withdraw from the Old
    School Presbytery of Oxford, Ohio, in favor of the New School
    Presbytery in Indianapolis.

Superiority of Religion Over the World, Isaiah, 40:28-31, LI, evening, September 23, 1838.

Humility, Matthew 5:3, LI, morning, September 30, 1838.

Covering Sin, Proverbs 28:13, LI, evening, September 30, 1838.

On Trust in God, Psalms 42:5, LI, morning, October 7, 1838.

[continuation of morning sermon], LI, evening, October 7, 1838.

Looking Unto Jesus, Hebrews 12:1-3, LI, morning, October 14, 1838.

Christ the Judge, Matthew 25:31-32, LI, evening, October 14, 1838.

God's Love for the Church, Isaiah 49:8-17, LI, morning, October 21, 1838.

[no title or text], LI, evening, October 21, 1838.

Jesus, Author and Finisher of Our Times, Hebrews 12:3, LI, morning, October 28, 1838.

Funeral Discourse [a woman committed suicide by drowning herself], Hebrews 3:17-18, LI, October 28, 1838.

Taking Offense at Christ, Matthew 11:16, LI, evening, October 28, 1838.

Duties of Pastors and Duties of Churches [pre-ordination sermon], Ephesians 4:8-13, LI, morning, November 4, 1838.

[continuation of morning sermon], LI, evening, November 4, 1838.

[Lyman Beecher, Henry's father, preached on atonement], LI, evening, November 8 [Thursday], 1838. Because a quorum was not present, Beecher was not ordained at this service.

John 14:27, LI, December 2, 1838.

Luke 2:13-14, LI, December 25, 1838.

Isaiah 1:2-3, LI, April, 1839.

I Chronicles 29:11, LI, May 4, 1839.

LI, July 28, 1839. [This was the last sermon Beecher delivered at Lawrenceburg.]

Luke 13:23-24, IND, September 22, 1839.

Behold I Stand at the Door and Knock, IND, November 8, 1839.

I Thessalonians 5:3, IND, November 10, 1839.

Ephesians 5:15-16, IND, January 5, 1840.

John 5:6, IND, March 25, 1840.

James 1:27, IND, May 10, 1840.

Platonean Society, Indiana Asbury University [now Depauw University], Greencastle, Indiana, September 18, 1840. [This was the first of Beecher's speeches to be published and it was issued in pamphlet form.]

Acts 26:28, IND, February 12, 1842.

Divinity of Christ, Terre Haute, Indiana, 1842; Indianapolis, Indiana, 1842; Madison, Indiana, 1842; Greenfield, Indiana, 1842; Lafayette, Indiana, March 1843; Springfield, Illinois, March 26, 1843; Fort Wayne, Indiana, July , 1843; Terre Haute, Indiana, July 9, 1843.

Political Duties of Christians, IND, August, 1842.

I John 2:2, IND, August 28, 1842.

The Strange Woman, IND, December 24, 1842.

Romans 7:12, IND, December 25, 1842.

I Corinthians 1:30, IND, 1843.

God Alwise, Lafayette, Indiana, February 19, 1843; Marion, Indiana, December 26, 1844; July 15, 1849.

Isaiah 53:11, IND, March 12, 1843.

Deuteronomy 13:19, IND, March 23, 1843.

Arguments for Christianity, Springfield, Illinois, June, 1843.

Matthew 5:20, IND, August 27, 1843.

Matthew 5:20, Lafayette, Indiana, October 17, 1843.

Matthew 4:17, Lafayette, Indiana, October 22, 1843.

Paul as Model for Teaching New Truth, IND, October 29, 1843.

Matthew 17:3-4, IND, December 3, 1843.

The Means of Securing Good Rulers, IND, 1844.

Unconverted Man, IND, 1844.

Galatians 5:6, IND, January, 1844.

Psalms 84:4, April 6, 1844.

Coming Short of Rest, IND, June, 1844; March 4, 1849.

Luke 16:8, IND, August, 1844

Genesis 40:14-23, IND, September, 1844.

Acts 26:28, IND, December 1, 1844.

A Dissuasive from Moral Indifference, Philomathean Society, Indiana University, Bloomington, Indiana, 1845.

Mark 10:13, IND, May 18, 1845.

Matthew 20:22-23, IND, June 22, 1845.

Except a Man Be Born Again, IND, December 1, 1844; Madison, Indiana, 1847.

Ezekiel 36:21-32, IND, December 12, 1845.

On Temperance, IND, 1846.

Exodus 20:5-6, IND, January 4, 1846.

Isaiah 13:11, January 11, 1846.

Divine Punishment, IND, January 17, 1846.

Isaiah 10:3, IND, January 28(4?), 1846.

Malachi 1:8, IND, February 8, 1846.

Matthew 6:21, IND, March 1, 1846.

Luke 24:5, IND, March 8, 1846.

Matthew 22:37-40, IND, April, 1846.

I Corinthians 10:31, IND, April 25, 1846.

On Slavery, IND, May 1, 1846.

On Slavery, IND, May, 1846.

On Slavery, IND, May, 1846.

Matthew 13:8, IND, May 28, 1846.

Isaiah 55:10-11, IND, June, 1846.

Matthew 5:20, IND, July, 1846.

John 13:34, IND, July, 1846.

Joshua 7:8-9, IND, July, 1846.

Hosea 4:17, IND, September, 1846.

Mark 1:24, IND, September, 1846.

As a Man Sows He Shall Reap, IND, September 1, 1846; March 28, 1849.

On Slavery, IND, October, 1846.

Luke 14:28-33, IND, Fall, 1846.

Psalms 89:46-47, IND, October 18, 1846.
Lecture to Union Literary Society, Indianapolis, Indiana, December 10, 1846.
Matthew 11:15, IND, 1847.
Acts 2:37, 41, 46, IND, March 1847.
Acts 13:45-46, IND, March 28, 1847.
Hebrews 12, May 31, 1847.
Matthew 26:66, IND, August 22, 1847.
Matthew 12:30, IND, September 13, 1847.
Hebrews 10:28-31, IND, October, 1847.
John 4:48, IND, October 10, 1847.
I Corinthians 1:17, IND, October 10, 1847. [Beecher's valedictory sermon at
    Second Presbyterian Church.]
Psalms 139:33-34, October 17, 1847. [First sermon in Plymouth Church.]
John 18:36, November, 1847.
Thanksgiving, November 25, 1847.
Romans 7:14-16, November 28, 1847.
Proverbs 9:12, December 1, 1847.
Luke 12:47, December 19, 1847.
Genesis 3:4, December 23, 1847.
John 11:45-46, IND, January 2, 1848.
Malachi 1:8, January 30, 1848.
Galatians 6:9, February 20, 1848.
Romans 2:4-5, February 27, 1848.
Goodnight Morning Dew, March 26, 1848; December 25, 1853; April, 1854.
Matthew 22:36-40, April, 1848
Ephesians 6:1, April 9, 1848.
Mathew 6:24-34, April 16, 1848.
Luke 10:30, April 16, 1848.
Matthew 4:17, April 23, 1848.
Against the Mexican War, April 27, 1848.
Romans 1:15-16, April 30, 1848.
John 15:15, May 7, 1848.
Job 42:5-6, May 14, 1848.
II Corinthians, 3:18, May 14, 1848.
Proverbs 5:14, May 28, 1848.
Matthew 13:31, June 11, 1848.
Matthew 13:31-32, June 18, 1848.
John 15:18-20, July 16, 1848
Matthew 13:31, August 26, 1848.
Revelation 14:2, 3, 5, September 3, 1948.
Job 1:16, September 10, 1848.
Revelation 4:11, September 24, 1848.
Mirthfulness [the data for this lecture is incomplete] November 4, 1848;
    March 22, 1859; New York City, April 25, 1859; Providence, Rhode
    Island, October 3, 1859.
Galatians 6:7, November 19, 1848.
Matthew 22:29, December 3, 1848.
Luke 9:55, December 10, 1848.

Romans 1:28, December 10, 1848.
I Peter 5:3, December 24, 1848.
Luke 15:7-10, December 31, 1848.
I Thessalonians 5:16, 1849.
Revelation 22:17, January 7, 1849.
Luke 19:44, January 21, 1849.
Luke 16:31, January 21, 1849.
Luke 9:59, February 4, 1849.
Matthew 5:13-16, February 17, 1849.
Romans 7:9-25, February 25, 1849.
John 15:22, February 25, 1849.
Luke 9:62, March 11, 1949.
[Beecher was ill and did not preach for over two months.]
Servant, June, 1849.
Matthew 22:42, July, 1849.
Hebrews 12:1-3, July, 1849.
Romans 6:1, September, 1849.
I Timothy 6:12, September, 1849.
Hebrews 12:15-17, September, 1849.
Exodus, 20:7, September 2, 1849.
Joshua 24:15, September 2, 1849.
Proverbs 22:1, September 23, 1849.
Psalms 42:5, October, 1849.
Isaiah 28:14-20, October, 1849.
Matthew 10:2-4, December 16, 1849.
Psalms 85:6, January 24, 1850.
Matthew 20:16, February 10, 1850.
John 7:24, February 14, 1850.
Luke 13:24, March 3, 1850.
Hebrews 11:27, April, 1850.
[At his congregation's expense, Beecher went to Europe for rest.]
Matthew 4:17, October, 1850.
Matthew 6:33, December, 1850
Proverbs 14:12, April, 1851.
Hosea 13:9, May 11, 1851.
Psalms 37:7, December 20, 1851.
Matthew 6:33, February 29, 1852.
Ephesians 4:13-14, April 11, 1852.
Philippians 2:12, May 25, 1852.
Galatians 4:9, June 6, 1852.
John 1:12-13, June 18, 1852.
I Peter 5:7, September 12, 1852.
Luke 10:25-28, April 10, 1853.
Romans 5:5, April 23, 1853.
Hebrews 12:7, July 3, 1853.
I Thessalonians, 4:11-12, Thanksgiving, 1853.
Philippians 3:13, January 2, 1854.
Hebrews 4:9, January 14, 1854.

Means of Grace are in Daily Life, July 24, 1854.

Identity or Imagination, Amherst College, Amherst, Massachuestts, August, 1853; Philadelphia, November 7, 1856; Newark, New Jersey, October 20, 1869.

Uses and Culture of Flowers, 1854.

Psalms 46:1, June, 1854.

A Man's Life in Christ, September 3, 1854.

Lecture, Matthew 13:31-33, Brown University, Providence, Rhode Island, September 5, 1854.

Lecture, Brooklyn, New York, October 29, 1854.

Patriotism [Beecher delivered this lecture twenty-nine times, but many dates and places are indecipherable] Portsmouth, New Hampshire, November 6, 1854; Worcester, Massachusetts, November 8, 1854; Newburyport, Massachusetts, November 9, 1854; Lynn, Massachusetts, November 10, 1854; Great Falls, New Hampshire, November 15, 1854; North Brookfield, Massachusetts, December 5, 1854; Hartford, Connecticut, December 12, 1854; Greenfield, Connecticut, December 14, 1854; Peekskill, New York, December 28, 1854; Boston, January 10, 1855; Salem, Massachusetts, January 12, 1955; Troy, New York, January 23, 1855; Utica, January 25, 1955; Watertown, New York, January 26, 1855; Springfield, Massachusetts, January 29, 1855; Westfield, Massachusetts, January 30, 1855; New York City, February 1, 1855; Elmira, New York, February 20, 1855; Syracuse, New York, February 26, 1855; Rochester, New York, March 6, 1855.

Conflict of Northern and Southern Theories of Man and Society, January 14, 1855.

Luke 18:8, February 4, 1855.

Romans 2:4, March, 1855.

Christians are Witnesses for Christ, March 1, 1855.

Hebrews 12:1-3, May 6, 1855.

Matthew 5:20, June, 1855.

Hebrews 5:35-36, June 17, 1855.

Job 19:27, July 15, 1855.

Dangers to be Guarded Against [the data for this lecture is incomplete] Rhinebeck, New York, December, 1855; Newark, New Jersey; [although undated, the following lectures were probably continued in 1856] Chicago, October 10, 1856; Milwaukee, Wisconsin, October 13, 1856; Rockford, Illinois, October 15, 1856; Bloomington, Illinois, October 17, 1856; Indianapolis, Indiana, October 20, 1856; Cleveland, October 24, 1856.

Hebrews 11:1 April 17, 1856.

Man and His Institutions, Tremont Temple, Boston, May 28, 1856.

Speech at Sumner Protest Meeting, Broadway Tabernacle, New York City, May 30, 1856.

Gradations of Personal Social Power [this lecture was delivered seven times during the 1856-57 season, but data is indecipherable except for following two cities] Morristown, New Jersey, Burlington, Vermont.

Philippians 2:5-9, September, 1856.

Deuteronomy 27:11-13, Fall, 1856.

Galatians 6:9-10, November 8, 1856.

Psalms 68:31, December, 1856.

How to Become a Christian, Burton's Old Theatre, New York City, March, 1857.

Deuteronomy, 33:25, May 30, 1857.

How to Become a Christin, March, 1858.

I Timothy 1:5, June, 1858.

Opening Public Park, Springfield, Massachusetts, Fall, 1858.

Luke 2:14, October 31, 1858.

Philippians 4:4, November 18, 1858.

Wastes and Burdens of Society, Providence, Rhode Island, December 20, 1858; Boston, December 22, 1858; Salem, Massachusetts, December 23, 1858; Cooper Institute, New York, January 7, 1859; Syrcause, New York, February 1, 1859; Buffalo, New York, February 2, 1859; Rochester, New York, February 4, 1859; Albany, New York, February 10, 1859; Hartford, Connecticut, February, 1859; Springfield, Massachusetts, February 18, 1859; Troy, New York, February 21, 1859; Castleton, New York, February 22, 1959; New York City, February 24, 1859; Westfield, Massachusetts, March 6, 1859; Utica, New York, March 7, 1859; Auburn, New York, March 9, 1859; Staten Island, New York, March 17, 1859; Springfield, Massachusetts, March 24, 1859; New Brunswick, New Jersey, March 28, 1959; Newark, New Jersey, March 29, 1859; Galesburg, Illinois, December 16, 1859; Chicago, December 18, 1859.

Matthew 6:13, January 23, 1959.

The Sympathy of Christ, Hebrews 4:14-15, HWBS-I, May 1, 1859.

John 16:33, July 3, 1859.

Love, the Fulfilling of the Law, Matthew 22:34-40, HWBS-II, Old School Presbyterian Church, Peekskill, New York, August 7, 1859.

The Christian Commonwealth, Cortland, New York, September 21, 1859.

Galatians, 5:7, September 18, 1859.

The Gentleness of God, II Corinthians, 10:1, HWBS-I, October 9, 1859.

Harper's Ferry Tragedy, October 10, 1859.

God's Husbandry, I Corinthians 3:9, HWBS-II, October 16, 1859.

The Incarnation of Christ, Hebrews 2:14-18, HWBS-II, October 23, 1859.

The Nation's Duty to Slavery, FWD, October 30, 1859.

Lecture Room Talk, December 1, 1859.

The Storm and Its Lessons, Isaiah 55:10-11, HWBS-I, December 4, 1859.

Thirteen Years in the Gospel Ministry: A Sermon of Ministerial Experience, I Corinthians 2:2-5, HWBS-I, January 8, 1860.

Women's Influence in Politics [also known as Woman Suffrage Man's Right], Cooper Institute, New York City, February 2, 1860.

The Lilies of the Field: A Study of Spring for the Careworn, Matthew 6:26, 28-29, HWBS-I, May 13, 1860.

The Divinity of Christ Maintained in a Consideration of His Relations to the Soul of Man, Ephesians, 1:15-23, HWBS-I, May 6, 1860.

The Sepulchre in the Garden, John 19:41-42, HWBS-I, July 1, 1860.

The Love of God, 1 John, 4:9-11, HWBS-I, October, 1860.

Lecture Room Talk, October 3, 1860.

Lecture Room Talk, November 13, 1860.

Lecture Room Talk, November 23, 1860.

Against A Compromise of Principle, FWD, November 29, 1860.

Puritanism, LO, Philadelphia, Pennsylvania, December 21, 1860.

Our Blameworthiness, FWD, January 4, 1861.

Lecture Room Talk, January 9, 1861.

Lecture Room Talk, March 21, 1861.

The Battle Set in Array, FWD, April 14, 1861 [delivered in reaction to the seige of Ft. Sumter].

The National Flag, FWD, April, 1861.

The Camp, Its Dangers and Duties, FWD, May, 1861.

Energy of Administration Demanded, FWD, June, 1861.

A Visit to Washington During the War, June 14, 1861; [Beecher delivered this modified sermon/lecture to a number of audiences, but he did not indicate where; therefore only dates are indicated] October 14, 1861; January 3, 1863; March 2, 1863; July 29, 1864; October 3, 1873; April 25, 1875; January 2, 1876; March 3, 1876; November 10, 1876; January 19, 1877; January 28, 1877; April 15, 1877; May 30, 1877; June 15, 1877; June 22, 1877; July 6, 1877; October 26, 1877; December 14, 1877.

Preaching Jesus Christ and Him Crucified, I Corinthians 2:1-2, HWBS-II, September 26, 1861.

The Necessity of Correct Belief, II Timothy 3:14-17, HWBS-II, October 6, 1861.

The Intercession of Christ, Hebrews 7:25, HWBS-II, Fall, 1861.

Mode and Duties of Emancipation, FWD, November 26, 1861.

Faithfulness in Little Things, Luke 16:10, HWBS-I, morning, December 22, 1861.

The Blind Restored to Sight, Mark 10:46-52, HWBS-I, evening, December 22, 1861.

Psalms 73:23-28, January 5, 1862.

The Churches Duty to Slavery, FWD, January 12, 1862.

Matthew 6:9-13, January 26, 1862.

The Long-Suffering of God, I Timothy 1:16, HWBS-II, February 23, 1862.

Springtime in Nature and in Experience, Song of Solomon, 2:11-13, HWBS-I, March 2, 1862.

The Beginning of Freedom, FWD, March 9, 1862 [delivered after the preliminary Emancipation Proclamation].

The Success of American Democracy, FWD, April 13, 1862.

The Immutability of God, Interpreted and Applied, Hebrews 13:8, HWBS-II, June 8, 1862.

Christianity in Government, FWD, June 29, 1862.

Speaking Evil of Dignitaries, FWD, July 16, 1862.

Divine Government of Nations as Displayed in the Slavery Question, September, 1862.

National Injustice and Penalty, FWD, September 23, 1862.

Opening of New Sunday School, November 16, 1862.
The Ground and Forms of Government, FWD, November 22, 1862.
Our Good Progress and Prospects, FWD, November 27, 1862.
Liberty under Laws, I Corinthians 8:9, FWD, December 28, 1862.
The Southern Babylon, FWD, January 4, 1863.
The Ministration of Suffering, Revelations 7:14, HWBS-II, March 22, 1863.
Moth Eaten Garments, James 5:2, HWBS-I, April 5, 1863.
A Conversation About Christ, Luke 24:13-15, HWBS-I, May 27, 1863.
[Beecher preached this sermon before he departed for Great Britain
for his vacation and subsequent speeches on the slavery question.]
[Beecher was in Europe and Great Britain from June through late November,
1863.]
Speech at Free Trade Hall, Manchester, England, AR, October 9, 1863.
Speech at Glasgow City Hall, Glasgow, Scotland, AR, October 13, 1863.
Speech at Free Church Assembly Hall, Edinburgh, Scotland, AR, October 14,
1863.
Speech at Philharmonic Hall, Liverpool, England, AR, October 16, 1863.
Speech at Exeter Hall, London, England, AR, October 20, 1863.
I Corinthians 1:18, November 21, 1863.
The Fatherhood of God, Romans 8:14-15, HWBS-I, December 20, 1863.
What Will you Do With Christ?, Matthew 27:22, HWBS-I, February, 1864.
The Patience of God, Micah 7:18, HWBS-II, April 17, 1864.
Romans 1:14-16, June 1, 1864.
Address at Fort Sumter, Charleston, South Carolina, April 14, 1865.
Christian Waiting, Psalms 37:3-9, Zion Church, Charleston, South Carolina,
HWBS-II, April 16, 1865.
Abraham Lincoln, Deuteronomy 34:1-5, LO, April 23, 1865.
The Life of Christ–Without, John 1:4-5, HWBS-I, October 1, 1865.
The Life of Christ–Within, John 12:24-25, HWBS-I, October 8, 1865.
Reconstruction on Principles National Not Sectional, Washington, D.C.,
December 13, 1865; Troy, New York, December 18, 1865; utica, New
York, December 19, 1865; Saratoga, New York, December 20, 1865;
Albany, New York, December 21, 1865; Buffalo, New York, January
9, 1866; Rochester, New York, January 10, 1866; Syracuse, New York,
January 11, 1866; Auburn, New York, January 12, 1866; Worcester,
Massachuestts, January 15, 1866; Boston, January 16, 1866; Portland,
Maine, January 17, 1866; Concord, New Hampshire, January 18, 1866;
New Haven, Connecticut, January 19, 1866; Norwalk, Connecticut,
January 22, 1866.
Visions, Acts 26:19, HWBS-II, January 15, 1866.
Fishers of Men, Matthew 4:18-19, HWB-S, February 15, 1866.
Three Eras in Life: God–Love–Grief; As Exemplified in the Experience of
Jacob, Genesis, 48:1-7, HWBS-I, February 22, 1866.
Life: Its Shadows and Its Substance, I Corinthians 7:29-32, HWBS-I, June 17,
1866.
The Hidden Manna and the White Stone, Revelations 2:17, HWBS-I, July 1,
1866.
Crowned Suffering, Mark 6:15-20, HWBS-I, October 28, 1866.

Martha and Mary; Or, Christian Workers and Thinkers, Luke 10:38-42, HWBS-I, December, 1866.

On the Decadence of Christianity, I Corinthians 1:22-24, HWBS-I, July 21, 1867.

Address at Adelphi Academy, New York City, July 23, 1867.

Grace Abounding, Ephesians 33:20-21, HWBS-II, Fall, 1867.

The State of Christianity To-Day, Romans 8:3, HWBS-II, Winter, 1867.

The Second Incarnation, Ephesians 1:22-23, HWBS-II, December 22, 1867.

Christian Character, John 1:12-13, HWBS-II, December 29, 1867.

Old Age, Ecclesiastes 12:1, HWBS-II, January 12, 1868.

The Teaching of Events, Acts 21:14, HWBS-II, January 19, 1868.

Christianity a Vital Force, John 6:63, HWBS-II, morning, March 22, 1868.

The Rich Fool, Luke 12:16-21, HWBS-II, evening, March 22, 1868.

Jacob's Ladder, Genesis 28:10-13, HWBS-II, April 15, 1868.

The Duty of Using One's Life for Others, Titus 2:14, OPP-I, September 20, 1868.

The God of Comfort, II Corinthians 1:3-4, OPP-I, September 27, 1868.

The Nobility of Confession, Matthew 3:5-6, OPP-I, October 4, 1868.

Self-Control Possible to All, I Corinthians 9:25, OPP-I, October 11, 1868.

Pilate, and his Modern Imitations, Matthew 27:24-25, OPP-I, October 18, 1868.

The Strong to Bear with the Weak, Romans 15:1, OPP-I, October 25, 1868.

Growth in the Knowledge of God, II Peter 3:18, OPP-I, November 1, 1868.

Contentment in All Things, Philippians 4:11-12, OPP-I, November 8, 1868.

Privileges of the Christian, Hebrews 12:22-24, OPP-I, morning, November 15, 1868.

Abhorrence of Evil, Romans 12:9, OPP-I, evening, November 15, 1868.

The Love of Money, I Timothy 6:9-11, OPP-I, morning, November 22, 1868.

Unprofitable Servants, Luke 17:10, OPP-VII, November 22, 1868.

The Family as an American Institution, Genesis 18:18-19, OPP-I, November 26, 1868.

Divine Influence on the Human Soul, Romans 8:26, OPP-I, morning, November 29, 1868.

Malign Spiritual Influences, I Peter 5:8-9, OPP-I, evening, November 29, 1868.

Moral Affinity, the True Ground of Unity, Matthew 12:46-50, OPP-I, December 6, 1868.

The Value of Deep Feeling, Luke 7:47, OPP-I, December 13, 1868.

Works Meet for Repentance, Acts 19:8-20, OPP-I, December 20, 1868.

Self-Conceit in Morals, Matthew 21:31, OPP-I, morning, January 3, 1869.

The Old and the New, Hebrews 9:15, OPP-I, evening, January 3, 1869.

The Hidden Christ, Luke 24:31, OPP-I, January 10, 1869.

Well-Wishing, Not Well-Doing, Matthew 21:30, OPP-I, morning, January 17, 1869.

The Crime of Degrading Man, Matthew 18:6-7, OPP-I, evening, January 17, 1869.

Sphere of the Christian Minister, Acts 27:10-11, OPP-I, January 24, 1869.

Suffering, the Measure of Worth, I Corinthians 8:11-12, OPP-I, January 31, 1869.

The Victory of Hope in Sorrow, I Thessolonians 4:13, OPP-I, February 7, 1869.

The Trinity, Ephesians 4:20, morning, OPP-I, February 28, 1869.

Morality, the Basis of Piety, Ephesians 4:22-30, OPP-I, evening, February 24, 1869.

The Power of Love, Ephesians 6:24, OPP-II, March 7, 1869.

The Way of Coming to Christ, Matthew 11:25-30, OPP-II, March 14, 1869.

Conduct, the Index of Feeling, John 15:10-16, OPP-II, March 21, 1869.

The Sympathy of Christ, Hebrews 4:14-16, OPP-II, morning, March 28, 1869.

The Supreme Allegiance, Matthew 10: 37-38, OPP-II, evening, March 28, 1869.

Retribution and Reformation, Genesis 32, OPP-II, April 4, 1869.

Counting the Cost, Luke 14:28, OPP-II, April 11, 1869.

Scope and Function of a Christian Life, Ephesians 6:11-18, OPP-II, April 18, 1869.

Human Ideas of God, Matthew 10:6, OPP-II, April 25, 1869.

The Graciousness of Christ, Hebrews 2:11, OPP-II, May 2, 1869.

Evils of Anxious Forethought, Matthew 6:27, OPP-II, May 9, 1869.

The Beauty of Moral Qualities, Matthew 5:16, OPP-II, morning, May 16, 1869.

Watchfulness, Mark 14:38, OPP-III, HWBS-III, evening, May 16, 1869.

The Problem of Joy and Suffering in Life, Proverbs 3:3, OPP-II, morning, May 23, 1869.

Authority of Right over Wrong, Matthew 8:29, OPP-II, evening, May 23, 1869.

The Apostalic Theory of Preaching, Philippians 1:15-18, OPP-II, May 30, 1869.

The Right and the Wrong Way of Giving Pleasure, Romans 15:2, OPP-II, June 6, 1869.

The Perfect Manhood, Ephesians 4:13, OPP-II, West Point, New York, June 13, 1869.

Dissimulating Love, Romans 12:9, OPP-II, morning, June 20, 1869.

Hindrances on the Threshold, John 5:6, OPP-II, evening, June 20, 1869.

The Door, John 10:9, OPP-II, morning, June 27, 1869.

The Preciousness of Christ, I Peter 2:7, OPP-II, evening, June 27, 1869.

Moral Theory of Civil Liberty, II Peter 2:19, OPP-II, morning, July 4, 1869.

Discouragements and Comforts in Christian Life, OPP-II, Hebrews 10: 35-37, evening, July 4, 1869.

Peaceableness, Romans 12:18, OPP-II, July 11, 1869.

Soul-Drifting, Hebrews 6:19, OPP-II, July 19, 1869.

The Hidden Life, Colossians 3:3, OPP-II, July 25, 1969.

Paul and Demetrius, Acts 19:23-41, OPP-III, HWBS-III, July 25, 1869.

Consolations of the Suffering of Christ, II Corinthians 1:5, OPP-III, HWBS-III, September 26, 1869.

Treasure that Cannot be Stolen, Matthew 6:19-20, OPP-III, HWBS-III, October 3, 1869.

Bearing, But Not Overborne, John 10:17, OPP-III, HWBS-III, October 10, 1869.

The Holy Spirit, Acts 19:6, OPP-III, HWBS-III, morning, October 17, 1869.

Sin's Recompense, Proverbs 5:11-13, OPP-V, evening, October 17, 1869.

Ideal Standards of Duty, Romans 3:4, OPP-III, HWBS-III, morning, October 24, 1869.

The Growth of Christ in Us, Galatians 4:19, OPP-V, evening, October 24, 1869.

Faults, James 5:16, OPP-III, HWBS-III, October 31, 1869.

The Comforting God, II Thessalonians 2:16-17, OPP-III, HWBS-III, November 7, 1869.

The Name Above Every Name, Philomen 2:9, OPP-III, HWBS-III, November 14, 1869.

National Unity, Isaiah 11:12-13, OPP-III, HWBS-III, November 18, 1869.

Social Obstacles to Religion, Matthew 10:36, OPP-III, HWBS-III, November 21, 1869.

Christ, the Deliverer, Romans 7:24-25, OPP-III, HWBS-III, December 5, 1869.

The God of Pity, Psalms 103:13-14, OPP-III, HWBS-III, December 12, 1869.

Sin Against the Holy Ghost, Matthew 12:31-32, OPP-III, HWBS-III, morning, December 19, 1869.

The Danger of Tampering with Sin, II Kings 8:7-15, OPP-IV, evening, December 19, 1869.

Inheritance of the Meek, Matthew 5:5, OPP-III, HWBS-III, December 26, 1869.

Memorials of Divine Mercy, I Samuel 7:12, OPP-III, HWBS-III, January 2, 1870.

The Victorious Power of Faith, Luke 17:5, OPP-III, HWBS-III, January 9, 1870.

The Peace of God, Philomen 4:7, OPP-III, HWBS-III, January 16, 1870.

Coming to One's Self, Luke 15:17, OPP-III, HWBS-III, morning, January 23, 1870.

Fragments of Instruction, John 6:12, OPP-III, HWBS-III, evening, January 23, 1870.

The Substance of Christianity, Ephesians 3:17-19, OPP-III, HWBS-III, February 6, 1870.

Spiritual Blindness, II Corinthians 4:3-4, OPP-III, HWBS-III, February 13, 1870.

Perfect Peace, I Peter 1:8-9, OPP-III, HWBS-III, February 20, 1870.

Preparation for Death, I Peter 1:8-9, OPP-III, HWBS-III, morning, February 27, 1870.

Moral Constitution of Man, Romans 2:13-15, OPP-IV, evening, February 27, 1870.

Fidelity to Conviction, John 9:35-38, OPP-III, HWBS-III, March 6, 1870.

Borrowing Trouble, Matthew 6:34, OPP-IV, March 13, 1870.

Witnessing for Christ, Mark 5:19, OPP-IV, morning, March 20, 1870.

Desiring and Choosing, Hebrews 11:25, OPP-IV, evening, March 20, 1870.

The Reward of Loving, Romans 8:28, OPP-VII, March 27, 1870.

Spiritual Stumbling Blocks, Isaiah 57:14, OPP-IV, April 3, 1870.

Beauty, Zechariah 9:17, OPP-IV, morning, April 10, 1870.

Conceit, Proverbs 22:1-6, OPP-IV, evening, April 10, 1870.

All Hail! Matthew 28:9-10, OPP-IV, April 17, 1870.

The True Economy of Living, Matthew 10:39, OPP-IV, morning, April 24, 1870.

Night and Darkness, Ephesians 5:11, OPP-IV, evening, April 24, 1870.

Law of Hereditary Influence, Exodus 39:7, OPP-IV, May 1, 1870.

The True Religion, Matthew 22:36-40, OPP-IV, May 15, 1870.

The Ideal of Christian Experience, Jonah 14:22-23, OPP-IV, May 22, 1870.

Observance of the Lord's Day, Isaiah 58:13-14, OPP-IV, May 29, 1870.

Sympathy of the Divine Spirit, Romans 8:26, OPP-IV, June 5, 1870.

Conflicts of the Christian Life, I Peter 1:6-7, OPP-IV, morning, June 12, 1870.

Merchant Clerks of Our Cities, Proverbs 23:19-23, OPP-IV, evening, June 12, 1870

Earthly Immortality, Hebrews 11:4, OPP-IV, June 19, 1870.

Follow Thou Me, Jonah 21:20-22, OPP-IV, morning, July 10, 1870.

The Christian Life a New Life, Jonah 3, OPP-IV, evening, July 10, 1870.

War, James 4:1-2, OPP-IV, July 17, 1870.

Patience, Hebrews 10:36, OPP-IV, morning, July 24, 1870.

Testimony against Evil, Romans 12:9, OPP-IV, evening, July 24, 1870.

Fiery Darts, Ephesians 6:16, OPP-IV, morning, July 31, 1870.

My Yoke is Easy, I John 5:3, OPP-IV, evening, July 31, 1870.

The Sufficiency of Jesus, Hebrews 12:2, OPP-V, September 25, 1870.

God's Love Specific and Personal, Galatians 2:20, OPP-V, October 2, 1870.

The Heavenly State, Matthew 22:30, OPP-V, October 9, 1870.

Future Punishment, Matthew 25:46, OPP-V, October 16, 1870.

The Ministration of Pain, Romans 7:18, OPP-V, October 23, 1870.

Selfish Morality, Luke 15:11-13, OPP-V, morning, October 30, 1870.

The Privilege of Working, Ephesians 3:8, OPP-VI, October 30, 1870.

The Importance of Little Things, Samuel 14:43-44, OPP-V, November 6, 1870.

The Training of Children, Ephesians 6:4, OPP-V, November 13, 1870.

Watching with Christ, Matthew 26:40, OPP-V, November 20, 1870.

The Tendencies of American Progress, Isaiah 55, OPP-V, November 24, 1870.

The Higher Spiritual Life, Luke 4:14-15, OPP-V, November 27, 1870.

The Ground of Salvation, Ephesians 2:4-8, OPP-V, morning, December 4, 1870.

Remnants, Romans 9:27, OPP-VI, evening, December 4, 1870.

Individual Responsibility, Mark 8:17-18, OPP-V, December 11, 1870.

The Era of Joy, Luke 2:10-11, OPP-V, December 25, 1870.

Intensity of the Spirit, Matthew 15:25, OPP-V, January 1, 1871.

Man's Will and God's Love, John 15:5, OPP-V, January 8, 1871.

Making Others Happy, Romans 15:2-3, OPP-V, January 15, 1871.

The Power of Humble Fidelity, Mark 12:41-44, OPP-V, morning, January 22, 1871.

Working Out Our Own Salvation, Philippians 2:12-13, OPP-VI, evening, January 22, 1871.

Isaiah 43:7, January 25, 1871.

The New Birth, John 3:5-7, OPP-VI, morning, January 29, 1871.

A Plea for Good Works, Titus 3:8-14, OPP-V, evening, January 29, 1871.

The Central Principle of Character, Matthew 19:22, OPP-VII, January 30, 1871.

The Harmony of Justice and Love, I Timothy 1:15, OPP-V, February 5, 1871.

Common Sense for Young Men on the Subject of Temperance, February 5, 1871.

Spiritual Hunger, Matthew 5:6, OPP-VIII, February 11, 1871.

The Preacher's Commission, Matthew 28:19-20, OPP-VI, morning, February 12, 1871.

Love, the Common Law of the Universe, I Timothy 1:5, evening, February 12, 1871.

Self-Care and Care for Others, Philippians 2:4, OPP-V, February 19, 1871.

The Lord's Prayer, OPP-VI, morning, February 26, 1871.

Labor and Harvest, Luke 7:11-35, OPP-V, evening, February 26, 1871.

Ignorance and Helplessness in Prayer, Romans 8:26, OPP-V, March 5, 1871.

A Safe Guide for Young men, Genesis 28:20-22, OPP-VI, March 12, 1871.

God's Disinterestedness, Matthew 5:48, OPP-VI, March 21, 1871.

The Liberty of the Gospel, Acts 21:15-26, OPP-VI, March 19, 1871.

Love-Service, Galatians 5:13-14, OPP-VI, March 26, 1871.

The Social Principles in Religion, Ephesians 2:19-22, OPP-VI, April 2, 1871.

The Faith of Love, John 20:29, OPP-VI, April 9, 1871.

Special Divine Providence, Matthew 6:33, OPP-VI, April 16, 1871.

The Law of Benevolence, Galatians 6:10, OPP-VI, morning, April 23, 1871.

The Two Revelations, Romans 2:14-16, OPP-VI, evening, April 23, 1871.

The Ages to Come, Ephesians 2:7, OPP-VI, April 30, 1871.

God's Workmanship in Man, Ephesians 2:8-10, OPP-VI, May 14, 1871.

The Name of Jesus, Philippians 2:9-11, OPP-VI, May 21, 1871.

Suspended Moral Convictions, John 12:42-43, OPP-VI, morning, May 28, 1871.

The Lesson from Paris, Revelations 18:7-8, OPP-VI, evening, May 28, 1871.

The Glory of Jehovah, Exodus 34:5-7, OPP-VI, morning, June 11, 1871.

Truthfulness, Colissians 3:9-10, OPP-VI, evening, June 11, 1871.

Heart-Conviction, Romans 10:10, OPP-VI, June 18, 1871.

The Heart-Power of the Gospel, Romans 1:16, OPP-VI, June 25, 1871.

Religious Fervor, Romans 12:11, OPP-VI, morning, July 2, 1871.

Soul-Building, I Corinthians 3:10-11, OPP-VI, evening, July 2, 1871.

The Cause and Cure of Corruption in Public Affairs, Proverbs 2:2-22, OPP-VII, October 1, 1871.

Working with God, I Corinthians 3:9, OPP-VII, October 8, 1871.

Lessons from the Great Chicago Fire, Psalms 36:6, OPP-VII, October 15, 1871.

Sovereignty and Permanence of Love, I Corinthians 13;13, OPP-VII, morning, October 22, 1871.

The Duty of Living Peaceably, Romans 12:18, OPP-IX, evening, October 22, 1871.

Physical Hindrances in Spiritual Life, Matthew 26:41, OPP-VII, October 29, 1871.

Relations of Physical Causes to Spiritual States, Matthew 26:41, OPP-VII, November 5, 1871.

Redemption of the Ballot, OPP-VII, November 12, 1871.

The Unity of Man, Acts 17:26-27, OPP-VII, November 19, 1871.

The Fruit of the Spirit, Galatians 5:22-23, OPP-VII, November 12, 1871.

Measurements of Manhood, Romans 12:3, OPP-VII, December 3, 1871.

The Inspiration of Scripture, II Timothy 3:14-17, OPP-VII, morning, December 10, 1871.

Other Men's Consciences, I Corinthians 10:29, OPP-VII, evening, December 10, 1871.

Practical Ethics for the Young, Matthew 13:52, OPP-VII, December 17, 1871.

The New Incarnation, John 1:14, OPP-VII, morning, December 24, 1871.

The Sigificance and Effect of Christ's Birth, Luke 2:11, OPP-VIII, evening, December 24, 1871.

The Worth of Suffering, Hebrews 12, OPP-VII, December 31, 1871.

God's Character Viewed through Man's Higher Nature, Luke 11:13, OPP-VII, January 7, 1872.

The True Law of the Household, Luke 14:12-14, OPP-VII, January 21, 1872.

Other Men's Failings, Galatians 6:2, OPP-VII, January 28, 1872.

Waiting Upon God, James 5:7-8, OPP-VII, February 4, 1872.

Do the Scriptures Forbid Women To Preach? I Corinthians 14:34-35, OPP-VII, February 11, 1872.

God First, Matthew 8:19-22, OPP-VII, February 18, 1872.

The Burning of the Books, Acts 19:11-13, OPP-VII, February 25, 1872.

Prayer for Others, I Timothy 2:1-2, OPP-VII, March 3, 1872.

The Hereafter, I Corinthians 13:13, OPP-VIII, March 10, 1872.

The True Value of Morality, Titus 2:9-15, OPP-IX, February 18, 1872.

The Deceitfulness of Riches, Matthew 13:22, OPP-VIII, February 25, 1872.

The Realm of Restfulness, Hebrews 1:17, OPP-VIII, March 24, 1872.

How to Learn About God, Jeremiah 9:23-24, OPP-VIII, March 17, 1872.

The Church of the Future, John 4:20-29, OPP-VIII, morning, April 7, 1872.

Our Father, the King: Brotherhood, the Kingdom, Matthew 6:9-10, OPP-VIII, evening, April 7, 1872.

God's Will Is Good Will, Philippians 4:4-7, OPP-VIII, April 21, 1872.

Should the Public Libraries Be Opened on Sunday? Cooper Union Hall, New York City, April 22, 1872.

The Conflicts of Life, Ephesians 6:10-18, OPP-VIII, morning, April 21, 1872.

The Aims and Methods of Christian Life, Acts 3:19-20, OPP-VIII, evening, April 21, 1872.

The Unity of Men, Hebrews 12:22-24, OPP-VIII, May 5, 1872.

Apostolic Christianity, II Peter 1:2-11, OPP-VIII, May 12, 1872.

The Battle of Benevolence, Matthew 5:11-12, 16, OPP-VIII, morning, May 19, 1872.

Signs of the Times, Matthew 16:2-3, OPP-VIII, evening, May 19, 1872.

The Law of Liberty, Galatians 5:1-18, OPP-VIII, morning, May 26, 1872.

Faith in Prayer, Mark 7:24-30, OPP-IX, May 26, 1872.

Bearing One Another's Burdens, Romans 15:1, Galatians 6:2-3, OPP-VIII, June 2, 1872.

The Indwelling of Christ, Colossians 1:27, OPP-VIII, morning, June 9, 1872.

Trustworthiness, Psalms 12:1, OPP-VIII, evening, June 9, 1872.

Spiritual Fruit-Culture, John 4:15, OPP-VIII, evening, June 16, 1872.

Thoughts of Death, John 9:4, OPP-VIII, June 16, 1872.

The Religious Uses of Music, Ephesians, 5:19, OPP-VIII, June 23, 1872.

Peaceable Living, Romans 12:18, OPP-VIII, June 30, 1872.

The Religion of Hope, Romans 8:24, OPP-VIII, morning, July 7, 1872.

What Is the Profit of Godliness? I Timothy 4:8, OPP-VIII, evening, July 7, 1872.

What Is Salvation? Ephesians 1:15-23, OPP-IX, September 29, 1872.

"As to the Lord," Colossians 3:22-24, OPP-IX, October 6, 1872.

The Past and the Future, Philippians 3:12-15, OPP-IX, October 13, 1872.

Moral Honesty and Moral Earnestness, John 14:6, OPP-IX, October 20, 1872.

Soul-Sight, John 20:29, OPP-IX, October 27, 1872.

Exterior and Interior Divine Providence, Philippians 2:13, OPP-IX, morning, November 3, 1872.

Faithfulness to Conviction, The Basis of Right Action, Romans 14:5, OPP-X, evening, November 3, 1872.

Boston Fire Sermon, morning, November 10, 1872.

The Use of Ideals, I Corinthians 1:28-31, OPP-IX, evening, November 10, 1872.

Earning a Livelihood, Ephesians 4:28, OPP-IX, November 17, 1872.

Waves and Cycles of National Life and Thought, Springfield, Massachusetts, November 18, 1872; Portland, Maine, November 19, 1872; Wakefield, Massachusetts, November 20, 1872; Boston, November 21, 1872; Providence, Rhode Island, November 22, 1872; Hartford, December 16, 1872; Bridgewater, Massachusetts, December 17, 1872,; Salem, Massachusetts, December 19, 1872; Charleston, Massachusetts, December 20, 1872; New York City, January 9, 1873; Harrisburg, Pennsylvania, February 17, 1873; Cincinnatti, Ohio, n.d.; St. Louis, Missouri, n.d., Chicago, March 3, 1873; Middletown, New York, February 17, 1875; Norwich, New York, February 18, 1875, Utica, New York, February 19, 1875; New London, Connecticut, April 18, 1876; Brattleboro, Massachusetts, April 19, 1876; Boston, April 20, 1876; [the following cities in Massachusetts were listed but without dates but delivered in 1876] New Bedford, Fall River, Lowell, Clinton, Newburyport, and North Haverhill.

Motives of Action, I Corinthians 10:31, OPP-IX, morning, November 24, 1872.

Paul and Silas in Prison, Acts 16:16-18, OPP-X, evening, November 24, 1872.

War and Peace, Isaiah 2:3-14, OPP-IX, December 1, 1872.

The Spirit of God, John 3:8, OPP-VIII, December 3, 1872.

True Christian Toleration, Acts 21:17-26, OPP-IX, December 8, 1872.

Forelookings, Proverbs 14:12, PPS-I, morning, December 15, 1872.

The Remnants of Society, Isaiah 10:20-23, OPP-IX, evening, December 15, 1872.

Morality Not Enough, Matthew 5:20, OPP-IX, December 22, 1872.
Unconscious Influence, Acts 5:15-16, OPP-IX, December 29, 1872.
True Knowledge of God, Ephesians 3:17-19, January 5, 1873.
The Nature and Power of Humility, Philippians 2:3-11, OPP-IX, Janury 12, 1872.
The Nature of Liberty, John 15:15, OPP-IX, morning, January 19, 1873.
The Love of Praise, Matthew 6:16-18, OPP-IX, evening, January 19, 1873.
Weak Hours, Genesis 25:29-34, OPP-IX, January 26, 1873.
The Test of Love, Matthew 7:21, OPP-IX, February 2, 1873.
Religion in Daily Life, Romans 12:11, PPS-I, morning, February 9, 1873.
Saved by Hope, Romans 7:9-25, OPP-IX, evening, February 9, 1873.
The Power of God's Truth, Isaiah 55:10-11, OPP-IX, morning, February 16, 1873.
Through Fear to Love, I John 4:18, OPP-IX, evening, February 16, 1873.
Spirituality and Morality, Matthew 22:37-40, OPP-X, March 9, 1873.
The Spread of Christian manhood in America, I Corinthians 1:18, OPP-X, March 16, 1873.
The Altars of Childhoo Rebuilt, I Kings 18, OPP-X, morning, March 23, 1873.
Crime and Its Remedy, Ecclesiastes 8:11, OPP-X, evening, March 23, 1873.
Reason in Religion, Hebrews 5:12-14, OPP-X, March 30, 1873.
The Discipline of Trouble, Hebrews 12:11, OPP-X, April 6, 1873.
Immortality, I Corinthians 15:19, OPP-X, morning, April 13, 1873.
God's Mercy Independent of Sects or Churches, Acts 22: 21-23, OPP-X, evening, April 13, 1873.
The Soul's Victory, I John 5:4-5, morning, April 20, 1873.
Heroism, Mark 12:41-44; 14: 8-9, PPS-I, evening, April 20, 1873.
The Narrow Way; The Light Burden, Matthew 11:28-30, OPP-X, morning, April 27, 1873.
Healing Virtue in Christ, Mark 5:24-34, OPP-X, evening, April 27, 1873.
Possibilities of the Future, I John 3:2, OPP-X, May 4, 1873.
Children, Matthew 18:10, OPP-X, May 11, 1873.
The Bible To Be Spiritually Interpreted, II Corinthians 3:6, OPP-X, May 18, 1873.
The Nature and Sources of Temptation, James 1:13-14, OPP-X, morning, May 25, 1873.
Revelation a Stimulus to Human Reason, Romans 7:6, OPP-X, evening, May 25, 1873.
The Sense of an Ever-Present God, Hebrews 11:27, OPP-X, June 1, 1873.
The Paternal Government of God, Matthew 6:9, OPP-X, morning, June 15, 1873.
The Christian Use of the Tongue, Colossians 3:17, OPP-X, evening, June 15, 1873.
The Nature, Importance and Liberties of Belief, John 9:35-38, OPP-X, morning, June 22, 1873.
Salvation by Hope, Romans 8:24, OPP-X, evening, June 22, 1873.
The Mercifulness of the Bible, Psalms 119:64, OPP-X, June 29, 1873.

This Life Completed in the Life to Come, Hebrews 13:14, OPP-X, morning, July 6, 1873.
The Temporal Advantages of Religion, I Timothy 4:8, OPP-X, evening, July 6, 1873.
The New Testament Theory of Evolution, I John 3:2-3, PPS-I, October 5, 1873.
The Prodigal Son, Luke 15:11-32, PPS-IV, (evening?), October 5, 1873.
The Atoning of God, Hebrews 4:14-16, PPS-I, October 12, 1873.
Prayer, I Timothy 2:1-2, PPS-I, October 19, 1873.
Mark 8:34, October 19, 1873.
Man's Two Natures, I Corinthians 2:14-15, PPS-I, October 26, 1873.
All-Sidedness in Christian Life, Ephesians 6:13, PPS-I, November 2, 1873.
Fact and Fancy, II Corinthians 4:18, PPS-I, November 9, 1873.
Cuba, and the Brotherhood of Nations, Galatians 3:28, PPS-I, November 16, 1873.
The Moral Teaching of Suffering, Romans 5:6-8, PPS-I, November 23, 1873.
How Goes the Battle?, Matthew 11:12, PPS-I, November 27, 1873.
The Nature of Christ, Hebrews 2:17-18; Heb. 4:16, PPS-I, December 7, 1873.
The Working and Waiting, Ephesians 6:13, PPS-I, December 14, 1873.
What is Christ to Me?, Colossians 1:10, PPS-I, December 21, 1873.
The Science of Right Living, Ephesians 4:31-32, PPS-I, December 28, 1873.
Religious Constancy, Hosea 6:3-4, PPS-I, January 4, 1874.
Soul Power, I Corinthians 12:3; PPS-I, January 11, 1874.
The Riches of God, Ephesians 2:4-7, PPS-I, January 18, 1874.
St. Paul's Creed, Philemon 4:8, PPS-I, January 25, 1974.
The Departed Christ, John 16:7, PPS-I, February 1, 1874.
The Naturalness of Faith, II Corinthians 5:7, PPS-I, February 8, 1874.
Spiritual Manhood, II Corinthians 12:10, PPS-I, February 15, 1874.
The Debt of Strength, Romans 1:14-15, PPS-I, February 22, 1874.
Special Providence, Matthew 6:19-34, PPS-I, March 1, 1874.
Keeping the Faith, Hebrews 10:35-36, PPS-I, March 8, 1874.
Resolving and Doing, Philemon 2:12-13, PPS-II, March 8, 1874.
Charles Sumner, Isaiah 1:26, PPS-II and LO, March 15, 1874.
Saved by the Rope, Romans 8:24-25, PPS-II, March 22, 1874.
The Primacy of Love, I Corinthians 1:18-24, PPS-II, March 29, 1874.
Faint-heartedness, Numbers 13 and 14, PPS-III, April 4, 1874.
Foretokens of Resurrection, Colossians 3:1-4, April 5, 1874.
Following Christ, Matthew 4:17-22, PPS-II, April 9, 1874.
Summer in the Soul, Luke 17:21, PPS-II, April 12, 1874.
The Temperance Question, I Corinthians 6:19-20, PPS-II, April 12, 1874.
Hindering Christianity, Galatians 5:22-26, PPS-II, April 19, 1874.
Soul-Relationship, Galatians 3:26-29; Ephesians 2:10-22, PPS-II, April 26, 1874.
Christian Joyfulness, Romans 12:12, PPS-II, May 3, 1874.
Liberty in the Churches, I Corinthians 12:31, PPS-II, May 10, 1874.
The Lord's Ministers, n.p., May 11, 1874.
Prayer and Providence, Matthew 6:19-21, PPS-II, May 17, 1874.
Truth-Speaking, Ephesians 4:25, PPS-II, May 17, 1874.

God's Grace, Ephesians 2:8, PPS-II, May 24, 1874.
The Secret of the Cross, I Corinthians 2:1-5, PPS-II, May 24, 1874.
Ideal Christianity, II Peter 2:1-4, PPS-II, May 31, 1874.
The Problem of Life, I John 3:2-3; Rom. 8: 18-21, PPS-II, June 7, 1874.
Unjust Judgments, Matthew 7:1, PPS-II, June 14, 1874.
The Triumph of Goodness, Revelations 15:3-4, PPS-II, June 14, 1874.
The Immortality of Good Work, Romans 14:13, PPS-II, June 21, 1874.
The Universal Heart of God, Isaiah 54:5, PPS-II, June 28, 1874.
The Delight of Self-Sacrifice, Matthew 20:28, PPS-II, July 5, 1874.
What Is Religion?, II Timothy 2:19, PPS-II, Twin Mountain House, White
    Mountain, New Hampshire, August 23, 1874.
Christian Sympathy, Romans 12:4-5, PPS-II, Twin Mountain House, White
    Mountain, New Hampshire, August 30, 1874.
Luminous Hours, Luke 9:28-42, PPS-II, Twin Mountain House, White
    Mountain, New Hampshire, September 6, 1874.
Law and Liberty, Galatians 5:13-18, PPS-III, Twin Mountain House, White
    Mountain, New Hampshire, September 13, 1874.
As a Little Child, Matthew 18:1-4, Twin Mountain House, White Mountain,
    New Hampshire, September 20, 1874.
God's Will, Matthew 6:10, PPS-III, October 4, 1874.
Present Use of Immortality, Hebrews 4:9, PPS-III, October 4, 1874.
The Test of Church Worth, Ephesians 4:20-24, PPS-III, October 18, 1874.
Peace in Christ, Romans 7:25; Romans 8:1, PPS-III, October 25, 1874.
The Indwelling of Christ, Matthew 28:18-20, PPS-III, November 1, 1874.
The End and the Means, Matthew 10:34-38, PPS-II, November 8, 1874.
Saved by Grace, Ephesians 2:8, PPS-III, November 15, 1874.
Soul-Rest, Matthew 11:28, PPS-III, November 22, 1874.
The Worlds' Growth, I Corinthians 4:20, PPS-III, November 26, 1874.
Foundation Work, Romans 15:20, PPS-III, December 6, 1874.
The Bible, II Timothy 3:14-17, PPS-III, December 13, 1874.
The Work of Patience, James 1:3-4, PPS-III, December 20, 1874.
The Divine Love, John 13:1, PPS-III, December 27, 1874.
Romans 14:7-8, 1875.
Unworthy Pursuits, Matthew 26:8, PPS-III, January 3, 1875.
The Divine Indwelling, John 14:23, PPS-IV, January 5, 1875.
True Rightousness, Philomen 3:9, PPS-III, January 10, 1875.
Things of the Spirit, II Peter 1:2-11, PPS-III, January 17, 1875.
Christian Contentment, Philomen 4:11-13, PPS-III, January 24, 1875.
Moral Standards, Romans 13:8-10; Gal. 5: 14, PPS-III, January 31, 1875.
Trials of Faith, I Peter 1:7, PPS-III, February 7, 1875.
The Old Paths, Jeremiah 6:16; Jeremiah 18:15, PPS-III, February 14, 1875.
Meekness, a Power, Matthew 5:5, PPS-III, February 21, 1875.
Extent of the Divine Law, Romans 8:10, PPS-III, February 28, 1875.
Soul-Growth, Isaiah 40:31, PPS-III, March 7, 1875.
Christ Life, Colossians 1:27, PPS-IV, March 14, 1875.
Good Deeds Memorable, Proverbs 10:6-7, PPS-IV, March 15, 1875.
The Courtesy of Conscience, I Corinthians 10:28-29, PPS-IV, March 21, 1875.
Love, the Key to Religion, John 14:15-17, PPS-IV, March 28, 1875.

Christianity Social, II Corinthians 4:14, PPS-IV, April 4, 1875.
Morality and Religion, Luke 10:27, PPS-IV, April 11, 1875.
The Law of Soul-Growth, Hebrews 5:14, PPS-IV, April 18, 1875.
Sources and Uses of Suffering, II Corinthians 1:3-5, PPS-IV, April 25, 1875.
God's Dear Children, Ephesians 5:1-2, PPS-IV, May 2, 1875.
Grieving the Spirit, Ephesians 5:30, PPS-IV, May 9, 1875.
Working and Waiting, Ephesians 4:30, PPS-IV, May 16, 1875.
The Sure Foundation, II Timothy 2:19, PPS-IV, May 23, 1875.
Nurture of Noble Impulse, Matthew 21:28-31, PPS-IV, May 30, 1875.
Sowing and Reaping, Romans 2:6-11, PPS-IV, June 6, 1875.
Soul-Statistics, II Peter 3:18, PPS-IV, June 13, 1875.
The Communion of Saints, Hebrews 12:1, PPS-IV, June 27, 1875.
Secret of Christ's Power, I Corinthians 2:2, PPS-IV, June 30, 1875.
Economy in Small Things, John 6:12, PPS-IV, (evening?) June 30, 1875.
The Christian Life a Struggle, Hebrews 12:2-3, PPS-IV, morning, July 4, 1875.
Universality of the Gospel, Matthew 28:18, PPS-IV, evening, July 4, 1875.
The Claims of the Spirit, John 33:56, PPS-IV, Twin Mountain House, White
    Mountain, New Hampshire, August 15, 1875.
The Kingdom Within, Romans 14:17, PPS-IV, Twin Mountain House, White
    Mountain, New Hampshire, August 15, 1875.
The New Birth, John 3:7, PPS-IV, Twin Mountain House, White Mountain,
    New Hampshire, August 22, 1875.
Perfection Through Love, Matthew 5:48, PPS-IV, Twin Mountain House,
    White Mountain, New Hampshire, August 29, 1875.
Revelation 22:4-5, April 2, 1876.
Romans 7:9, April 9, 1876.
I Corinthians 13:8-13, May 28, 1876.
Oratory, National School of Oratory, American Academy of Music,
    Philadelphia, Pennsylvania, May 29, 1876.
Ephesians 6:5-8, June 4, 1876.
Advance of a Century, Peekskill, New York, July 4, 1876.
Acts 20:21, October 8, 1876.
Fellowship within the Church, April 15, 1877.
Address to Grand Army of the Republic, June 5, 1877.
Acts 19:34, June 24, 1877.
Psalms 18:43, July 22, 1877.
Lecture Room Talk, November 24, 1877.
Past Perils and the Peril of Today, November 29, 1877.
The Wastes and Burdens of Society [this lecture evidently was begun in
    November, 1877, but Beecher did not keep complete records: when
    data is missing, he did not supply it] Warren, Massachusetts, 1877;
    Springfield, Massachusetts; Lancaster, Pennsylvania; Pittsburgh,
    Pennsylvania; North Attleboro, Massachusetts, November, 1877;
    Holbrook, Massachusetts; Philadelphia, December 3, 1877; West
    Chester, Pennsylvania, December 5, 1877; Salem, Massachusetts,
    December, 1877; Providence, Rhode Island, December, 1877;
    Manchester, New Hampshire, December, 1877; Pittsfield,
    Massachusetts, December, 1877; Elmira, New York; December 24,

1877; Titusville, New York, December 25, 1877; Ashtabula, Ohio, December 27, 1877; Newark, New Jersey, 1878; Wilmington, Delaware, 1878; Baltimore, January 16, 1878; Belfast, Maine, 1878.

Romans 8:20-22, January 20, 1878.

On the Bible and Personal Experience, March 19, 1878.

Lecture Room Talk, May 10, 1878.

Early Marriages, Permament Moralities, November 24, 1878.

Lecture Room Talk, October 17, 1879.

William Ellery Channing, LO, Boston, April 7, 1880.

Love and Hate, April 18, 1880.

A Statement of Belief, July 11, 1880.

Assassination of President Garfield, July 3, 1881.

Death of President Garfield, September 25, 1881.

Lecture on Evolution, Chicago, Illinois, February 7, 1883.

Address at Seventieth Birthday Celebration, New York City, June 25, 1883.

Lecture on Evolution, Denver, Colorado, September 17, 1883.

A Circle of the Continent, November 29, 1883; Home for Consumptives, Brooklyn, New York, January 16, 1884.

Wendell Phillips, Psalms 41:1-2, LO, February 10, 1884.

Thanksgiving Sermon, November 27, 1884.

Job 37:6, December 21, 1884.

The Sign of The Times, Matthew 16:2-3, E&R, May 17, 1885.

Evolution in Human Consciousness of the Idea of God, John 17: 3:2; II Peter 3:18, E&R, May 24, 1885.

The Two Revelations, John 1:3, E&R, May 31, 1885.

The Inspiration of the Bible, II Timothy 3:16, E&R, June 7, 1885.

The Sinfulness of Man, Romans 8:19-22, E&R, June 14, 1885.

The New Birth, John 33:3, E&R, June 21, 1885.

Divine Providence and Design, Isaiah 46:5, E&R, June 28, 1885.

Evolution and the Church, John 11:43-44, E&R, July 5, 1885.

Lecture Room Talk, July 27, 1885.

Eulogy on Grant, LO, Tremont Temple, Boston, October 22, 1885.

Romans 8:35-39, March 7, 1886.

City Temple, London, July 4, 1886.

Christian Self-Denial, Matthew 16:24, City Temple, London, July 8, 1886.

Sermon, Union Chapel, London, July 11, 1886.

Sermon, Westminster Chapel, London, July 18, 1886.

Lecture, Exeter Hall, London, July 19, 1886.

Sermon, London, July 25, 1886.

Lecture, Exeter Hall, London, August 5, 1886.

Sermon, Bradford, England, August 8, 1886.

Sermon, Liverpool, England, August 15, 1886.

Sermon, Carlisle, England, August 22, 1886.

Sermon [location in Great Britain unknown], Matthew 5:16, August 28, 1886.

Sermon, Glasgow, Scotland, August 29, 1886.

Lecture, Aberdeen, Scotland, September 2, 1886.

Lecture, Aberdeen, Scotland, September 3, 1886.

Sermon, Edingburgh, Scotland, September 5, 1886.

Sermon, Scarboro, England, September 12, 1886.

Sermon, Y.M.C.A., Torquay, England, September 19, 1886.

Sermon, Christ's Heroism in Suffering, Brighton, England, September 26, 1886.

Lecture, Union Chapel, London, October 1, 1886.

Sermon, Public Hall, London, October 3, 1886.

Lecture, Public Hall, London, October 4, 1886.

Conscience, City Temple, London, October 8, 1886.

Sermon, Harecourt Chapel, London, October 10, 1886.

Address, School for Ministers' Sons, Caterham, England, October 12, 1886.

Address, City Temple, London, October 15, 1886.

Address, Freedmen's Missions Aid Society, Westminster Chapel, London, October 16, 1886.

Farewell Sermon, City Temple, London, October 17, 1886.

Lecture, Liverpool, England, October 18, 1886.

Mark 5:28, February 27, 1887.

Luke 16:4, February 27, 1887.

Lecture Room Talk, February 28, 1887.

Lecture, Society for Ethical Culture, Chickering Hall, New York City, April 2, 1887.

3. Calendar of Sermons and Speeches By Title Only

On Abraham
Abuses of the Beautiful
On Accepting Christ
Against Clerical Manners
Against Doctrinal Preaching
On the Aim and Design of Preaching
Aims of the Bible
On Alcohol
American Board of Commissioners for Foreign Missions
On American Civilization
The American Colonies
Art of Happiness
The Atonement
On the Atonement
On Backsliding
On Beauty
Benefits of Economic Depression
On Benevolence
Burgess, Daniel, Funeral Sermon
Changing Religious Thought
On Character
On the Character of God
Charity and Justice
On Charity Towards Foreign Immigrants
On Cheerfulness

The Chinese Question
On Choosing Christ
Christ the Living Redeemer
Christ the Master
On Christian Charity
On Christian Witness
On Church Membership
Address, Common Sense
Conditions of Continental Europe
Conditions of the South
On Conscience and Conduct
On Conscience as a Force in New England's History
On Conversion
Conversion not Easy or Cheap
On Cooperation Among Christian Sects
Cornelius and Peter
On Creeds
The Cultural Determinants of Belief
Death and the Future State
Deceitfulness of Riches
On the Difficulty of Attaining Religion
On Divine Government
Doctrinal Difficulties and Individual Cases
The Doctrine of Faith and Works
Doings One's Duty
On Education
Education of Conscience
The Elements of Happiness
The Emancipator
Encyclopedias
On Eternity
The Exceeding Lawlessness of Our Nation
Exemplars of Virtue and Vice
Fitness for the Ministry
Free Trade Lecture
Fruits of Religion
The Function of the Gospel
Future Punishment
The Gates of Prayer
On Gluttony
God the Father
On God's Mercies
God's Poor
Greeley, Horace
On Habits
On Heaven
On Heedlessness
Historical View of Man's Sinfulness

Home Missions
Home Missions in Oregon and California
How Far May We Cooperate with Bad Men in the Promotion of Good
    Objects
The Human Element in the Bible
Imagination
Importance of Teaching the Young
The Industry of Idleness
The Influence of Modern Science on Religious Beliefs
On Innocent Vs. Dangerous Amusement
Inspiration in the Bible
Is Suffering an Evil?
Judgment Day
Knowledge is Power
Knowledge of God Through Growth in Grace
On Labor
The Language of the Bible
The Laws Governing Human Conduct
Lessons of the New Testament Contrasted with the Old
On Love and Humanity
On Love of the Beautiful
Lower Vs. Higher Natures
A Man's Liberty in the Use of the Bible
On Man's Sinfulness and Danger
Man's Strength and Weakness
On the Martyrdom of Prophets and Reformers
Address, Mechanics' Association
On the Measure of Duty
Ministerial Labors in the Mississippi Valley
The Ministry
On Miracle
On Moody and Sankey
Moral Truth in the Bible
Nature and Operation of Love
October
On Oratory
Our Country
Outworkings of Love
On Overzealous Clergymen
Paul and His Writings
On Paul's Epistle to the Romans
Paul's Theology
Peace and Prosperity
On Personal Religion
On Political Corruption
Political Excitement
Postwar Prosperity
The Power of an Active Ministry and Church

On Praise in Worship
On Preaching
Preaching on Secular Topics
Present Conditions of the World
On the Prodigal Son
Prophesy of Destruction of Jerusalem
The Prosperity of New England
On Public Duties
Railroads
On Reconstruction
Relation of Ideality to Morals
Religion of North American Indians
Religious Gains of the Past Century
Religion in the Home
Religious Thought in America
On Repentance
On Republicanism
On Resolutions
Retraction of Statement Made in Previous Sermon
On Revivals
On the Rise of the Laboring and Commercial Classes
On the Sabbath
On Self-Denial
To Skeptics of Religion
On Slavery
Society
Address, Society for Promoting Collegiate Education at the West
The Source of our National Troubles
Spiritual Development
Spirituality and Religious Study
The State of Religion
The Subjection of Women
On Temperance
The Tendency of the Creation Towards Happiness
On Toleration
On the True Gospel
The Voice of God
Vicious Men Reformers
On Waiting God's Time
What Will You Do With Christ?
On Women's Suffrage
On the World's Final Evangelization
On Work
On Worshipping Christ
Wrongdoing and Punishment
Address, Y.M.C.A.
The Young America

Bibliography

The Beecher Family Papers, Sterling Library, Yale University, New Haven Connecticut, contain the collected papers of Henry Ward Beecher. These sources include the following kinds of rhetorical materials: drafts of speeches, ranging from sketchy notes to complete texts; sermon notes of varying lengths; texts of sermons that range from fragments to complete texts; sermon notebooks, which vary in detail; miscellaneous materials from the Plymouth Church: texts of speeches, printed copies of some sermons, and newspaper accounts of some sermons and speeches; and a photographic file of Beecher and his family. The Library maintains helpful finding aids to the collection.

The Bibliography is divided into two sections. The first part lists the books that Henry Ward Beecher wrote (for a chronological listing of Beecher's sermons and speeches, see "Chronology of Sermons and Speeches"). The second part lists books, articles, and dissertations about Beecher.

Works by Henry Ward Beecher (arranged chronologically)

Lectures to Young Men. Salem: J. P. Jewett, 1846.
Industry and Idleness. Philadelphia: William S. Young, 1850.
Star Papers. Boston: J. C. Derby, 1855.
Defence of Kansas. Washington, D.C.: Buell and Blanchard, 1856.
Life Thoughts. Edited by Edna Dean Proctor. Boston: Phillip, Sampson & Co., 1858.
New Star Papers. New York: Derby and Jackson, 1859.
Plain and Pleasant Talk About Fruits, Flowers, and Farming. New York: Derby and Jackson, 1859.
War and Emancipation. Philadelphia: T. B. Peterson, 1861.
Eyes and Ears. Boston: Ticknor and Fields, 1862.
Freedom and War Discourses. Boston: Ticknor and Fields, 1863.
American Rebellion: Report of the Speeches of the Rev. Henry Ward Beecher. London: Samspon Low and Son, 1864.

Royal Truths. Boston: Ticknor and Fields, 1866.
Norwood: Or Village Life in New England. New York: Fords, Howard, and
     Hulbert, 1867.
Yale Lectures on Preaching. New York: J. B. Ford, 1872-74.
The Life of Jesus, the Christ. New York: J. B. Ford, 1872.
Should Libraries Be Open On Sunday? New York: J. B. Ford, 1872.
Lecture Room Talks. New York: J. B. Ford, 1874.
God Unknowable, and How to Know Him. London: James Clarke, 1876.
Twelve Lectures to Young Men. New York: Fords, Howard, and Hulbert,
     1879.
"Progress of Thought in the Church." *North American Review* 135 (August,
     1882): 99-117.
Cleveland Letters. n.p., 1884.
A Circuit of the Continent. New York: Fords, Howard, and Hulbert, 1884.
Comforting Thoughts. Edited Irene Ovington. New York: Fords, Howard,
     and Hulbert, 1885.
A Summer in England with Henry Ward Beecher. Edited by James B. Pond.
     New York: Fords, Howard, and Hulbert, 1887.
Last Sermons. London, 1887.
Patriotic Address. Edited by John R. Howard. New York: Fords, Howard,
     and Hulbert, 1887.
Bible Studies. Edited by John R. Howard. New York: Fords, Howard, and
     Hulbert, 1893.
Autobiographical Reminiscences of Henry Ward Beecher. Edited T. J.
     Ellinwood. New York: F. A. Stokes Co., 1898.
Lecture and Orations by Henry Ward Beecher. Edited by Newell Dwight Hillis.
     New York: Fleming H. Revell Company, 1913.

Works About Henry Ward Beecher

Abbott, Lyman. *Henry Ward Beecher*. Hartford: American Publishing
     Company, 1887.
Adams, Douglas Glenn. "Humor in the Pulpit from George Whitefield
     through Henry Ward Beecher." Th.D. diss., Graduate Theological
     Union, 1974.
Addison, Daniel Dulany. *The Clergy in American Life and Letters*. London:
     The Macmillan Company, 1900.
American Public Address: 1740-1952. Edited by A. Craig Baird. New York:
     McGraw-Hill, 1956.
Barrows, John Henry. *Henry Ward Beecher: The Shakespeare of the Pulpit*.
     New York: Funk and Wagnalls, 1893.
Batsell, B. Baxter. "An Analysis of the Basic Elements of Persuasion in the
     Yale Lectures on Preaching." Ph.D. diss., University of Southern
     California, 1944.
Beecher as a Humorist. Compiled by Elaenor Kirk. New York: Ford,
     Howard and Hulbert, 1887.

Beecher, William Constantine. *A Biography of Rev. Henry Ward Beecher.* New York: Charles L. Webster, 1888.

Bernhardt, Roger B. "Henry Ward Beecher's Application of His Own Theories of Persuasion." M.S. thesis, University of Wisconsin, 1947.

Buckley, J. M. "Beecher at Liverpool." *Century Magazine*, November, 1888, pp. 240-43.

Burns, Robert Elwood. "A Development of Criteria for Effective Preaching from an Analysis of the Preaching of Henry Ward Beecher." S.T.D. diss., Garrett-Evangelical Theological Seminary, 1975.

Chesebrough, David Bruce. "The Call to Battle: The Stances of Parker, Finney, Beecher, and Brooks on the Great Issues Surrounding the Civil War and a Comparison of Those Stances with Other Clergy in the Nation." D.A. diss., Illinois State University, 1988.

Clark, Clifford Edward, Jr. "Henry Ward Beecher: Revivalist and Anti-Slavery Leader–1813-1867." Ph.D. diss., Harvard University, 1968.

_____. *Henry Ward Beecher: Spokesman for a Middle-Class America.* Urbana: University of Illinois Press, 1978.

Covington, Robert Cooper. "A Critical Study of the Preaching of Henry Ward Beecher Based on his Published Sermons." Ph.D. diss., New Orleans Baptist Theological Seminary, 1960.

Crocker, Lionel. "Beecher and Fosdick." *Central States Speech Journal* 12 (1961): 100-105.

_____. "Henry Ward Beecher." In *History and Criticism of American Public Address.* Edited by William Norwood Brigance. New York: McGraw-Hill, 1943.

_____. "Henry Ward Beecher and the English Press of 1863." *Speech Monographs* 6 (1939): 20-43.

_____. "Henry Ward Beecher at Fort Sumter, April 14, 1865." *Southern Speech Communication Journal* 27 (1962): 149-59.

_____. *Henry Ward Beecher's Art of Preaching.* Chicago: University of Chicago Press, 1934.

_____. *Henry Ward Beecher's Speaking Art.* New York: Fleming H. Revell, 1937.

_____. "Lincoln and Beecher." *Southern Speech Communication Journal* 26 (1960): 149-59.

_____. "The Rhetorical Influence of Henry Ward Beecher." *Quarterly Journal of Speech* 18 (1932): 82-87.

_____. "The Voice Element in Prose." *Quarterly Journal of Speech* 12 (1926): 168-75.

Duduit, James Michael. "Henry Ward Beecher and the Political Pulpit." Ph.D. diss., The Florida State University, 1983.

Elsmere, Jane Shaffer. *Henry Ward Beecher: The Indianapolis Years, 1837-47.* Indianapolis: Indiana Historical Society, 1973.

Garff, Royal L. "A Study of Henry Ward Beecher's Methods of Controlling Hostile Audiences." Ph.D. diss., University of Southern California, 1944.

Goodell, John. "The Triumph of Moralism in New England Piety: A Study of Lyman Beecher, Harriet Beecher Stowe, and Henry Ward Beecher." Ph.D. diss., The Pennsylvania State University, 1976.

Gossard, John Harvey. "The New York City Congregational Cluster, 1848-1871: Congregationalism and Antislavery in the Careers of Henry Ward Beecher, George B. Cheever, Richard S. Storrs, and Joseph P. Thompson." Ph.D. diss., Bowling Green State University, 1986.

Griswold, Stephen M. *Sixty years with Plymouth Church.* New York: F. H. Revell, 1907.

Hendrikson, Ernest H.   "Rhetorical Elements of Beecher's English Addresses." M.A. thesis, State University of Iowa, 1929.

Henricksen, E. H.   "Elements of Persuasion in Henry Ward Beecher's Speeches in England in 1863." M.A. thesis, University of Iowa, 1929.

"Henry Ward Beecher." *Atlantic Monthly,* May, 1858, pp. 862-70.

Hertz, Emanuel. *Pew 89: Lincoln and Beecher.* n.p., 1929.

Hibben, Paxton. *Henry Ward Beecher: An American Portrait.* New York: George H. Doran Company, 1927.

Hillis, Newell Dwight.   "The Ruling Ideas of Henry Ward Beecher's Sermons." *The Congregationalist and Christian World,* January 2, 1904, pp. 11-12.

Holmes, Oliver Wendell. "The Minister Plenipotentiary." *Atlantic Monthly* 13 (1864): 106-12.

Howard, Joseph. *Life of Henry Ward Beecher.* Philadelphia: Hubbard Brothers, 1887.

_____, and T. J. Ellinwood. *Sermon Briefs of Henry Ward Beecher.* Boston: Pilgrim Press, 1905.

Knox, T. W. *Life of Beecher.* Cincinatti: W. E. Dibble, 1887.

Metaphors, Similes, and other Characteristic Sayings of Henry Ward Beecher. Compiled by T. J. Ellinwood. New York: Andrew J. Graham & Co., 1895.

McLoughlin, William Gerald. *The Meaning of Henry Ward Beecher: An Essay on the Shifting Values of Mid-Victorian America.* New York: Alfred A. Knopf, 1970.

"Mr. Beecher in Great Britain." *New York Times,* November 4, 1863, p. 4.

Oliver, Robert T. *History of Public Speaking in America.* Boston: Allyn and Bacon, 1965.

"Preacher Beecher." *Time,* October 3, 1927, pp. 47-48.

"Rev. Henry Ward Beecher." *The Practical Christian Life Illustrated,* August, 1886, pp. 1-2.

Rourke, Constance Mayfield.   "Henry Ward Beecher." *Woman's Home Companion,* November, 1926, pp. 25-176.

_____. *Trumpets of Jubilee.* New York: Harcourt, Brace, and Company, 1927.

Ryan, Halford R. "Henry Ward Beecher." *American Orators Before 1900: Critical Studies and Sources.* Edited by Bernard K. Duffy and Halford R. Ryan. Westport: Greenwood Press, 1987.

Sermons in American History. Edited by DeWitte Holland. Nashville: Abingdon Press, 1971.

Shaplen, Robert. *Free Love and Heavenly Sinners*. New York: Knopf, 1954.
"'Sold' by Beecher in '60, Slave Girl Revisits Church." *New York Herald Tribune*, January 8, 1927, p. 13.
Stowe, Harriet Beecher. *Men of Our Times*. Hartford: Hartford Publishing Company, 1868.
Stowe, Lyman Beecher. *Saints, Sinners, and Beechers*. Indianapolis: Bobbs Merrill Company, 1934.
Thompson, Noyes L. *The History of Plymouth Church*. New York: G. W. Carleton, 1873.
Waller, Altina Laura. "The Beecher-Tilton Adultery Scandal: Family, Religion, and Politics in Brooklyn, 1865-1875." Ph.D. diss., University of Massachusetts, 1980.
_____. *Reverend Beecher and Mrs. Tilton*. Amherst: University of Massachusetts Press, 1982.
Walters, C. H. "A Quantitative Study of the Oratorical Style of Henry Ward Beecher." M.A. thesis, University of Wisconsin, 1930.

Index

ABOUT THE AUTHOR

Halford Ryan is professor of public speaking at Washington and Lee University, Lexington, Virginia. He teaches undergraduate courses in the history and criticism of American public address.

He is a graduate of Wabash College, A.B., 1966, and the University of Illinois, M.A., 1968, and Ph.D., 1972. He studied at Princeton Theological Seminary on a Rockefeller Theological Fellowship, 1966-67.

Ryan is author, editor, or co-editor, of seven books, the most recent of which is *Harry Emerson Fosdick: Persuasive Preacher*.

Great American Orators

Defender of the Union: The Oratory of Daniel Webster
Craig R. Smith

Harry Emerson Fosdick: Persuasive Preacher
Halford R. Ryan

Eugene Talmadge: Rhetoric and Response
Calvin McLeod Logue

The Search of Self-Sovereignty: The Oratory of Elizabeth Cady Stanton
Beth M. Waggenspack

Richard Nixon: Rhetorical Strategist
Hal W. Bochin